NERO

&

PAUL

NERO & PAUL

HOW THE GOSPEL OF GRACE DEFEATED THE RULER OF ROME

KATHIE LEE GIFFORD WITH
DR. BRYAN LITFIN

W Publishing Group
An Imprint of Thomas Nelson

Nero and Paul

Published by W Publishing, an imprint of Thomas Nelson, 501 Nelson Place, Nashville, TN 37214, USA.

Thomas Nelson titles may be purchased in bulk for educational, business, fundraising, or sales promotional use. For information, please email SpecialMarkets@ThomasNelson.com.

Emphasis in Scripture quotations has been added by the authors.

ISBN 978-1-4003-3669-2 (audiobook)
ISBN 978-1-4003-3668-5 (ePub)
ISBN 978-1-4003-5566-2 (ITPE)
ISBN 978-1-4003-3666-1 (HC)

HarperCollins Publishers, Macken House, 39/40 Mayor Street Upper, Dublin 1, D01 C9W8, Ireland (https://www.harpercollins.com)

Library of Congress Control Number: 2025946310

Art Direction: Meg Schmidt
Cover Design: Tim Green at Faceout Studio
Interior Design: Sara Colley

I dedicate this book to my beloved grandchildren,
with a prayer that they will always walk in the
footsteps of their Messiah, Yeshua.

KATHIE LEE GIFFORD

CONTENTS

FIRST CENTURY CHRONOLOGY

27 BC	Octavian is given the title of Emperor Caesar Augustus; the Roman Republic becomes the Roman Empire
AD 14	Caesar Augustus dies; Tiberius becomes the second emperor
AD 33	Jesus Christ is crucified, resurrected, and ascends to heaven
AD 34	Stephen is stoned; Saul (Paul) is converted on the road to Damascus
AD 37	Nero is born; Caligula becomes the third emperor; Paul finishes his Arabian ministry and returns to Jerusalem, then goes home to Tarsus and lives quietly for about nine years
AD 39	Plot against Caligula is discovered; Agrippina is exiled
AD 40	Nero's father, Ahenobarbus, dies
AD 41	Caligula is assassinated; Claudius becomes the fourth emperor; Agrippina is brought back from exile
AD 46	Paul embarks on his First Missionary Journey
AD 48	Messalina has an affair and is executed; Paul writes Galatians
AD 49	Claudius marries Agrippina, expels Jews from Rome; Seneca becomes Nero's tutor; Paul attends Jerusalem Council, then embarks on his Second Missionary Journey

AD 50	Claudius adopts Nero; Paul writes 1 and 2 Thessalonians
AD 51	Thirteen-year-old Nero publicly adopts the toga of manhood
AD 52	Disaster occurs at the opening of the lake floodgate; Paul embarks on his Third Missionary Journey
AD 53	Nero marries Octavia
AD 54	Claudius is poisoned by Agrippina; Nero becomes the fifth emperor
AD 55	Agrippina and Nero have conflict about Acte; Nero murders Britannicus; Paul writes 1 Corinthians, has a "painful visit" in Corinth, then writes 2 Corinthians
AD 56	Paul spends the winter in Corinth
AD 57	Paul writes Romans from Corinth, travels to Jerusalem, is arrested there and imprisoned in Caesarea for two years
AD 58	Nero begins a relationship with Poppaea Sabina
AD 59	Nero has his mother, Agrippina, assassinated; Paul is tried before Festus, departs Caesarea as a prisoner, and is shipwrecked on Malta
AD 60	Nero establishes the Five Year Games; Paul finally arrives at Rome, where he is put under house arrest for two years
AD 61	Paul writes the Prison Epistles: Ephesians, Philippians, Colossians, and Philemon
AD 62	Nero divorces and executes Octavia; Nero marries Poppaea; Paul has his first trial before Nero and Poppaea; Paul is released as innocent and goes to Spain
AD 63	Paul is back in the Aegean Sea area, traveling and ministering for two years; writes 1 Timothy and Titus; spends the winter of 63–64 in Corinth

AD 64	Great Fire of Rome (July); Paul gets word of the fire and begins his journey to Rome, but winters in Nicopolis
AD 65	Nero stages the second Five Year Games in Rome; begins construction of the Golden House; kicks Poppaea to death; a coup is attempted against Nero; Seneca is forced to commit suicide; Peter is martyred at the Circus of Nero on the Vatican Hill and is buried nearby; Paul arrives in Rome
AD 66	Jewish revolt against Rome begins in Jerusalem; Paul is arrested and imprisoned in the Carcer; writes 2 Timothy; is condemned at a second trial with Nero; is martyred on the Ostian Way; Nero departs for a "victory tour" in Greece
AD 67	Nero wins prizes in Greece for singing and chariot racing; marries the boy Sporus
AD 68	Nero returns from Greece and soon learns of a Spanish uprising against him; almost everyone abandons him; he commits suicide; three successive men briefly reign as emperors
AD 69	Vespasian fights to suppress the Jewish revolt in Jerusalem; is proclaimed emperor in the eastern provinces
AD 70	Vespasian returns to Rome and is confirmed by the Senate as emperor; his son Titus conquers Jerusalem and destroys the Jewish Temple

JULIO-CLAUDIAN FAMILY TREE

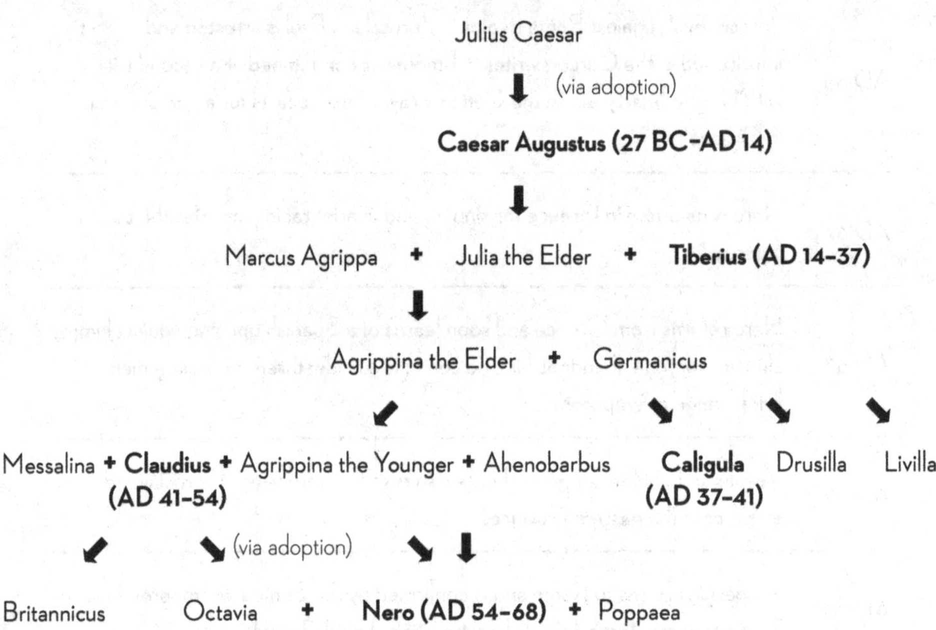

+ = MARRIAGE

⬇ = OFFSPRING

Simplified depiction. Some persons and family relationships are omitted.

Servian wall
Circus of Caligula and Nero
Amphitheater
Via Salaria
Pratetorian Camp
Temple of Isis and Serapis
Baths of Nero
Baths of Agrippa
Theater of Pompey
Temple of Juno
Capitoline
Via Labicana
Theater of Balbus
Forum
Nero's Golden House
Palatine
Servian wall
Via Aurelia
Imperial Palaces
N
Tiber Island
Temple of Jupiter
Tiber River
Circus Maximus
Via Appia
Theater of Marcellus
Via Ostia
Paul's Burial Site

GALLIA
GERMANIA
DACIA
ILLYRICUM (DALMATIA)
MOESIA
THRACE
ITALY
Adriatic Sea
Black Sea
Corsica
Rome
Forum of Appius
Three Taverns
Puteoli
Sardinia
Tyrrhenian Sea
MACEDONIA
Amphipolis
Philippi
Thessalonica
Neapolis
Samothrace
Berea
Apollonia?
BITHYNIA & PONTUS
Mt. Olympus
EPIRUS
Ionian Sea
Aegean Sea
Troas
Assos
Mitylene
MYSIA
ASIA
Pergamum
Thyatira
Sardis
GALATIA
CAPPADOCIA
Delphi
Chios
LYDIA
Smyrna
Ephesus
LYCAONIA
Antioch (Pisidian)
COMMAGENE
Sicily
Rhegium
Athens
Philadelphia
PISIDIA
Iconium
ACHAIA
Cenchreae
Corinth
Samos
Laodicea
Colossae
PAMPHYLIA
Euphrates R.
Syracuse
Miletus
Lystra
Derbe
CILICIA
NUMIDIA
Sparta
Patmos
LYCIA
Attalia
Tarsus
Issus
Kos
Cnidus
Seleucia Pieria
SYRIA
AFRICA
Malta
Patara
Aleppo
Antioch (Syrian)
Crete
Rhodes
Myra
Perga
Phoenix
Salmone
Lasea
Cyprus
Cauda
Salamis
Fair Havens
Paphos
ABILENE
Mediterranean Sea
PHOENICIA
Sidon
Tyre
Ptolemais
Damascus
JUDEA
Caesarea
Jordan R.
Jerusalem
Dead Sea
TRIPOLITANIA
CYRENAICA
ARABIA
EGYPT
Nile R.
Red Sea
First missionary journey (AD 46–48)
Second missionary journey (AD 49–51)
Third missionary journey (AD 52–57)
Trip to Rome (AD 59–60)
0 200 km.
0 200 miles
10,000 ft 3050 m
5000 ft 1525 m
2000 ft 610 m
1000 ft 305 m
0 (sea level) 0 (sea level)
-1640 ft -500 m
Maps by International Mapping.
Copyright © 2008 by Zondervan. All rights reserved. NIVv0524.

HISTORICAL NOTE

Like the first book in the Ancient Evil, Living Hope series, *Herod and Mary*, the story of Nero and Paul presents two intertwined lives: a godly hero and an evil villain. Written as narrative nonfiction, it's grounded in ancient writings and drawn from contemporary scholarship. Many of the quotations come directly from modern English editions of the original sources—sometimes slightly adapted or perhaps retranslated from Greek or Latin if that seemed best—but always recorded with the utmost historical accuracy.

Of course, this book is meant to be more than just bare-bones history. It is a page-turning story! To make it vivid and fascinating for the reader, I have sometimes used my novelist's background to imagine what the events might have been like for the original participants. In those cases, I have employed fiction-writing techniques such as dialogue or scene-setting to help ancient history come alive. Although those scenes require imagination and creativity, they are always grounded in the best available sources that give a framework for what actually happened.

When it comes to history, some level of imagination is always required, because none of us was an eyewitness to the original events. Even the most reliable ancient writers had agendas that colored how they presented their material. Ancient people didn't feel the need to be as accurate and objective as today's historians. This is why the trend among many modern scholars is to question—and often debunk—everything the ancient writers reported, then rewrite the story of a figure like Nero in a new light. By discounting the criticisms of Nero as the result of ancient biases against him, modern scholars are freed to instead describe what they think the true narrative should be.

The problem with that approach is many of those negative things aren't implausible. They fit perfectly with the pattern of insane madmen in history, whether in ancient Rome, or some other historical empire, or evil regimes around the world today. Often, those negative accounts are corroborated by other sources, so when taken together, they reflect widespread opinions at the time. Those opinions deserve to be given more credence than modern scholarly reconstructions. Therefore, Kathie Lee and I have presented in this book *the Nero who is found in the ancient sources*, not the Nero of our own creation.

What are the ancient sources about Nero? The big three are

- Tacitus, *Annals*, Books 12–16 (translated in the Loeb Classical Library series and the Oxford World's Classics series),
- Suetonius, *Lives of the Caesars*, Nero (translated in the Loeb Classical Library series and the Oxford World's Classics series), and
- Dio Cassius, *Roman History*, Books 61–63 (translated in the Loeb Classical Library series).

These sources provide a wealth of information about Nero, along with the many other characters who swirled around his glamorous, iniquitous, outrageous, and often dangerous orbit.

When it comes to the apostle Paul, the main historical source is, of course, the New Testament. This source has the benefit of being entirely trustworthy, since it came directly from God. Nevertheless, though the biblical text is without error, it still requires interpretation. Many aspects of Paul's biography—not to mention his theology—have divided scholarly opinion over the years. The story we have written for you represents our best reconstruction of the facts as we can discern them, though other scholars might quibble about a few matters.

Our baseline Bible translation in this book is the New King James Version. If something in that translation didn't seem clear enough, we have also used the New International Version, the English Standard Version, and the New Living Translation. At times, we've also paraphrased verses, putting them in our own conversational words (and indicated as such in the footnotes). We encourage you to look up these references in your Bible and see how each one connects to what you're reading!

A few modern resources about Nero and Paul deserve to be mentioned because I found them helpful and relied on them often, even if I didn't always agree with their conclusions. They are

Shadi Bartsch, Kirk Freudenburg, and Cedric Littlewood, eds., *The Cambridge Companion to the Age of Nero* (Cambridge University Press, 2017),
F. F. Bruce, *Paul: Apostle of the Heart Set Free* (Eerdmans, 1977),
Edward Champlin, *Nero* (Harvard University Press, 2005),
John F. Drinkwater, *Nero: Emperor and Court* (Cambridge University Press, 2019),
David L. Eastman, *Paul the Martyr: The Cult of the Apostle in the Latin West* (Society of Biblical Literature, 2011),
Anthony Everitt and Roddy Ashworth, *Nero: Matricide, Music, and Murder in Imperial Rome* (Random House, 2023), and
N. T. Wright, *Paul: A Biography* (HarperOne, 2018).

Kathie Lee and I worked closely on this project as we envisioned, plotted, and wrote the story in a constant back-and-forth editorial process. Before setting down any words on the page, we talked about the big ideas we wanted to communicate. We settled on the central theme of God's expansion of Israel's gospel to the ends of the earth.

Through faith in Jesus, people everywhere can become temples of God's Holy Spirit. The apostle Paul made it his life's mission to spread this message to Jews and Gentiles alike. Nero, in contrast, wanted all the attention—and eventually, worship—to focus on himself. His selfishness, cruelty, and egomania flowed out of Rome's agenda of power, pride, and plunder. *Nero and Paul* tells the story of their two conflicting visions for rightful lordship over the ancient world.

Since I did most of the typing for this manuscript, the codas after each chapter offer a window into Kathie Lee's insights. The ideas in this book are hers as well as mine, for we shared our views and understandings continually until our minds converged on the final approach and message. Then, as we talked through various questions about each chapter, we made recordings that we turned into edited transcripts. Kathie Lee is far too lively and engaging not to have her own voice included! Together, the chapters and codas convey our shared vision for *Nero and Paul.*

We hope you will find both of these characters fascinating (though for very different reasons). Most importantly, we pray that through their stories you will encounter the Divine Story that stands behind it all.

Dr. Bryan M. Litfin
Lynchburg, VA

PROLOGUE

THE EXIT OF THE SPIRIT

"It is finished," declared the man whose broken body had been nailed to wooden beams.[1] His gut-wrenching words tumbled from his lips along with his final gasps, "Father, into your hands I commit my spirit!"[2] At that moment, his spirit left him.

The dead man's friends called him Yeshua.

Today, most people know him as Jesus.

Was Yeshua alone when he finally perished on the Roman cross? Certainly, in the extremity of his sufferings, he had felt abandoned. Hanging suspended by the nails, he had cried out in his native tongue of Aramaic, *Eli, Eli, lema sabachthani?* "My God, my God, why have you forsaken me?"[3] As Yeshua took upon himself the sins of the world, the Lamb of God felt the separation from his Father.

Yet some faithful companions had remained nearby. Glancing in their direction as his life ebbed away, Yeshua could discern through blood-drenched eyes the comforters who had stayed with him. Among them was his mother, Miriam of Nazareth, known to us as Mary. Two other women stood there as well, each also named Mary, along with a lone man, the apostle John. He later

---

1. John 19:30.
2. Luke 23:46 ESV.
3. Matthew 27:46 NIV.

recorded in his gospel, "There stood by the cross of Jesus His mother, and His mother's sister, Mary the wife of Clopas, and Mary Magdalene."[4] Yeshua called out to John, commanding his beloved disciple to take his mother into his care. Then, after drinking sour wine in fulfillment of a Hebrew psalm, Yeshua gave up his spirit.

Because his suffering had been extreme, death came as a relief to the Savior's battered body. The Romans knew how to inflict pain, knew it in exquisite detail. In crucifixion, they had perfected their diabolical craft. The cross forced a terrible, repetitive choice: either lift the body's weight against three iron nails or suffocate in breathless panic. Searing pain in the victim's hands and feet alternated with desperate asphyxiation in a never-ending cycle. The extremity of the anguish was beyond human endurance, yet it was impossible to escape, sometimes for days on end.

Yeshua had endured it for about six hours, pulling with wearied arms and pushing with weakened legs against the agony of the nails, elevating his body just enough to snatch an elusive gasp, then collapsing in exhaustion. But there would not be, *could* not be, any rest on a Roman cross, because a moment later the desperate need for air required doing it all again. Yeshua kept up the struggle until, at last, he had drained the cup of suffering all the way to the bottom. Then he relinquished his spirit and died.

Like any mother watching her child suffer, Mary wept at the agonizing death of her son, grieving from the depths of her soul. She had pondered the meaning of Yeshua's life even before he was born.[5] She had suckled her infant with her breasts.[6] She had seen the crimson blood of his circumcision, the sign of Moses' covenant.[7] Now her precious son had been brutally killed by a trio of enemies: the nation's corrupt leaders, the cruel and domineering Romans, and the devilish serpent himself. Perhaps Mary struggled with deep despair at what she had just witnessed. If so, she can be forgiven. The other disciples would suffer their own crises of faith.

Yet God was up to something big, something far greater than the forlorn disciples could have imagined. He had a purpose behind the pain. Yeshua was

---

4. John 19:25.
5. Luke 2:19.
6. Luke 11:27.
7. Luke 2:21.

no helpless victim of Rome. "No one can take my life from me. I sacrifice it voluntarily," the King of kings had declared. "For I have the authority to lay it down when I want to and also to take it up again."[8] That was why Yeshua exclaimed "It is finished!"—not a pitiful whimper of defeat but a victorious shout from a Son who had completed his Father's task. His meaning was "It is accomplished! I have carried out what needed to be done!"

No sooner had Yeshua exhaled his victory cry than great things sprang into motion. The world was about to change, never to be the same again. Unknown to Mary and the weeping disciples on the hill of Golgotha, a place of carnage and death outside Jerusalem's walls, the two hands of God had just accomplished a life-giving deed inside the city. The supposed tragedy atop the hill of crucifixion—its crags shaped like a skull—had just resulted in a victorious event on Jerusalem's highest summit. There, the Jewish temple rose toward the sky from the lofty platform called the Temple Mount.

King Herod had built the temple out of brilliant white stone and trimmed it with gleaming gold. It towered over Jerusalem, rising 150 feet above its hilltop setting. Huge pillars flanked its massive central doors. Above the doors, beneath an overhanging porch, golden grape clusters dangled, each as large as a man. A magnificent curtain hung at the entrance. The temple's facade faced east, greeting the rising sun each day. The reflected rays served as a beacon to all the earth. "Let the peoples praise You, O God," the temple proclaimed. "Let the nations be glad and sing for joy!"[9]

This lighthouse architecture was just as it should be, for Israel's temple—and the story it represented—proclaimed the good news of the world's salvation. The great Hebrew prophet Isaiah had declared that "the sons of the foreigner who join themselves to the Lord, to serve Him and to love the name of the Lord, to be His servants . . . even them I will bring to My holy mountain and make them joyful in My house of prayer . . . For My house shall be called a house of prayer for all nations."[10] Along with the Jews, the Gentiles were invited to find God at the temple. It stood in Jerusalem not only as a focal point of Israel's worship but as a lodestar for the whole world. People from everywhere could come to the temple and encounter the one true God.

---

8. John 10:18 NLT.
9. Psalm 67:3–4.
10. Isaiah 56:6–7.

When Yeshua exhaled his final breath upon the cross, inside the temple God demonstrated the power that had just been unleashed. Its inner sanctum, the Most Holy Place, was guarded by a magnificent veil that hung from the ceiling to the floor. As soon as the Savior uttered his final words and exhaled his last breath, the mighty hands of God ripped the temple's veil in two. Clearly, this was God's doing, for the veil was torn from top to bottom. Other divine miracles occurred as well. The sun stopped shining and darkness fell upon the land. The gospel of Matthew vividly describes the scene:

> Then, behold, the veil of the temple was torn in two from top to bottom; and the earth quaked, and the rocks were split, and the graves were opened; and many bodies of the saints who had fallen asleep were raised; and coming out of the graves after His resurrection, they went into the holy city and appeared to many. So when the centurion and those with him, who were guarding Jesus, saw the earthquake and the things that had happened, they feared greatly, saying, "Truly this was the Son of God!"[11]

The Mishnah, the first written collection of rabbinic literature, provides some details about the veil that hung in Herod's temple. It recorded that the fabric's thickness was a "handbreadth"—that is, the width of a man's palm at the thumb, or about four inches—quite a hefty piece of cloth! The veil stood sixty feet high and thirty feet wide. Creating such an enormous curtain required eighty-two young girls to serve as weavers. Their duty was to make two new veils every year. Each one was so heavy that when it needed to be removed for cleaning, its transport required three hundred hardworking priests! But a job mere men found laborious presented no obstacle to the creator of the universe. With a great rush of wind and a loud ripping sound, God himself tore the veil wide open.

All afternoon, while the enormous veil hung divided, cleft in two, Yeshua's gashed body hung lifeless on the cross. The corpse stayed there until dusk began to set in. Finally, a rich man named Joseph received permission to take it away. He wrapped the body in a linen shroud and placed it in his own rock-cut tomb. Shaped like a little cave, the tomb was located in a garden that had once

11. Matthew 27:51–54.

been a quarry but had returned to green space. A large, round stone could be rolled across the tomb's entrance to seal it.

In ancient Jewish culture, women were the ones to clean a dead body, anoint it with spices and ointments, and prepare it for long-term burial. Yeshua's female followers (no doubt including his mother) prepared for the task by gathering the needed supplies. Yet as the sun started to go down that Friday night and the Jewish Sabbath began, the women realized they could no longer work. The job of anointing Yeshua's blessed body would have to wait until Sunday morning. Little did they know that God had something different in mind!

It was Yeshua himself, the Anointed One, gloriously risen from the dead, who appeared to the faithful women at dawn that first Easter morning, then to his twelve disciples, then to hundreds more.[12] Yeshua "presented himself alive after His suffering by many infallible proofs, being seen by [His followers] during forty days and speaking of the things pertaining to the kingdom of God."[13] Finally, with all his work accomplished, Yeshua returned to the heavenly home from which he had come.

And then a wonderful thing happened: The Spirit of God took up residence in a new Most Holy Place! The Spirit's mysterious and unexpected outpouring fulfilled what the temple's torn veil had signified—the ripped opening wasn't an entrance into God's presence but an exit to let him out. No longer would God dwell in a golden room in Jerusalem. Now his Holy Spirit had rushed out of the temple to fill the entire world!

Mary, the mother of Jesus, experienced the Spirit's arrival along with the other disciples.[14] They had all assembled in the upper room, a guest chamber in a Jerusalem house where Yeshua's followers had tended to gather. Mary gasped as she discerned tongues of flame leaping over her friends' heads. Then something filled her body, transforming and enlivening it, not in a physical way, yet discernible nonetheless. The only word to describe it was *power*, for that is what her Son had promised. The Spirit of Jesus would empower his followers to take his message from Jerusalem "to the end of the earth."[15]

---

12. Mark 16:1–8; 1 Corinthians 15:6.
13. Acts 1:3.
14. Acts 1:14.
15. Acts 1:8.

Mary knew this feeling of empowerment better than any of the disciples because the Spirit of God had descended on her once before. At that time, God had overshadowed her womb and made her pregnant.[16] Now the Spirit had come again—but this time his presence was permanent, never to depart. Mary could feel her Son's warm love infusing her. Clearly, the Holy Spirit came from him. She knew Yeshua intimately, so she recognized his inner touch. "I am with you always," he had promised, "even to the end of the age."[17] The Spirit of Yeshua was his gift, an abiding presence by which God would energize his people.

Then Mary understood. Many years before, she had brought her newborn infant to the temple for a dedication sacrifice. A prophet named Simeon had predicted her future pain—the sword-piercing agony of watching Yeshua writhe upon the cross. Yet Simeon had also spoken words of praise to God: "For my eyes have seen Your salvation, which You have prepared before the face of all peoples." Mary had learned her precious Son would be "a light to bring revelation to the Gentiles, and the glory of Your people Israel."[18]

That's it! No longer is the temple the only place of God's presence on earth. Now he dwells within people of all nations. Mary marveled to think God had done such an amazing thing through her Son. *Because of Yeshua, people of every race can become the Most Holy Place of the Lord!*

Of course, the followers of this new Way didn't reject the Jerusalem temple. Its fundamental meaning was the same as ever, though now it extended into flesh and blood instead of mere blocks of stone. Under the leadership of James, the new believers were "continuing daily with one accord in the temple, and breaking bread from house to house, they ate their food with gladness and simplicity of heart."[19] These faithful Jews stood in favor with all the residents of Jerusalem.

Yet one vile man lurked in the shadows, a Jew from foreign parts. The young fellow watched the fanatical followers of Yeshua with a hateful eye. Malevolence seeped from him, invisible, yet all too real. Mary noticed him from time to time—a dark presence who seemed to exude evil from his heart.

---

16. Luke 1:35.
17. Matthew 28:20.
18. Luke 2:30–32.
19. Acts 2:46.

She didn't know his name. She hoped she would never meet him. He was someone to avoid at all costs.

Little did Mary know this man's life would soon be transformed in a radical fashion. Her fearsome enemy would perceive the meaning of the temple's ripped veil better than anyone else. "Do you not know you are the temple of God," he would one day write to fellow believers, "and that the Spirit of God dwells in you?"[20] One day, those profound words would define the destiny of this zealous Jew. Although Mary didn't yet know it, his name was Saul of Tarsus, and he was destined to change the world.

CODA

After each chapter, we (Kathie and Bryan) have included a transcription of our conversations about what we have learned. As you reflect on this chapter, our prayer is that you see Jesus through the eyes of his mother, Mary—a connection point to our previous book, *Herod and Mary*. She can be a model for parents who walk with their children through suffering. We also want to emphasize the new way that God is working: no longer through a man-made temple in a certain location, but in a new kind of temple—the people of God in whom the Spirit lives because of what Jesus has accomplished. This new intimacy with God will be a key element of Paul's gospel proclamation.

BRYAN: The opening scenes of this book may seem a surprising place to begin, but it's exactly where it should start—with Mary at the foot of the cross, in great despair over the horrendous suffering of her Son, Jesus. It's fitting, isn't it?

KATHIE: It's perfect. It's the way our first book ended, with Mary, and the baby Jesus, not in her womb, but holding him, lifting him up to the man suffering on the cross. It couldn't be more perfect.

BRYAN: Our readers may want to go back and review *Herod and Mary*, if they haven't yet, maybe even before they read *Nero and Paul*. Both are written as narrative nonfiction but in the telling we reveal the fascinating historical

20. 1 Corinthians 3:16.

background. So yes, it's perfect, but hard, too, because here's a mother watching her Son suffer greatly. Maybe we talk about that. Kathie, what do you think it was like for Mary to stand there at the foot of the cross? We know from Scripture she was there with John. What was that like? Because it wasn't like he was way up high, thirty feet above the ground.

KATHIE: No, she was able to look him right in the eyes. As a mother myself, I can't even imagine the agony she was experiencing.

BRYAN: Right in the eyes, yeah. People were crucified down low, at street level. What do you think that was like for her as a mother?

KATHIE: Agony. Jesus was going through agony as well of course but it was a different kind of agony. Jesus was never a parent, he didn't have the experience of having had children, yet he was also the creator of the universe. So he obviously understood things that we don't understand. But as a mother who received the message from the angel and believed it, Mary didn't battle it and didn't fight against it. She just surrendered to it. And she "treasured up all these things and pondered them in her heart."[21] All these things. She'd been told by the different people that she met, that had prayed over him, that she would have to go through this. It was all very prophetic stuff. So she knew what was coming. She also knew the Torah. She knew what it said, that the Messiah would suffer. I get the feeling she was brilliant—a brilliant and instinctively beautiful human being. And she knew her child was unique. But now here he was, suffering such terrible agony, right before her eyes.

BRYAN: I wonder if Mary thought of that scripture where it says, "They will look on Me whom they pierced."[22] I wonder if that came to her mind as she looked upon her Son who was pierced.

KATHIE: How would one ever even prepare for that, Bryan? Jesus is about thirty-three years old. My son, Cody, is about to turn thirty-five next week. I can't even imagine looking into the face of my son who's not only suffering right now but has just been tortured with whips. His eyes . . . he was such a beautiful human being. In my mind and imagination Jesus was beautiful and people were attracted to him because of his kindness and gentleness. He only became unrecognizable after he was tortured. And Mary gave birth to him, to

---

21. Luke 2:19.
22. Zechariah 12:10.

God. I mean, nobody in history can ever say that, right? And that's what is so interesting about our story about Nero. Compare it to his mother, Agrippina. She gave birth to a man who called himself a god. But Mary actually gave birth to God himself!

BRYAN: Yeah, that's a great comparison. I love that. We will see in this book that there's these two mothers, too, right? It's not just Nero and Paul. It's also Agrippina and Mary.

KATHIE: And you know, one of them had goals for her son that were simply evil because she wanted power. Everything was about the lust for power. But Mary knew the Torah. She knew that the name Immanuel means "God with us," and the name Jesus meant he was going to save humankind for all time.

BRYAN: Yes, he's the true Savior, but the emperors were also called "savior." At least they were hailed as "lord and savior." Those are biblical words, but they were applying them to the emperor—falsely, of course.

KATHIE: I love the biblical word you taught me recently. I've almost memorized it.

BRYAN: *Skubala!* It's from Philippians 3:8, where Paul says he counts all things as "rubbish" compared to knowing Christ. But really, it can mean something gross, like "dung" or "crap."

KATHIE: Anyone else who's trying to be the world's savior is full of crap! Emperor Nero was full of *skubala*!

BRYAN: That's for sure! And some people knew from the start who the real Savior was, but the world didn't recognize him at first. Scripture says that when Mary took the baby Jesus to the temple, he was prophesied over.[23]

KATHIE: Yes! Both Simeon and Anna prophesied over him.

BRYAN: Simeon said, "You will be pierced."[24] He was saying to Mary that she will be pierced with suffering. And now here she is looking on the one who was pierced prophetically. So she felt the piercing in her gut as she looked at her Son's piercings. And that's nearly impossible for a mother. Do you have any advice for a parent who might be going through a trial and watching their children suffer?

---

23. Luke 2:25–38.
24. Luke 2:35, author's paraphrase.

KATHIE: You've been there. So have I. As hard as it is to suffer yourself, there is nothing more profoundly crushing than to watch someone you love suffer. You'd take their place in an instant if you could. I remember that with my father and my mother when they were dying. I'd say, "Just end their suffering, Lord!" And Frank, even though he wasn't suffering terribly from what he was going through with chronic traumatic encephalopathy, CTE, from all the microconcussions from playing football, he *was* suffering. And you just say, "Well, Lord, end it, then. It's not your will that any of us should suffer." But I would gladly take their place. I don't know that I could ever say, "I'll get up on that cross, Lord, and hang naked in front of people" and all of that. I don't think I could do it, but I would want the suffering to end.

BRYAN: And I can imagine if Mary could have done it, she would want that. Imagine if somehow she took Jesus down from the cross, healed his wounds, and he went on to live the rest of his life. She would be happy in one sense that she rescued him. But all of us would lose our salvation.

KATHIE: But she didn't do that. She knew what the endgame was. Somebody told me years ago that the meaning of what Jesus said on the cross at the end was not "It is finished" but "It is accomplished." I mean, he still had work to do. He was going to be buried, he was going to be resurrected, and then work with the apostles and the disciples, and then be ascended. And then all the work that's done in sanctification with the Holy Spirit. In that sense, it is not yet finished. But on the cross, "It is accomplished" was what he was saying. He's the only human being ever born with the singular goal of dying. The purpose of Jesus being born was so he would die. He was the ultimate, perfect sacrifice, a blood sacrifice for sin. And when he died, he said, "It is accomplished. I died. That was my purpose."

BRYAN: Our book opens with "It is finished" because you read that in the Bible. The verb means to bring something to an end. Yet the meaning goes beyond that. And by the end of that scene, we point it out.

KATHIE: Yes. It was just a section of his life and purpose that he finished, a season of suffering. When I heard about "It is accomplished," it helped me understand he was saying, "This part of my journey is done. God, my Father, sent me to die. He sent me to be born to die." And I've never gotten over that. The whole concept is the hope that Jesus brought. Mary kept that stored in her heart. She knew the Torah. It's so important to keep emphasizing that.

She knew that the Messiah would come and would suffer and would save the Jewish people and even the Gentiles. She knew that part of it too. And there were no Gentiles, I don't think, at the crucifixion, except for maybe the centurion at the end who said, "Surely he was was the Son of God."[25] He might have been the first convert, you know.

BRYAN: Right, he might have been, that's a great point. In fact, that's kind of the segue to the second scene that we have in the prologue. He sees the earthquake and the dark sun. And the centurion is not only a Gentile, but he's the ultimate representative of Rome standing there.

KATHIE: And the ultimate eyewitness. But he doesn't know what happened to the temple veil.

BRYAN: The ultimate eyewitness, right. And because the temple veil is torn, and because God's presence has gone out, like you're saying, he very well might be the first Gentile convert. And it's interesting that in the Gospels or the book of Acts, it's often centurions who convert, like Cornelius. So the Gentiles, even the military men, even the violent men, even the ultimate Romans are bowing the knee to the true Son of God, all because the Holy Spirit has come out of the temple. But here's the question, Kathie: What if that centurion was the man with the hammer who had nailed Christ up to that cross? What if he was the same man now saying, "That was the Son of God, whom I just put on the cross." That's sobering to think about.

KATHIE: Yes! And maybe he said, "What have I done?" Or did Judas say, "What have I done?" Judas knew the minute they gave him the silver, "Oh, my God, what have I done?"

BRYAN: Mary was in the upper room when the torn veil brought power, when it allowed the shekinah presence of God, the Holy Spirit of God, to fill the church. She was there when that presence descended on her.

KATHIE: The mother of God received the Holy Spirit of God. All the disciples did. With the tongues of flame.

BRYAN: And so all the disciples realized, including Mary, this is prophecy being fulfilled in our midst. The temple is across town in Jerusalem, but here we are in the upper room, and we're seeing the fire, which was the fire that led the Israelites in the wilderness, the fire of God, the flaming shekinah that

25. Matthew 27:54 NIV.

once dwelled in the temple. It is now right here above us. That was big news to everybody! That is the idea of the temple veil being torn. I mean, really, it's sort of universalizing the gospel. It's Paul's message, right?

KATHIE: It's Paul's gospel, yes. And I think we are very clear about that. The gospel is the good news that all people have been looking for since the dawn of humankind.

BRYAN: So those believers are called on a mission and the new temple is not the upper room and it's not Herod's temple—which our first book was so much about. We talked about the beauty of that building, which, by the way, at the end of this book, is destroyed.

KATHIE: Right. They were all confused about where to go. "We've got to be over here or over there to know God." But the beautiful thing is that God is in so many places, and he said, "I will be with you, I will come alongside you."[26] We don't need man-made religion. This is *my* message—the gospel! I want nothing to do with religion. I want everything to do with the living God! I can't stand religion, and I can't stand what it does to people. It puts us in chains. Jesus came along to free us from all of it. And yet some people prefer it. I mean, the Pharisees and the Sadducees, they wanted it. It controlled their environment. It controlled the money. And it's so often about power and the money. But God didn't come to give us rules for religion and power. He came to give us a relationship with him.

BRYAN: You sound like the apostle Paul because you're proclaiming his message! It's not about rule keeping and man-made religion. It's about Yeshua, the Savior, indwelling you as the temple of God. Kathie, you just encapsulated the whole message of this book! You sound like the apostle Paul when you're saying these things.

KATHIE: Well, I'm better looking. He was apparently quite homely. [Gestures to self.] He didn't look like all this, baby!

BRYAN: They say he had a bald head and a unibrow. A single eyebrow grown together.

KATHIE: Oh, I take care of that every day!

---

26. Isaiah 41:10, author's paraphrase.

ONE

THE ZEAL OF SAUL

Sweat dripped from Paul's forehead and soaked his dirty, ragged tunic. The air in the dungeon felt close, sultry, heavy. Though the summer sun beat down on the stone walls of the Carcer in Rome, the prison where he awaited his execution, the burning rays didn't offer the gift of illumination. The tightly locked door and lack of windows saw to that. Only the sun's oppressive heat reminded him of its presence outside. Despite being a frail old man, Paul, who had been known as Saul before he became an apostle, was incarcerated in Rome's darkest and most terrifying jail—the very thing he had done to the followers of Yeshua many years before. Now, like them, Paul endured harsh imprisonment while waiting for the mercy of God. Though we don't know all the details, the infamous horrors of the Carcer provide a vivid picture of what it must have been like for Paul.

As if the heat wasn't bad enough, the place reeked of sewage. A bucket in the corner supposedly served the prisoners' toilet needs, but since the soldiers never emptied it, the bucket had long since overflowed and no one bothered to use it anymore. Two other convicts were chained with Paul, both emaciated and hopeless. Though he had explained the gospel to the suffering men, their fogged minds gave no evidence they had understood. *May God have mercy on their souls*, Paul prayed.

Occasionally, a desolate wail arose from a hole in the prison's floor. A second cell was located below the main level—the fearsome Tullianum, a pit from which no one emerged alive. Down there, a lone prisoner languished in utter darkness, gradually starving to death. The main-level Carcer had been built by Rome's fourth king, seven hundred years before the time of Paul. But it was Rome's sixth king who had made the place even worse by turning an old cistern below the floor into the second, subterranean cell. That king was Servius Tullius, whose ancient name the Tullianum now bore. He had installed a sewer to drain the spring waters that naturally bubbled into the cistern. Now the Tullianum was a dank, cold dungeon where convicts awaited a terrible death. If starvation was taking too long, a quick strangulation could finish the job. Then the corpse could be dumped down the sewer and the victim would never be spoken of again.

Paul didn't believe such a lingering fate would await him. As a Roman citizen, his death, if decreed, would be cleaner. Perhaps he could avoid the Tullianum. *I hope so*, he thought. *It is a fearsome place!*

A creaking sound, accompanied by a sudden rush of blinding light, indicated the Carcer's door had been opened. The two other forlorn prisoners stirred in their chains and drew back to the walls, terrified and trembling, for the door's opening usually meant bad things. Perhaps they would be dumped into the Tullianum, or be beaten, or be strangled where they lay. Maybe they would be tortured for the soldiers' amusement. Or they might be dragged outside and put on trial, leading to an inevitable sentence of crucifixion. Only rarely did the soldiers bring any food. The opening of the door normally brought trouble.

Paul, however, didn't move, for he was unafraid. He wasn't ashamed of his chains, nor did he want anyone to think he was. As for death, it held no power over him. "To live is Christ, and to die is gain" was his confident motto.[1] In the darkness of the Carcer he reminded himself of it often.

Two legionaries stepped into the gloom, helmeted and clad in armor. Though their swords remained sheathed, both men carried spears in case the prisoners grew unruly. Then Paul discerned a third man behind them, a visitor whose identity was unclear as he stood silhouetted against the doorway. But when he crossed the threshold, Paul's heart leapt with joy. *Onesiphorus!* He was a visitor from Ephesus, one of Paul's dearest friends. A bribe had allowed him entrance into the cell. He walked in with a leather satchel slung over his shoulder. Precious things would surely be inside it.

---

1. Philippians 1:21.

"Don't stay too long," one of the soldiers said gruffly as he shoved Onesiphorus toward Paul, who reclined on a straw mat. Both guards exited the prison, leaving the door ajar.

Onesiphorus kneeled beside the mat and greeted Paul in the name of the Lord. After the two exchanged warm expressions of brotherly affection, Onesiphorus opened his satchel and withdrew a barley loaf, a jar of olives, and three sardines wrapped in vine leaves. Immediately, Paul divided the food into thirds and had Onesiphorus distribute two of the portions to the foul-smelling prisoners nearby. They snatched the food and wolfed it down with no words of gratitude. A jug of watered wine also helped to slake their terrible thirst. As for the man in the Tullianum below, no food or drink was given to him. Even if he could somehow find it in the darkness, it would only prolong his suffering.

Onesiphorus returned to Paul's side and once again reached into his satchel. "I have something else that will please you," he said with a smile on his bearded lips. Then he withdrew his second gift.

"Parchments!" Paul exclaimed. "And ink! And reed pens!"

Onesiphorus set the items on the dungeon floor, then added a clay lamp, a sealed jar of olive oil, and a fire striker with some tinder. "Now, my brother, you can write words of hope, even in this place of darkness and fear."

"Yes," Paul agreed, clutching Onesiphorus's arm, "the Word of God must shine forth. I have so many things to say to the brethren. And first among them, I shall write to my beloved Timothy."

After Onesiphorus departed, Paul didn't immediately light his lamp. A tiny bit of sunlight crept around the frame of the door, as well as through a few cracks in the walls, providing just enough light to see by during the day. It was nighttime that terrified the prisoners the most. Then everything was utterly black—the deep darkness of the blind. The long nights stretched on and on, slowly creeping by, like sand through an hourglass, often without the relief of sleep. Paul thought he would prefer to save his lamp for those dreadful times.

Gradually, his drifting thoughts returned to the early days in Jerusalem, to his first encounter with the followers of the Way. *How I hated those people! Oh Lord, forgive me!* Memories of his acts of persecution often assaulted Paul, causing vivid dreams in which he murdered God's people while the ugly demons around him laughed. He would gasp and wake up in a cold sweat from those nightmares, even in the muggy confines of the Carcer. "You are the chief of sinners!" the demons would screech. Only the remembrance of the gospel would banish their fearsome accusations.

Why had he persecuted the followers of the Way? He could picture each of them so clearly: how James, the Lord's brother, would preach the Torah from the temple's steps; how Mary, the Lord's mother, would offer tender memories of her Son; how Peter, the Lord's leading disciple, would explain the contours of the gospel. *They all offended me so terribly. Zeal for the Lord's house consumed me—but I did not yet understand!*

The term *zeal* was an important one for Paul. It had defined his life before he met Yeshua. "I advanced in Judaism beyond many of my contemporaries in my own nation, being more exceedingly zealous for the traditions of my fathers."[2] Paul's Greek word was *zelotes*, describing a person with great concern for the Torah and the temple. A party of especially devoted men had started calling themselves "Zealots." In fact, even one of Yeshua's own disciples was known as Simon the Zealot to distinguish him from Simon Peter. Simon the Zealot's devotion to God's Word was intense, uncompromising, and very sincere.

Sometimes, the excessive zeal of these men could erupt into violence. They believed God alone, not any human figure, should be their ruler and Lord. Earlier that summer, some Zealots in Jerusalem had taken a leading role in riots that had broken out when a Roman governor had stolen money from the temple treasury—an act to which the Zealots objected, since that money belonged to God. In the mayhem, several imperial soldiers were lynched, then the Romans retaliated with crucifixions. The violence quickly spiraled into outright rebellion against Rome. From the dark confines inside the prison walls, Paul now wondered whether the war was still continuing in Jerusalem.

Though he wasn't a member of the Zealots, the same kind of zealous spirit had animated him, leading him to persecute the movement called the Way. Later, he explained himself to his Israelite brethren like this: "I am indeed a Jew, born in Tarsus of Cilicia, but brought up in this city [Jerusalem] at the

2. Galatians 1:14.

feet of Gamaliel, taught according to the strictness of our fathers' law, and was *zealous toward God* as you all are today."[3]

Likewise, he explained to the Philippians that if anyone should have put confidence in having intense zeal for the Torah, it was him. He was "circumcised the eighth day, of the stock of Israel, of the tribe of Benjamin, a Hebrew of the Hebrews; concerning the law, a Pharisee; *concerning zeal, persecuting the church*; concerning the righteousness which is in the law, blameless."[4] Although Paul later considered his persecution of the church to be a terrible sin, before his conversion he thought he was doing God's work. If zeal for the divine law required pruning some dead branches off Israel's tree—the supposed heretics who had accepted the false prophet named Yeshua—he didn't mind serving as the pruning shears in the hands of the Lord.

As Paul's mind sifted the painful memories from his persecuting days, he recalled that the first branch to be snipped from Israel's vine by his misguided shears was a holy man named Stephen who had been debating the Jews in Jerusalem, trying to show the true meaning of God's Torah and the temple. Stephen announced that everything had come together in the person of Jesus of Nazareth. But false witnesses slandered Stephen, forcing him to defend himself against charges of blasphemy before the Jewish council called the Sanhedrin. "Are these accusations true?" the high priest had asked him. Filled with the Holy Spirit, Stephen replied by proclaiming the story of Israel.

Stephen's account began with the Jewish patriarch Abraham. God called him from his distant home to the promised land of Israel—an inheritance intended for his innumerable offspring. Yet Abraham's grandson Jacob found himself forced to immigrate to Egypt because of a famine. For four hundred years, his descendants, the Israelites, endured harsh slavery in that country, until God raised up Moses as a deliverer. After God revealed himself to Moses at the burning bush, Moses drew courage and led God's people out of Egypt. During their wilderness sojourn, they worshiped at their movable tabernacle.

3. Acts 22:3.
4. Philippians 3:5–6.

But once they had entered the promised land, a mere tent no longer sufficed to house the Lord's holy presence. Eventually, King David decided to build a permanent dwelling place for the God of Jacob. Yet it was his son Solomon who achieved it.

So far, Stephen's explanation had provided a perfectly acceptable narrative to the Jewish leaders of the Sanhedrin. It was their own story, the biblical story, the one they knew and loved. But things took a sudden, dangerous turn when Stephen made a new proclamation to these men whose temple served as their base of power. "The Most High does not dwell in temples made with hands," Stephen announced, then quoted God's statement to Isaiah to back up his words: "'Heaven is My throne, and earth is My footstool. What house will you build for Me?' says the Lord, 'Or what is the place of My rest? Has My hand not made all these things [in creation]?'"[5]

After proclaiming the new, universal form of worship—no longer limited to a man-made building—Stephen fiercely accused the Sanhedrin of spiritual blindness. He called them stiff-necked toward God and the children of forefathers who had slain the prophets. Now they had betrayed and murdered the Righteous One, totally disregarding the true meaning of the Torah.

The leaders flew into a rage at these words and gnashed their teeth at Stephen like wild animals. When he gazed up into heaven and announced that he saw Yeshua standing in glory at God's right hand, the national leaders howled, stopped their ears, and leapt into action. Their minions dragged Stephen outside the city and surrounded him. They stripped him of his clothing, leaving him naked and defenseless. He stood in their midst with his hands bound behind his back. Though Rome forbade capital punishment, the enraged mob couldn't be stopped. Stephen had to be killed! To free their arms for hurling heavy rocks, they laid their cloaks and robes in a pile to be guarded by a watchman. His name was Saul of Tarsus.

As the elderly apostle reclined on the floor of the Carcer in Rome, the horrific memories of Stephen's martyrdom came flooding into his mind, just as they

---

5. Acts 7:48–50.

often did in his nightmares. We can imagine how vividly he must have remembered the vicious spirit that took hold of the mob that day. Stephen stood upright in holy tranquility, gazing toward the clouds where he had claimed to see his Lord. But stoning was a violent death that would break the martyr's tranquil pose. The goal of stoning was to make the death communal. Everyone participated. The community as a whole rejected the victim. No one could say whose stone had dealt the final blow. All the participants held collective responsibility for the death. Together, they were cleansing the filth from the nation's midst.

Paul grimaced as he recalled the violence of the first stone striking the church's original martyr. It was a melon-sized chunk, jagged along its edges. With a dull thud, it hit Stephen in the ribs, shattering them in a spray of blood. Many others followed, each ripping his skin and breaking his bones. Though he tried to remain standing, the hail of rocks rained down on him like the devil's firestorm. "Lord Jesus, receive my spirit!" Stephen cried as he fell to his knees.[6]

More stones hammered into the kneeling martyr, tearing his flesh in each place they struck. Like a butchered piece of meat, a glossy redness covered Stephen's body. As the mob's rage surged, they seized even larger stones, raising them above their heads with two hands before hurling them down with murderous fire in their eyes.

A weak voice came from the torn and battered victim as he succumbed to the onslaught. He swayed on his knees, barely able to remain upright. "Lord, do not charge them with this sin," he whispered.[7]

The next chunk of limestone struck Stephen square in the face. Gore flew into the air as he toppled over. Rocks cascaded onto the helpless figure lying prone in the blood-drenched sand. At last, he no longer moved or spoke. No breath stirred his mutilated frame. His twitching ceased. The job was done. Stephen was dead. Israel had been cleansed.

Praise be to God, the zealot Saul prayed as he stood over the garments of the frenzied mob. *The blasphemer has received what he deserved. May every follower of Yeshua receive the same!*

---

6. Acts 7:59.
7. Acts 7:60.

CODA

In this conversation, we emphasize the help that a friend's encouragement can provide in dark times. So often, God's grace is mediated to his people through friends. We also try to find the line between being zealous for God's glory yet not being harsh. And we consider Stephen's martyrdom as an example of the sacrifices that have to be made to follow God to the utmost.

BRYAN: In this first chapter we flash forward to the time when Paul is not called by his Jewish Hebrew name Saul anymore, but Paul, his Gentile name. It's also when he's no longer the evil figure Mary saw in the early days. We drop in on him as he is nearing death in the Carcer. We get the word *incarcerated* from that; you are literally "in the Carcer." He's in jail, like in a dungeon. And yet Onesiphorus comes and ministers to him. And so let's just think about that for a minute.

KATHIE: Why did they let him in?

BRYAN: At that time you would give a little money, a little bribe. The soldiers expected to make money off the prisoners because they didn't give them rations or food. So whoever was your friend would have to come and bring you food. And, of course, a little extra for the soldiers' pockets, and they would let you in. That's the only reason. The ancient church collected offerings, and often the money, among other things, was for visiting the imprisoned. And so here's an imagined scene of them doing that. Let's maybe think a little bit about the question: Have you ever been down in the dark dungeon of life, and then some friend comes and encourages you? It's very meaningful, isn't it?

KATHIE: It is a light that brings you up out of the darkness. It gives you hope in the darkness. And his friend brings him a little oil lamp and a parchment.

BRYAN: Yes, parchments so he can write to Timothy, because he writes to Timothy from the dungeon, so he would have to have gotten parchments from somewhere. Then in that letter Paul asks him, "Hey, by the way, can you pick up the Scriptures and the parchments and bring them to me? Because I've got more writing I want to do."[8]

KATHIE: He's on fire at this time—on fire for the gospel! We try to bring those scenes to life in our book, scenes that are so beautiful, because we're

---

8. 2 Timothy 4:13, author's paraphrase.

seeing the exact opposite with the abundance of bestiality and everything on the Roman side, and the orgies and the food and the wine and the drunkenness on the side of Nero. But here's Paul, with nothing but the presence of God in his life, truly, truly. And he has written a lot about his suffering, but he always says, "I deserved it. I was the worst of sinners."[9] But I'd say Nero was worse than him. I'm sorry, but he was! That's amazing, isn't it? Paul killed believers. But Nero did too. Nero, once he got to doing that, he didn't hold back. Yet Paul said he was the "chief of sinners."[10]

BRYAN: We all have to think that way, don't we? I mean, it's easy to say, "Hitler was worse, or, you know, somebody else, they're bad. I'm kind of medium." But everybody needs to think, "I am the chief of sinners, yet the Chief of saviors has come and saved me."

KATHIE: That's right. That's right. And there is no condemnation in him.[11]

BRYAN: Paul has to get you to that place of being the chief of sinners before you are really gonna accept the gospel, because you can too easily accept halfway gospels. Like, I'm pretty good, and if God gives me a boost of grace, I'll kind of do some decent stuff. You gotta get to that lowest of low points, and Paul felt it himself, where he said, "I am nothing, Christ is everything."[12]

KATHIE: And we talk so much in this chapter about how he really had this zealousness for God. He thought everything he was doing was justified.

BRYAN: What do you think of that word *zealous*, like when he says, "I was zealous for the law"? That's the thing he talks about the most from before his conversion, before the road to Damascus. *Zealous* is his favorite word. Do you think of it as positive or negative?

KATHIE: He felt that it was positive. I think he was probably trying to get a place in the Sanhedrin. This was an ambitious man, and he was making a big name for himself. So were the other rabbis; they were all trying in their own way to be the next high priest. That's what I think Paul thought: This way of behaving will get me some brownie points.

BRYAN: But should we be zealous today? Is that something Christians should say about themselves?

---

9. 1 Timothy 1:15, author's paraphrase.
10. 1 Timothy 1:15, author's paraphrase.
11. Romans 8:1.
12. Galatians 2:20, author's paraphrase.

KATHIE: I don't like the word. I don't like extremism. To me, it sounds incredibly religious, and I avoid those terms.

BRYAN: Yeah, me too. But you know what's interesting is while it can have that connotation of extremism, when Jesus drove out the money changers with the whip, which was an act of social disobedience, what Scripture verse was quoted about him? "His disciples remembered that it is written: 'Zeal for your house will consume me.'"[13]

KATHIE: So that kind of zeal, yeah, maybe that's good. It's like a fire for God, having a fire for his Word, or being on fire for God.

BRYAN: That's a cleansing thing, isn't it? A cleansing fire.

KATHIE: Right. It doesn't feel good when it's on fire, but when it's done, beauty comes from the ashes of it. So that is my preferred word. But at the same time, I was not Paul. We were not raised that way. His world was a completely different place. We were not under the control of the Romans. Nor the rabbis who added laws. There were about six hundred more laws put on them that they had to keep. How did the people do it? They even had to tithe on their spices, you know? Just a few flakes of spice. I mean, are you kidding?

BRYAN: Again, you sound just like Paul, because that was his message: The law came not because you could keep it but to teach you that you certainly can't keep it apart from God's grace. Bottom line, it all has to be about grace. But there were differences back then, too, just like with all people. It's like today—the Presbyterians and the Baptists both love Jesus, but one will say baptize a baby and one doesn't. There are these different ways of following Christ. And then, of course, there are heresies too. Some teachings are just plain false.

KATHIE: We should call the Pharisees "the Scarisees" because they're scary. I can't stand being around the Scarisees!

BRYAN: Me either! As we finish chapter 1, at the end we have a final scene where Paul is indeed scary, and he displays his zeal, right? He's like, "I'm so zealous, I'm so much a cleansing fire that I need to cleanse Israel from false prophets." So he thinks this guy, Stephen, who follows this supposedly false messiah, has to be cleansed or pruned off the bush of Israel, as we say. But they mean to murder him. So what about Stephen and his martyrdom? We talked about Jesus and his suffering on the cross. Can you imagine death by stoning?

---

13. John 2:17 NIV.

KATHIE: You know, everything in Stephen's life—and we don't know that much about him—but I think everything was preparing him for that moment. Jesus was right there with him.

BRYAN: All the Christian martyrs always say, "When I'm suffering, Christ is suffering in me."[14] It's true. He is right there in the midst of the suffering. So is martyrdom ugly and satanic? Or a martyrdom like Stephen's, is it beautiful? Or somehow both?

KATHIE: It's both. It's ugly. It's evil. I can't even imagine it. I would be a very bad martyr. I would hope God would give me grace. But I have no doubt that what comes from it is the beauty we know comes from ashes. I just think about a Joan of Arc scenario, you know, literally ashes. You think about someone who is burned at the stake. You think about what Nero did to the believers, the horrendous story we include at the end of the book, right? We have to trust that Jesus would never leave us or forsake us, ever. Stephen knew it because he knew Jesus personally. Or maybe he never actually met him. We don't know. But he might have.

BRYAN: The Bible says there were over five hundred disciples that knew him and saw the risen Christ.[15] So maybe Stephen was one of those. The martyrdom of Stephen ends with Paul standing there supervising the cloaks, and he's approving it. Which is interesting because he later becomes a martyr as well. What an irony that at the beginning of our book the wicked Saul, who is unsaved at that point, is looking with hatred on a Christian martyr, but his destiny is to someday become a Christian martyr himself.

KATHIE: And I think the death of Stephen must have inflamed him all the more to go to Damascus. He is saying, "Now I'm going after those other misguided followers outside of Jerusalem. They're trying to hide, they're trying to get away, but they can't. We will find them, and we will destroy them, and destroy this false messiah."

BRYAN: That's a good transition, because, yes, Stephen's martyrdom leads Paul to Damascus. But first we need to bring Nero into the story!

TWO

THE "GOSPELS" OF ROME AND ISRAEL

Emperor Nero felt his heart begin to race as he approached the naked woman's corpse. It lay upon a couch beneath a shroud of linen. The thin cloth rose and fell along the contours of her body from her forehead to her toes. Bloodstains, so fresh their redness hadn't yet faded to rust, marked the shroud like pustules on a leper's skin. The biggest stain lay over the woman's belly, the place where she had been stabbed the deepest. Yet it was just one wound of many. Numerous blows had been required to kill her.

We can imagine that Nero must have sat for a long time in the dimly lit bedroom and stared at the corpse. He remained unmoving, not because he was emotionless, but because the turbulence of his emotions made him afraid to act. At last, he gathered his courage and managed to say, "Remove it." His command had no regal force behind it, for his voice cracked and his words came out like a schoolboy caught red-handed in mischief. Nevertheless, the slave obeyed immediately, laying bare the woman who would never again rise from her couch.

Her skin was pale, yet not so much as to suggest death's pallor had taken full control. No rigidity had yet seized her limbs. The wounds had been hurriedly washed, removing at least some of their gore lest it offend Nero's noble eyes. A tiny bit of warmth rose from the woman's skin as Nero's hand hovered over her wrist. *Do I dare touch it?* Instead of making a mental decision, an inner compulsion answered the question for him. He caressed the wrist, then lifted the arm. When he released the limb, it flopped back onto the couch with the familiar limpness of a cadaver. *She's truly dead.* The thought was at once comforting and horrific.

Nero's eyes strayed across the woman's body. He bent over the wound in her belly and gave it a close inspection. After starting to extend his finger, he drew it back, then renewed his determination and touched the gash. He told himself the gentle probing was a scientific verification, not a defiling desecration. Though he wanted to bend his ear close to the woman's breast and listen for a heartbeat, even an emperor had his limits. The slave would see the intimate gesture and word would get out. People would find him repulsive, tarnishing his reputation even further. So Nero resisted the urge and gave the woman's body one last sweep with his eyes. Then he spun away.

"I did not know she was so beautiful," he said.

No one dared reply to the macabre observation, but that didn't matter. Nero hadn't addressed the words to the slave, or to the frightened morticians who stood in the corner, but simply to the cosmos. Perhaps the Furies would hear it—those goddesses who wreaked vengeance upon evildoers. Perhaps they would go lightly on him with their punishments. Nero's mind recoiled as he anticipated how their mental whips would soon assail him. *You did the right thing,* he told himself. Yet his reassurance felt fake, so comfort remained elusive. He gestured to the morticians, snapping his fingers to punctuate his command: "Take her away and cremate her. Do it this very night. Then never speak of it again." The men jumped into action as Nero left the room.

Over the next week, the guilt-ridden emperor could barely eat or sleep. Tears of regret came often, but frequent rages consumed him as well. Long bouts of comatose silence separated those extremes. Food of any kind sickened him, so he always pushed away the plate after a few bites. Whenever he managed to fall into a doze, the lightest of disturbances would awaken him. Sometimes, Nero shot up from his bed from no cause at all, his heart racing and his body drenched in sweat. Other times, he would hear trumpets in the distance. He knew it must be a funeral march of the dead, a fanfare played by ghostly fingers on behalf of a woman falsely accused. *No—not falsely! Guilty! She deserved it!* Despite that thought, it still felt wrong.

A fearsome task lay before Nero, one he dreaded because it would seal his fate in one direction or another. For now, he remained in limbo, living quietly in his seaside villa at Baiae. The people of this sleepy resort town wouldn't pass judgment on him. They possessed insufficient power to raise a revolt. But not so in Rome. The citizenry there could unite into a vast mob that no single man could resist, especially not if the Praetorian Guard abandoned him. And that didn't even factor in the Senate. Such an august, patrician body from the days of old had enough power—if its members could muster a unified political will—to take out an emperor and replace him with a better one. Nero feared that once the senators laid eyes on him, they would do just that.

At last Nero determined to return to the capital and meet his fate. As the day approached, he sent a letter ahead to the Senate. It had one main purpose: to absolve him of guilt for any wrongdoing. The murder was necessary, he claimed. The woman was a conspirator who had sent an assassin. She refused to keep her female place, instead stirring up political intrigues. The whole empire had been in danger of collapse unless drastic action had been taken, so no crime had been committed. On the contrary, a mortal enemy of the state had been eliminated. Surely the gods rejoiced!

The sea voyage from Baiae to Ostia, the port of Rome, took two days. As Nero passed through the Porta Trigemina, the triple gate by which the Ostian Way entered Rome, a feeling of dread made his body tense up. He could hear the roar of a mob in the streets. Would it be friendly or hostile? Not until his eyes fell upon the people's faces did Nero receive his answer. *Smiles! Good cheer! Approval! Happiness all around!* A flood of relief washed over him. He was saved! His life had been redeemed. The people were treating him like a conquering hero, a victor bringing good news for all mankind. Nero was no criminal, but an evangelist with glad tidings for the world. Tyranny had been defeated. Now the Roman Empire could flourish!

Proceeding directly to the Senate House, Nero found the elite aristocrats united in his favor. Only one senator, a man of principle, had dared to make any criticism. He had removed himself from the day's gathering with the words "Nero might be able to kill me, but he cannot harm me." *I can do both,* Nero thought. *And I most certainly will.*

For the next several days the whole city celebrated Nero. Again and again the Senate showered him with honors and passed laws of which they knew he approved. Though some disturbing omens occurred, Nero did his best to dismiss them. An eclipse darkened the sky so much that the stars could be seen by day. Then the elephants that drew his chariot into the Circus Maximus refused to walk past the senators in their boxes. Worst of all, a lightning bolt struck Nero's garden party, destroying his banquet like a vengeful eagle snatching away its prey. *No matter*, Nero assured himself. *The gods approve of me. They have hidden my crime from the public. Everyone believes I hold only good things in store for them!*

At dawn one morning, while Nero dreamed upon his bed about his divine favor, two imperial clerks descended from his palace and entered the Forum. An infant's wail caught their attention, so they walked over to a covered basket. Inside it was a baby wrapped in cloths—a waif abandoned by an impoverished mother who had no means to care for it.

The clerks noticed a tag affixed to the infant's basket. One of them bent down and read the words, then turned to his companion with widened eyes. "We mustn't let Caesar hear of this!"

The other man could sense the fear in his friend's voice. "Why not? What does it say?"

"It is a rebuke," the first man replied. "The mother says she cannot raise this child, lest it do to her what Nero has done."

Now the second man, equally frightened, nodded his agreement. He snatched the tag and threw it down a sewer grate. "Let us speak no more of this," he whispered in urgent tones. "There is no greater crime than for a son to slay his mother."

Among Nero's many atrocities recorded in history, his flagrant matricide, which we've just dramatized, stands out as one of the worst. His mother, Agrippina the Younger, certainly wasn't popular, nor was she innocent. Yet no one believed Nero should have killed her.

Nevertheless, when he returned to Rome after committing the evil deed, he turned his walk of shame into a triumphal entry that brought a saving message to the city. In Nero's way of thinking, he had just defeated the forces of darkness. Victory had been achieved. New prosperity was on its way. Could this be called a message of salvation? Could it even be characterized as a "gospel"?

Modern people tend to think of evangelism as a purely Christian concept. For example, the good news of Yeshua spread across the ancient world after Saul supervised Stephen's martyrdom. Acts 8:1 says, "At that time a great persecution arose against the church which was at Jerusalem; and they were all scattered throughout the regions of Judea and Samaria." Even as Saul began ravaging the church, dragging many believers to jail, God had an evangelistic purpose behind the persecution: "Therefore those who were scattered went everywhere preaching the word."[1] Was this the first-ever proclamation of a gospel message? Far from it. Long before the Christians began to proclaim salvation, the Romans had been articulating their own promise of happiness, security, and abundant life. Like the Christians, they, too, called it "good news." It was an announcement of the blessings their king had to offer.

When Caesar Augustus rose to power in 31 BC, the new ruler took pride in all his accomplishments. Toward the end of his life, he wanted everyone to know what he had done. He composed a lengthy proclamation of his many achievements, titled *Things Accomplished by the Deified Augustus.* In his will, he commanded the Senate to inscribe the text on two bronze plaques to hang on his mausoleum. Although those have been lost, many copies of the decree were made across the empire. Several transcriptions have survived, so the text can be read today.

The *Things Accomplished* begins with Augustus at age nineteen. It recites a litany of his glorious deeds in politics, government, and war. He received numerous ovations and triumphal parades. Many people—even whole provinces—swore oaths of loyalty to him. He constructed temples, aqueducts, bridges, and roads; founded new colonies; and distributed lavish public donations from the spoils of war or his own personal funds. For entertainment purposes, he put on gladiator shows, naval reenactments, and animal fights (in which a total of 3,500 African beasts were slain by professional hunters). The empire's boundaries expanded as the legions conquered new lands and brought foreign rulers under Rome's dominion. The Senate declared him first in rank out of all men, earning him the name "Father of the Fatherland." Augustus ushered in a golden age known as the Pax Romana, or Roman peace.

1. Acts 8:4.

Though the emperor's prideful decree might not sound like a gospel message to those accustomed to Christian terminology, that is exactly what it was. He wanted his people to hear the good news offered by a victorious king. The secular Greek word for "good news," *euangelion*, is exactly the same word the Bible uses for the gospel. It consists of two parts: the prefix *eu-*, "good," and *angelia*, "announcement." In Latin, the parallel word was *evangelium*. An evangelistic message announced the good things a triumphant king could do for you. Once that king took over, a splendid new age had arrived.

But the roots of this word go back even further than the time of Caesar Augustus. Long before it was a Roman or Christian word, it was a Hebrew word, a Jewish word, an Israelite word. The story of God bringing good news to earth, promising blessing through his chosen servant, goes all the way back to the garden of Eden. Then the chapters of God's story played themselves out in the pages of the Hebrew Scriptures as his people lost their way, found deliverance, and renewed their expectation for a coming King who would put to right all that had gone wrong in the world.

This was precisely the story that an observant Jew like Saul of Tarsus had been reared upon. He had studied it in depth at the feet of the greatest rabbis of his age. The only thing Saul lacked was the knowledge that Yeshua the Messiah formed the climax of God's saga. Stephen had proclaimed this very message in Saul's hearing, but the vicious persecutor didn't have the eyes to see it. Only divine intervention could make the misguided Pharisee understand.

At first, Saul hoped that, with enough zeal for the Torah and the temple, God's people would receive the glorious kingdom that would banish Rome forever. If some Jewish heretics with a false messiah had to be pruned away with bloodshed, so be it. That was Saul's zealous desire as a young man. He couldn't understand how a crucified criminal could be the Prince of Peace. Soon, though, he would come face-to-face with the real Yeshua—an encounter that would change his life forever. Only through Yeshua would the Israelite gospel rise up and replace the false gospel of Rome. Then the so-called Pax Romana would be replaced by the *shalom Yerushalayim*, the peace of Jerusalem God had offered to all humankind.

During the years when Saul's persecution prompted the followers of Yeshua to spread the message of good news, Nero wasn't yet in charge of the Roman Empire. Instead, the second emperor after Augustus, Tiberius, sat on the imperial throne—though only metaphorically, for he wasn't even living in the capital. He had retreated to the luxurious isle of Capri, where he was ignoring his political responsibilities and indulging in sexual depravity. The natural end of a gospel that offered only earthly gratification was extreme debauchery!

When Tiberius died, his successor picked up the trumpet of Rome's gospel. Tiberius had dragged his adopted son Caligula to Capri so he could keep an eye on him as the heir apparent. Some ancient accounts claim Caligula murdered Tiberius so he could seize the throne. Yet the third emperor proved to be no better than his hedonistic predecessor. Caligula's version of good news followed Tiberius's same path of murderous paranoia and extreme decadence. Holding on to imperial power through whatever means necessary—and enjoying its fleshly benefits—preoccupied Caligula's twisted mind.

But his sister had other ideas. At first, she cooperated with Caligula and played nice. In time, though, she began to conspire against her brother's rule. This devious conniver eventually became one of the most powerful women in all of Roman history.

In AD 37, she gave birth to a son. The noble boy would be her pathway to glory. She burned with ambition to rule the Roman Empire through her offspring. Someday, she fervently hoped, her son would be the king of kings!

The midwives laid the newborn child, wrapped in swaddling cloths, at his father's feet. Only when the father gathered the boy from the ground would he be guaranteed to live. The mother waited for her husband to accept their son. At last, he picked up the bawling infant and announced his name. "He shall be called Lucius Domitius Ahenobarbus," the father declared. And for a while, that was the boy's name.

But it wouldn't last. Eventually he took a new name, the one that would make him infamous through the ages. History knows this ill-fated boy as Nero (AD 37–68). As Agrippina the Younger cradled him close and examined his puckered face, she couldn't have guessed the baby in her arms would one day gaze upon her naked body and consign her corpse to the flames.

CODA

The themes discussed in this conversation reflect our awareness that even a terrible tyrant like Nero didn't start out horrible, but as a sweet child who was corrupted. Sin is universal in the human race, not just in evil dictators. The question is, What gospel will provide the solution? Rome had its message of how to find happiness in life. But the gospel of the true King provides the only real pathway to blessing. It's a message for everyone!

BRYAN: We start with a scene at a later point in Nero's life—just as we did with Paul's life—and then we roll back to the beginning and tell the story from the start.

KATHIE: I like that. Everybody loves a baby, right?

BRYAN: Right, but you don't love someone who just killed his mother, and that's where we begin.

KATHIE: I didn't know how bad his mother was, though. She was pretty bad.

BRYAN: She deserved it, if any woman ever did.

KATHIE: Wow, she sure did.

BRYAN: The sources are pretty clear that it was widely believed Nero inspected Agrippina's naked corpse. They say he came and looked at her body, and there's this kind of incestuous aspect to that as well.

KATHIE: "I never knew how beautiful she was." Is that what you're saying?

BRYAN: Yes, that's how he was quoted, as if he were discovering it for the first time. It might be that he's covering up the fact that he absolutely did know because of his incest, so he's acting innocent in front of whoever's in the room. People had warned him, saying the army's not gonna stand for you if you keep this up. So it was just weird. But why include that whole scene? Can you help us here? It might seem gratuitous or unnecessary. Why would we put in a scene right at the beginning—and we did this with Herod too—where we start with him in totally disgusting nastiness? But we're not trying to be gross in our book, right?

KATHIE: No, nothing's gratuitous, no. If I think about that, I realize you can be sexually intimate with somebody and never see their body. I mean, this woman is laid out there like a piece of art and he valued his own artistic thing. He thought he was an artist. I think there must have been something—although she'd been stabbed and all of that, she wasn't in her perfect form—but I'm sure she was seen as beautiful. People thought of beauty differently back then. Sex was just so, I don't know, what's the word for it? There was a violence to it. There was a violence about the culture. And if you see her just beautifully laid out and lying still, there's something peaceful, perhaps.

BRYAN: And we're putting it in the book, like you said, not to be gratuitous, but to introduce you to this character who's at the height of depravity. You have to see that while he eventually got there, he didn't start there. You have to go back to the beginning and see, like you said, everyone loves a baby. Baby Nero was sweet. He wasn't sinful, he hadn't done anything bad yet. So what happens to get him to the point where he's looking at his mother's corpse, whom he just killed? That's why our story lets the reader know you're going to get there. But at the beginning, he wasn't like that. What steps along the way caused him to descend into that sin, and ultimately into madness and false-god worship?

KATHIE: And unbelievable depravity.

BRYAN: Yeah, unbelievable. And that's the story we're trying to tell. It helps, I think, for our readers to know that.

KATHIE: Also, I don't think he had any shame about it.

BRYAN: But Paul had shame. He said, "I'm the chief of sinners."[2] But Nero said, "I'm the chief of artists."

KATHIE: I don't know if he was even sorry that he had murdered her. The same was true about Herod as with Nero. And if we consider other ancient rulers—it seems everybody got rid of anybody that stood in their way of fame and fortune and success. They just killed without remorse. They did anything they had to do to keep their power, until they no longer had a choice. They had to keep killing and killing. And that's when Jesus said, What does it cost? If you lose your very soul, even if you gain the whole world, what does it profit?[3] All these guys, every one of them, have gained the world—humanly speaking. We don't cover Julius Caesar, but his story would be the same too. It would be the same for all of them. And it could be anybody today who is murdering Christians. What does it matter what you have gained on earth? You've lost

---

2. 1 Timothy 1:15, author's paraphrase.
3. Mark 8:36, author's paraphrase.

everything that matters. And after that, eternity in hell. I totally believe in hell. If there's a heaven, then there's a hell. For every truth, there's a counterpart.

BRYAN: Jesus believed in it because he taught a lot about hell. But he also taught, and Paul taught, that victory comes in the gospel. So in this chapter, when Nero comes back to Rome from the seaside mansion where he killed his mother, he comes back to Rome and makes it a kind of victory tour.

KATHIE: Yeah, they welcomed him back. Whether they really respected him, I don't think they did, but they had to. He was still the power source, so they had to act like it.

BRYAN: The power source, exactly. And that raises the issue of gospels, the good news. One thing that maybe our readers didn't know, which we bring out in this chapter, is that Rome had a gospel too. They had their own good news that their king would give. Good news means something that a king gives, right?

KATHIE: I was just remembering from our first book that there was a lot of teaching on the fact that after Mariamne died, Herod had sex with her when she was a corpse.

BRYAN: Yeah, that's in one of the Jewish sources. It's in the Talmud.

KATHIE: And so the depravity of this kind of stuff is sicker than anything we can possibly imagine. That's why you need a gospel of good news, because life is full of so much bad news!

BRYAN: So the question is, What's the good news? Because a king like Herod, or a king like Nero, their gospel was about power and domination, but what was Jesus' gospel? It was the exact opposite. The antithesis. Jesus' is not about domination but about being the *dominus*, which means "lord," so in that sense his lordship is the gospel. But we don't dominate other people, right? That's the anti-gospel.

KATHIE: We can't dominate people and call ourselves believers in the Way. We can't do both.

BRYAN: We can only point them to the Lord, the *dominus* of the world.

KATHIE: And that's what we're trying to do through this book. My whole life is about that now—helping people know Jesus. Knowing him personally, not politics, not religion. I promised Billy Graham that I would never talk about politics. When I was in my twenties, Billy said, "Kathie, you're gonna have a huge career. You're gonna have such a powerful influence in the arts.

But if you start talking about politics, you'll lose half your audience, and that's what we want to keep: the audience. We want people to know God loves them and has a purpose for their life." And . . . hmm . . . there was a purpose for me bringing this up but now I don't remember what it was!

BRYAN: You're saying you're keeping yourself apart from politics. That's Rome's gospel: that through man's politics we can win. But the true gospel is the crucified and risen Christ.

KATHIE: Right! That's the story of it all. Everything I write about, everything we're trying to do in films, everything is like, "Yeah, you want religion? Or do you want a relationship with the living God? You decide, it's your choice."

BRYAN: So Rome had its gospel through its emperors, and many people would often think, "The Christian gospel starts with Jesus." But Israel had a gospel first, right?

KATHIE: Yes! It started with the calling of Abram. We know that out of Iraq, out of the land of Ur, God called Abram and Sarai. And I love the fact that when they did get to the Holy Land, God gave them an *h*. He changed their names, which is an interesting thing. He added the *h* to *Abraham*. He added the *h* to *Sarah*. In Judaism the *h* represents the breath of God. The *ruach* of God. A lot of people don't know why all of a sudden Saul was called Paul, you know?

BRYAN: He changed his Jewish name to a Greek one, because he had to go evangelize to the Gentiles.

KATHIE: That's exactly right. It's not unlike how we change our names because God changes our hearts.

BRYAN: That was his mission, and the fire that we talked about before. He thinks, "I'm all about purifying Israel!" until God tells him, "No, actually, you're about Gentiles."[4] Think how crazy that was for Paul, when he thinks he's all about purifying Judaism. But God's mission is "You gotta go to the goyim, the non-Jewish people, and hang out with them and love them as much as you think you should be loving Jews." That's very mind-blowing for a zealous ancient rabbi!

KATHIE: So completely and totally radical, just as much as it was when Jesus started loving women the way he did. Nothing was more radical than

4. Acts 13:47.

that! Women were not worthy, women were not valuable, women were not called daughters of Abraham. But Jesus said, "Oh, yes you are! With me there's neither Greek nor Roman. Not a slave nor free. Not male nor female. All of that is gone!"[5] Instead, there's this kind of broad inclusion of those who have been outcast, even in the temple. You know, you've got the court of the women and they can't go past it, or the court of the Gentiles. The ultimate plan of God is to break down these barriers. Get ahold of that veil, tear that veil down. Let the Spirit come out to everyone!

BRYAN: Right, because you're not trying to get into the holy of holies, you're letting the holy of holies come out to you.

KATHIE: Yeah. We *are* the holy of holies. His children are the holy of holies. He lives in us, through us, around us. "In him we live and move and have our being."[6]

BRYAN: And Paul, who understood that, when he was talking about sexual immorality, he said to the Corinthian church, "Do you not know that you are the temple of God?"[7] Like, would you go into a church—and I hate to be crude—but would you urinate on the pulpit or the altar? Of course not! Because it's holy.

KATHIE: Or fornicate on it.

BRYAN: Yeah, or fornicate in the holy place. You wouldn't do that. So then why would you fornicate on what the true church is, not buildings of brick and stone, but your own body? Why commit desecration against the place that is a temple of holiness, where the Holy Spirit lives?

KATHIE: Amen. Paul didn't understand that at first. But he learns.

BRYAN: Right. He learned it on the road to Damascus. And that's where we go in our next chapter.

---

5. Galatians 3:28, author's paraphrase.
6. Acts 17:28.
7. 1 Corinthians 3:16.

THREE

THE ROAD TO DAMASCUS

The Jewish Sabbath—called by its practitioners "Shabbat"—has been observed continuously by God's people for nearly thirty-five hundred years. How might a middle-class Jewish family in Jerusalem have celebrated Shabbat? And how might they have attempted to integrate the Way of Yeshua into their observances?

The oil lamps were lit as dusk arrived. The household father gathered his family for a shared meal. Instead of sitting in chairs, they reclined on low couches around a center table as was common in the Mediterranean world (later the Mishnah would make reclining at a Sabbath meal an obligation). The mother placed a jug of watered wine on the table. The stately patriarch poured some of the red liquid into an earthenware cup and said a blessing over it, then distributed more cups to his family members. Sacred meals in antiquity usually began with the sacrificial pouring of wine to a deity, called a libation; but in Jewish homes, a prayer was said instead. "Yeshua began his last Passover meal with thanksgiving for the cup before giving it out," the father explained.

The meal proceeded in solemn sobriety. Several courses were served, each in its turn, for this was no ordinary meal. The mother had prepared a great feast. The staple of bread was eaten first—unleavened, just as Scripture instructed—followed by a second course of stew made with chickpeas, lentils, and fish. But the most special treat was the third course: a leg of roasted lamb, expertly carved with an heirloom knife and served with bitter herbs. During each of the courses, two special loaves sat untouched on a tray to recall how, before each Shabbat, the Israelites in the wilderness collected a double portion of manna, the miraculous bread sent from heaven.

When the hearty meal was finished, a second phase began: a time of theological discussion and spiritual inquiry. The ancient Greeks often did something similar in their symposium, when intellectual philosophy was discussed after a meal—though drunkenness, erotic music, and dancing girls often marred those occasions. No such carnal practices would be happening in this devout Jewish home. Instead, the father would instruct his wife and children about the implications of God's "new covenant."

From the head of the table, he quoted from memory a passage in the book of Jeremiah:

> Behold, the days are coming, says the LORD, when *I will make a new covenant* with the house of Israel and with the house of Judah—not according to the covenant that I made with their fathers in the day that I took them by the hand to lead them out of the land of Egypt, My covenant which they broke, though I was a husband to them, says the LORD. But this is the covenant that I will make with the house of Israel after those days, says the LORD: *I will put My law in their minds, and write it on their hearts*; and I will be their God, and they shall be My people.[1]

The family's firstborn son spoke up with genuine curiosity. "What does this mean?" he asked. He was a serious boy of twelve years, just coming into manhood. "The Torah belongs on scrolls. It is written on parchment with ink. Can God's Word inhabit flesh and blood as well?"

"Think on this, my children," the father replied. "Where does the Scripture speak of God's Spirit residing in the human heart?"

The other child of the family, a feisty younger daughter, had a quick answer. She, too, had been steeped in Torah and could quote long passages from memory.

1. Jeremiah 31:31–33.

"The prophet Ezekiel speaks of this," she recalled. "God said, 'I will give you a new heart and put a new spirit within you; I will take the heart of stone out of your flesh and give you a heart of flesh. I will put My Spirit within you and cause you to walk in My statutes, and you will keep My judgments and do them.'"[2]

The mother nodded sagely at her daughter's words. "Did we not witness this very thing on the day of Pentecost, not long ago? Blessed Peter declared it to fulfill the words of the prophet Joel: 'And it shall come to pass in the last days,' says God, 'that I will pour out of My Spirit on all flesh. . . . And it shall come to pass that whoever calls on the name of the LORD shall be saved.'[3] You see? Scripture promises that even the Gentiles shall receive the Spirit!"

"Not likely," the boy muttered bitterly. "Surely not the wicked Romans." Even at his age, he had seen the soldiers' abuse of his people. Their cruelty made him long for the Messiah to bring deliverance from their domineering ways.

The kindly patriarch didn't chastise his son for his lack of grace but accepted the words with understanding. "The Lord may be doing a new thing," he remarked, "one that surprises us all. Be ready for a fresh wind to blow, my son."

Reaching across the table, he drew the jug of wine to himself, along with the family's best goblet. It was made of fine glass, adorned with a floral pattern. The two loaves of unleavened bread sat on a plate nearby. Assuming a more formal tone, the father said, "The presence of the Spirit within us marks the new covenant. This gift comes from God. Blessed be he."

"Amen," the family said in unison.

The father raised one of the loaves in his hands and declared, "The following account has been reported to me by Matthew himself. On the night of his betrayal, the Lord Yeshua took bread, blessed it, broke it, and gave it to the disciples. Then he said, 'Take, eat; this is my body.'"[4] With that, the father tore the bread in half and distributed pieces to his wife and two children. Together, they ate the flesh of the Messiah.

Next, the father poured the wine diluted with water into the beautiful household goblet. After looking into the eyes of each family member one by

2. Ezekiel 36:26–27.
3. Acts 2:17, 21.
4. Matthew 26:26.

one, he said, "Yeshua also took the cup and gave thanks, then passed it to the disciples, saying, 'Drink from it, all of you. For this is my blood of the new covenant, which is shed for many for the remission of sins.'"[5] The patriarch took a sip, then handed the cup to his wife. She had just put the goblet to her lips when a loud bang and harsh shouts shattered the *shalom* of the house. Everyone scrambled to their feet as intruders burst into the room.

"Stand where you are! Do not move!" ordered an authoritative voice. He was a burly captain of the temple guard, accompanied by three of his henchmen. All of them held long daggers. Behind the squad, the father discerned an even more fearsome figure: *Saul of Tarsus!* The high priest had given the zealous Pharisee the authority to arrest the followers of Yeshua and put them on trial. Banishment and property confiscation were the normal punishment. Even execution wasn't out of the question. If permission for capital punishment couldn't be obtained from the Romans, a lynch mob could be arranged.

"I am a man of peace," the father calmly told the captain. "Please, sir, put away your weapon."

"You are a heretic!" Saul countered, his voice screeching like a rusty nail being pried from a board. "It's prison for you! Guards, bind this man and take him away."

The mother and daughter clutched each other in the corner of the dining room, their eyes wide with fright. As the father stepped around his couch to offer himself to the guards, a hideous crime happened so quickly he could scarcely comprehend it. The son, moved by the impetuous fires of youth, snatched the heirloom carving knife from the table and brandished it at the captain. "You cannot have my father!" he screamed.

The muscular captain seized the boy by his wrist, immobilizing the knife. His own dagger loomed in his upraised hand, its blade pointed down. A single swift motion would plunge the dagger into the boy's breast. "Drop that weapon—now!" he barked.

"Do as he says," the father urged. But his son didn't relent. He kept struggling against his captor's grip. "You are no Israelite!" the boy accused. "The spirit of Rome is in you!"

"Silence, you blasphemer!" shouted Saul.

---

5. Matthew 26:27–28.

The angry boy tried to switch his knife to his free hand. As he made the move, the captain's raised arm descended. Though he could have stabbed the little rebel, there was no need to kill him. A hard blow would be enough to stun him, so the captain turned his wrist as the blade fell, striking his captive on the skull with the knob of the dagger's hilt.

The terrified daughter didn't perceive the turn of the captain's hand. "No!" she cried as she saw the knife begin to fall toward her brother's unprotected chest. Lurching out of her mother's grip, she leapt to the boy's side and tried to drag him from harm's way. As she reached him, the captain's flying blade caught her across the throat. The edge bit deep, slicing open an artery. She collapsed to the floor in a cascade of blood.

The mother shrieked and fell upon her daughter's body. With both hands pressed to the gushing wound, she begged God for help. The father tried to come help as well but the temple guards seized him before he could intervene. Ignoring his protests and struggles, they dragged him out the door.

As the daughter's precious lifeblood drained onto the floor at the foot of the Shabbat table, Saul surveyed the gruesome scene with his jaw clenched. Food lay scattered everywhere. The overturned goblet dribbled wine across the table. The grieving mother wept like an imbecile. The dazed boy moaned in the corner. And the little girl never moved again.

"I guess blasphemy has its price," Saul said with a shrug, then glanced upward. He lifted pious palms to the ceiling. "Even so, O Lord, may thy will be done." With those cold words, the church's foremost persecutor spun away from the shattered family and followed the guards outside.

There are no historical texts that record this family actually existed; it is an imagined scene. Yet events like these certainly happened to innocent believers as Saul tried to stamp out the emerging Way of Yeshua. Scripture calls his vicious activities a "great persecution."[6] Since the Greek word for "great" is *megas*, it could be called a mega-persecution.

6. Acts 8:1.

Saul "made havoc of the church, entering every house, and dragging off men and women, committing them to prison."[7] Clearly, Saul was enraged, so the early believers suffered under his lethal intent. He was "breathing threats and murder against the disciples of the Lord."[8] After he felt confident enough that Jerusalem had been brought under control, he turned his attention to the next big city, Damascus. Many believers had fled there for refuge.

Saul obtained official letters from the high priest granting him the right to arrest any heretics and haul them back to Jerusalem for trial, whether men or women. They would be compelled, by force if necessary, to curse the name of their Savior. The abuse these people would have endured is obvious. But Saul didn't care, for his zeal made him believe he was doing God's work. He later explained his mindset:

> I myself thought I must do many things contrary to the name of Jesus of Nazareth. This I also did in Jerusalem, and many of the saints I shut up in prison, having received authority from the chief priests; and when they were put to death, I cast my vote against them. And I punished them often in every synagogue and compelled them to blaspheme; and being exceedingly enraged against them, I persecuted them even to foreign cities.[9]

But unknown to Saul, things were about to change as he approached the great city of Damascus.

After journeying for eight days, Saul had walked 160 miles along the dusty highway from Jerusalem to Galilee, across the Jordan River, and northward toward the edge of the Arabian Desert. As morning dawned on the ninth day, the distant walls of Damascus, barely visible on the horizon, were now beckoning the weary travelers. Today they would arrive and begin executing their mission.

---

7. Acts 8:3.
8. Acts 9:1.
9. Acts 26:9–11.

Walking at the party's lead, Saul was followed by some temple guards selected because of their reputation for zeal, a couple of servants to take care of practicalities, and a pair of donkeys for the baggage. We can picture him with a satchel slung over his shoulder in which he carried the letters from the high priest that would allow him to make arrests and transport his prisoners to Jerusalem for trial. *And then their execution*, he hoped as he plodded along in the summer heat.

Around noontime, the group approached a scattering of palm trees for a rest in the shade. Just as they were about to reach the shelter, a light more blinding than the overhead sun blazed around them. Instantly, Saul's eyes went dark. He staggered and groped for balance. His men filled the air with cries of alarm. Saul might have stayed on his feet if not for the thunderous voice whose every word felt like a catapult stone striking his heart. The raw power of this vocal assault knocked him to the ground. He lay prone upon the highway as his addled mind finally registered what had just been said to him: "Saul! Saul! Why are you persecuting me?"

P-p-persecuting? No! It is . . . zeal for the Lord . . . his holiness . . .

The heavenly voice—so resonant with power, so authoritative, yet somehow also benign—demanded an answer. Paul licked his dirt-encrusted lips and stammered, "W-w-who are you, Lord?"

"I am Jesus," the voice in the light declared, "the one whom you are persecuting."

The words came as a shock to the zealous Pharisee. He trembled and moaned, not knowing what he should do. *If Jesus is alive . . . speaking to me . . . then what his followers claim is true. He is risen! And if I'm persecuting them . . . then I'm persecuting him! They are, in some way, part of him. The body of Messiah includes them!*

The implications of this startling revelation left Saul bewildered. Yet as the basic truth set in, a deep and dreadful fear seized Saul's soul. *I'm not zealous for God—I am his murderer! I'm guilty of deicide! What crime could be worse? What Jew could survive the wrath deserved for killing God's Anointed? Will Yahweh slay me this instant for such vicious and vile actions?*

As he lay flat upon the road, his eyes blind, his head spinning, Saul could only whisper, "Lord, what do you want me to do?"

"Arise and go into the city, and you will be told what you must do," Jesus replied. Then the light faded and he was gone.

Uneasily, Saul rose to his hands and knees. Sweat dripped from his nose onto the pavement. Even when he opened his scrunched eyes, he could see nothing. His companions rejoined him and helped him stand. Saul's legs shook and his knees felt weak. One of the most pious of the temple guards asked, "What did the heavenly voice say? We heard its rumble, but we could not make out the words."

"It was Jesus of Nazareth. He told me to follow him."

Rendered speechless by the startling declaration, Saul's companions took him by the hand and helped him trudge into the city. For three days and nights, he remained in utter darkness, neither eating nor drinking. It was as if he had died. His body lay motionless on his cot. His whole world shrunk to a tomb-like bedroom. Surely the judgment of death must be at hand.

But the Living God had something different in mind for Saul. Graciously, instead of blasting the persecutor with punishment, Jesus revealed his future mission. From then on, he would no longer murder believers in the Messiah but would work to expand their number—not only among the Jews but even among the Gentiles.

Knowing that bearing witness to the Son of God would entail danger, Jesus promised to deliver Saul from his future persecutors. It was to the pagan Gentiles that Saul should now go with the good news, "to open their eyes, in order to turn them from darkness to light, and from the power of Satan to God, that they may receive forgiveness of sins and an inheritance among those who are sanctified by faith in me."[10]

It seemed like too much to take in. But somehow, through the fog of confusion, Saul realized he had just been recommissioned. Instead of going to Damascus to kill Jews, his future would include traveling across the empire to shine a gospel light to the Gentiles.

Saul had been given a task, a divine repurposing of his ardent zeal. Through a sinful Jewish rabbi, whose heart was darkest of them all, the Light of the World was about to make all things new.

---

10. Acts 26:18.

CODA

We begin this conversation with a discussion of the Jewish Passover and how it points to Yeshua, or Jesus, the Messiah of Israel. But Paul couldn't see that truth because he was spiritually blind. Only his conversion on the road to Damascus, which blinded him so he could truly see, allowed him to discern the meaning of his Jewish faith. Everyone needs Jesus, the Light of the World, to rescue us from spiritual darkness and illumine the right way for us to walk in life.

BRYAN: In this chapter we have Saul's vision of Christ on the road to Damascus, but before we get there, let's drill down into just how much of a persecutor he was, because you really have to establish that before you can see his transformation on the road. Saul, or Paul, as we know him, was an evil, violent man. Not only did he stand over Stephen and supervise that stoning, he persecuted many believers. Let's envision this story of a family.

KATHIE: Yeah, when they're doing Shabbat.

BRYAN: Exactly. Maybe it touches the spirit a little bit. Now, of course, it's imagined, but we do that for the reader to picture it. Of course it's not totally made up, because we know Paul was a man of violence. He was "breathing threats and murder," and he persecuted the Way to death, both men and women.[11] So he actually did that kind of thing.

KATHIE: You know what it reminded me of, Bryan? Kristallnacht.

BRYAN: Tell the readers what Kristallnacht is.

KATHIE: It was the time in Germany when the Nazis went after the Jews—the good Jew, the bad Jew, they didn't care. You're a Jew? You're gone. They gathered them up and sent them away. It was a terrible sound when that siren would go off and the soldiers would show up to capture you. Kristallnacht was a November night, a crystal night, also known as a night of broken glass, when they started wiping out the Jews, collecting them and putting them on trains.

BRYAN: Right, *Kristallnacht* means the "night of crystal," or broken glass, from all the windows smashed in the rioting against the Jews.

KATHIE: Oh yes, they broke everything and just dragged them away, full families, taking the men to put them in concentration camps.

---

11. Acts 9:1, 22:4–5.

BRYAN: That's a great connection, Kathie. I'm so glad we're bringing this out because in the story that we tell with Saul and the Jewish family, there's this overturned table with a broken goblet. And I didn't even think of it as being like Kristallnacht, but your storytelling ability is imagining these connections.

KATHIE: I can't watch a movie about the Holocaust without hearing the sound from the siren. Then it would be the pounding of the doors, and the screaming. Same for the ancient Jews. "Open up in the name of Rome!" they would say.

BRYAN: The Nazis called themselves the Third Reich. They thought of themselves as the continuation of previous kingdoms, including the Romans.

KATHIE: That's what I mean by "nothing changes." What does it profit a person to gain all power but lose their soul?

BRYAN: And the Shabbat that they're celebrating, these people are followers of the Way. So talk a little bit about how Shabbat is meant to point to the broken body and shed blood of the Messiah. Do you think that's true?

KATHIE: Yes, I do believe it's true. I think of it as a Passover meal. I love the ancient aspect of it, and the modern as well. A friend of mine and I had Shabbat together this past Friday. For the first time in over a year, he said the prayers. And because he'd been living in a dark world this past year, he couldn't remember them. He learned them as a child. And he'd struggle a little, and I thought, wow, just one year and you forget. But it was such a joyful time, and it's beautiful because it's the ancient aspect of the Seder. We still do it today.

BRYAN: The Last Supper of Jesus was a Passover Seder. The bread that he broke was his own flesh, given for his disciples, for the whole world. Not all our readers will know that, right?

KATHIE: Yes, and I think it's beautiful.

BRYAN: And the wine is the blood of Christ.

KATHIE: You know, every Passover Seder is four glasses of alcoholic wine.

BRYAN: You actually have a farm, and a vineyard with vines in it. You have a wine business, called GIFFT.

KATHIE: I do have a wine business, and I drink it because it's good! But it's also because I'm Jewish, and I do what they did in Israel. Jesus said at that Seder that he wouldn't drink wine again until the final banquet as we celebrate his great victory over Satan,[12] and over sin, and we're all gathered there together.[13] It's going to be the most joyous feast!

BRYAN: It should be a time of great celebration, because he spilled his blood, but he didn't stay dead. He rose up! It's like the scriptures that Peter preaches in Acts. In his sermons, he is always showing that Israel's Scriptures point to a resurrected Messiah.

KATHIE: Always. People are willfully ignorant about it. They just are. But it's right there in front of them. And you know, it's one thing when you know something culturally or you know it religiously, but, too often, it hasn't made it to your heart.

BRYAN: Or in the case of bread and wine, to your stomach! You gotta bring Jesus all the way down inside. So that's a perfect segue to our final scene of chapter 3. We have imagined that Saul was hurting families. We know he was. And we know he watched Stephen's martyrdom. He's being willfully ignorant, like you said. So what does it take to break through willful ignorance? Sometimes, it's a blinding light from the presence of the risen Christ.

KATHIE: You have to be made blind so you can see.

BRYAN: Well said. He had to be made blind so he could see. Yeah, beautiful. And he gets blinded on the road to Damascus.

KATHIE: And he's the only one that heard the voice of Yeshua. He must have seemed like a madman. The people with him must have thought he was having a stroke or something, if they even knew that word back then. But all of a sudden, for him to be fine, and then a light blinded him, that was shocking! Was it like the sun? Or was it Jesus' own glory? And why didn't that kill him?

BRYAN: Not everybody who sees the risen Christ goes blind.

KATHIE: He is the Sun, *and* he's the Son of God. Yes, it was the Son that blinded Paul, or Saul, as he was called then. And Jesus asked him, "Why are you doing this? Why are you persecuting me?"[14]

BRYAN: Which is interesting, because Saul thought he was persecuting heretics, but the heretics were actually Jesus, right? They are himself. That's only true if the Holy Spirit has come out of the temple and he lives in you. It was stunning to Saul, and it threw him to the ground, threw his mind into confusion.

---

12. Revelation 19:9.
13. Matthew 26:29.
14. Acts 9:4, 22:7, 26:14, author's paraphrase.

KATHIE: Sometimes it just takes a sermon in a little Baptist church for somebody to come to know Jesus and walk forward to accept him. Other times, it takes something that literally blinds you physically so you can see spiritually.

BRYAN: And when you meet the risen Christ, you don't think, "Oh, he's so sweet," like how we have these sentimental pictures of him. "Oh, Jesus, I would want to stroke your soft little beard." No way. In the book of Revelation, when you look at Jesus—and that's who Saul was seeing on the road, the Jesus of the end times—that Jesus is actually scary.

KATHIE: He's the one that's gonna be riding on the white horse.

BRYAN: Paul did not see a tame stonemason from Nazareth.

KATHIE: He saw the risen Christ in all his glory, and that's what it took. That's the gospel, right there: *whatever it takes.* Jesus does what he needs to do. He leaves the ninety-nine sheep and goes after the lost one.[15] Praise God!

15. Luke 15:4–7.

FOUR

TWO BIRTHS

One night, deep into the quiet recesses of sleep, a citizen of Damascus woke up hearing his name being called by the Lord. "Ananias!"

"Yes, Lord," he answered.

"Go to the house of Judas on Straight Street and ask for a man from Tarsus named Saul, for he is praying. In a vision he has seen a man named Ananias come and place his hands on him to restore his sight."[1]

The command frightened Ananias. He realized this vision was telling him to visit the church's worst persecutor! What? Ananias had heard the reports about all the harm Saul had done to the saints in Jerusalem and that he had come to Damascus with the authority from the chief priests to arrest anyone who called on the name of Jesus.

Knowing he was fearful, the Lord revealed something important about Saul to comfort Ananias and to help calm him: No longer was Saul an enemy of the Way. Jesus said to Ananias, "Go! This man is my chosen instrument to proclaim my name to the Gentiles and their kings and to the people of Israel. I will show him how much he must suffer for my name."[2]

Saul had a new calling. God's mission for him was to go to the Gentiles and share the good news that Israel's message was for the entire human race. Saul was to carry the gospel to the ends of the earth.

---

1. Acts 9:11–12 NIV.
2. Acts 9:15–16 NIV.

But before all of that could happen, Ananias had to take his own step of faith.

On the morning after his vision, while sleepy Damascus was just beginning to stir, Ananias left his house and made his way to the city's main east–west thoroughfare, known as Straight Street. There he found the home to which Jesus had directed him. "I'm here to meet a man from Tarsus named Saul," he told the doorkeeper.

"He is expecting you," the servant replied.

Ananias was led to an enclosed garden at the rear of the house. The servant then gestured to a bedroom door adjoining the garden. "The man you seek is in there."

Ananias thanked the servant and approached the door. Despite the news that Saul had converted to the Way, trepidation made his heart race. *Will I soon be thrown into prison?* The thought made Ananias chide himself. A believer in Jesus should be willing to endure persecution. Dismissing his fears, he gave the door a threefold knock. A voice from inside told him to come in.

Saul was lying flat on a cot when Ananias entered. He was fully clothed, yet he seemed to be sleeping. His eyes remained shut as Ananias went to his bedside and took a seat on a stool. "Brother, I am sent to you from God."

"I know," the blind man answered. "He revealed that you would come and lay hands on me. I am ready."

No longer afraid, but now confident in God, Ananias extended his right hand and placed it on Saul's head. His words resonated with prophetic power as he spoke. "Brother Saul, the Lord Jesus, who appeared to you on the road as you came, has sent me that you may receive your sight and be filled with the Holy Spirit."[3]

At that moment, Ananias saw what looked like hard scales fall away from Saul's eyes. Focus and clarity came back to his gaze. As he fixed his attention on Ananias, he said, "Aha! At last, I can see."

Ananias realized his new brother was speaking both physically and spiritually. More words of prophecy welled up inside Ananias, so he let them flow out: "The God of our ancestors has chosen you to know his will and to see the

---

3. Acts 9:17.

Righteous One and to hear words from his mouth. You will be his witness to all people of what you have seen and heard."[4]

It was the radical new message of the Way. Instead of coming to God through a man-made building, all people could now encounter God through Jesus. The Messiah wasn't only for Israel; Jesus served as the universal light. His brilliance would blind those with dark hearts, but he would shine like a beacon to anyone who sought the Lord.

Enlivened and energized by the healing, Saul sat up on his bed, though he didn't yet stand. His sandals lay on the floor. Beside them, a Torah scroll protruded from a satchel. Both would be needed soon, for Saul's beautiful feet had been appointed to carry the good news of God to the ends of the earth.[5] Ananias leaned over and embraced him—a killer who had become a kinsman, a fiend who had become a friend.

Yet one vital task still needed to be done. Outside the bedroom, a decorative pool and fountain adorned the house's garden. The Holy Spirit gave Ananias a final prophetic message. "And now why are you waiting?" he said to Saul. "Arise and be baptized, and wash away your sins, calling on the name of the Lord!"[6]

At this command, Saul rose from the bed and let Ananias lead him outside. The sacred ritual would complete his conversion to Jesus and forever display its truth. Saul instinctively understood the symbolic value of the water. In order for him to be restored, he had to be reborn.

Just as human gestation begins in water, and childbirth is signaled by its flow, so also, spiritual rebirth in God is signed with water. Since Saul had been reborn by an inner and outer washing, he adopted a new name. In addition to the Jewish name of his origins, he started using the Roman name of his worldwide mission: *Paulus*, or Paul.[7] The Latin word *paulus* means "small," and, by extension, "humble." The name fit Paul's altered reality. He felt reduced and

4. Acts 22:14–15 NIV.
5. Isaiah 52:7; Romans 10:15.
6. Acts 22:16.
7. Acts 13:9.

humbled by his overpowering experience on the Damascus road. As a newborn babe in Christ, he knew full well what Jesus had meant when he said, "Unless you are converted and become as little children, you will by no means enter the kingdom of heaven."[8]

When Paul believed in Jesus and accepted baptism at the hands of Ananias, he didn't just accept a new set of theological ideas. His transformation wasn't purely mental; it was spiritual and organic. Everything about Paul was different. The Spirit had taken up residence within him. His life had to be restarted from scratch because Jesus had just called him to a whole new sense of self. Now the task for the reborn Paul—like any child who must grow into adulthood—was to understand his identity, own it personally, and determine his life's future direction.

Not much is known about Paul's metaphorical "teenage years" except that he spent them in the remote desert of Arabia—the home of Mount Sinai. After turning to Jesus, Paul realized he needed to completely rethink the meaning of God's Torah. Previously, he had gotten it wrong—terribly wrong! He had even persecuted faithful Israelites to their deaths! It was time for a category shift about the person of Jesus and his place in God's plan.

To do such heavy-duty rethinking, Paul had to go where it all began. He needed to be like a new Moses, coming down from God's mountain with divine revelation that would change the world. To understand this hidden and mystical time in Paul's life, it is best to let him describe it in his own words. He wrote, "But when he who had set me apart before I was born, and who called me by his grace, was pleased to reveal his Son to me, in order that I might preach him among the Gentiles, I did not immediately consult with anyone; nor did I go up to Jerusalem to those who were apostles before me, but I went away into Arabia, and returned again to Damascus."[9] Only at the foot of Mount Sinai, where Moses had received God's law, could Paul discern the true meaning of the Torah that Jesus had revealed.

---

8. Matthew 18:3.
9. Galatians 1:15–17 ESV.

Though Paul's Arabian experience lasted a couple of years, he probably didn't dwell in the desert like a reclusive hermit for the entire time. He was a man of cities, a productive citizen who earned his living as a maker of tents and awnings. Paul felt more at home in an urban environment than out in the arid wastes. Eventually, he made his way back to the bustling capital of Damascus, where he ran into trouble with the authorities—the first of many times he would experience such danger.

While evangelizing Gentiles in the villages of Arabia, Paul had aroused the anger of the local king. The king ordered his governor in Damascus to lock down the city and arrest the illegal preacher. The local Jewish authorities also opposed Paul, watching the city gates so they could kill him before he escaped. As he hid in the very house where his blinded eyes had been healed, and where he had been baptized in the garden pool, Paul prayed that Jesus would deliver him from the soldiers who had surrounded the building. They pounded on the front door, demanding his surrender. *Lord! How can I proclaim the gospel to the world if I'm locked in a cell?*

Some of Paul's converts, who knew the Scriptures well, proposed a biblical means of escape. "Recall the story of Rahab at Jericho," one of them said. "She let down the Hebrew spies through the wall. This house also adjoins the city wall!"

"Let's try it," Paul agreed.

As night fell, his friends took him to an upstairs bedroom. A large wicker basket sat upon the windowsill, attached to a hemp rope. After Paul climbed into it, six burly believers took the rope in their fists and began to lower him. The brisk breeze wasn't a pleasant comfort but a source of fear as it made the basket sway back and forth. The ground lay far below, for the terrain sloped away from the wall into a deep defensive ditch. In the distance, a few traders approached the city gate and the guards stopped them. Paul prayed they wouldn't notice the strange pendulum dangling from the window.

Finally, the basket bumped against the dirt. Paul climbed out, ducked his head to keep a low profile, and crept beneath the pale moonlight to a nearby copse of trees. A godly friend met him there with a travel satchel full of food.

"May God speed you, my brother," he said as Paul started toward the southbound highway.

"May God speed the gospel," Paul replied.

After escaping from Damascus in the basket, Paul finally returned to Jerusalem. There he met with Peter and James, the two foremost leaders of the early church. He didn't need to get their approval of his mission, for he knew his gospel had been revealed by the Messiah himself. Yet he wanted to forge bonds of cooperation and unity with the original apostles. Their mutual friend Barnabas had arranged the meeting after assuring Peter and James that Paul, the former persecutor, had been truly converted to faith in the risen Lord.

So it was that in the year AD 37 Paul found himself ready for whatever lay ahead. He had believed in Jesus and been baptized with water and the Spirit. He had endured trials and travails. He had gone to the mountain of God to attain growth and maturity. Most importantly, he had received divine revelation about the universal gospel, the message to be proclaimed to the ends of the earth. For this vital task, Paul's repurposed zeal would stand him in good stead. His spiritual rebirth was complete. Now it was time for him to fulfill his divine calling.

Unknown to Paul, another important birth took place in the year 37. It didn't happen in Jerusalem, or Damascus, or the wilds of Arabia, but in a luxurious seaside villa in Italy. The resort town was known as Antium. There, Agrippina the Younger, the great-granddaughter of one emperor, the sister of another, and the niece and future wife of a third, had just become the mother of a fourth: Nero, her one and only son.

Nero was born at dawn, "just as the sun rose, so that he was touched by its rays almost before he could be laid upon the ground." Though childbirth at sunrise was considered a good sign, it was accompanied by a bad one. Nero was born feetfirst, a breech delivery everyone took as a malignant omen. The same thing had happened to Caligula, his mother's brother, and he didn't turn out well. Both emperors ended up on the wrong side of history.

Yet the gods, so it was said, protected the young Nero. At one point, rival family members realized the child could be an heir to the imperial throne, so they sought to kill him. The opportunity came one day when Nero was taking his noontime nap. When the assassins drew near to the sleeping boy, a snake darted from beneath his pillow and scared the killers away. Then the snake shed its skin and left it behind. Agrippina had the snakeskin enclosed in a golden bracelet, which Nero wore for a long time afterward. He only quit wearing the bracelet around the time he ordered her murder. Ancient Romans believed that baby vipers ate their way out of their mothers' sides, killing them in the process. Matricide became the defining crime of the future emperor.

Today's popular imagination depicts Nero as a depraved maniac with blood always dripping from his hands. His contemporaries in the Roman aristocracy, as well as his ancient biographers, reviled him with exactly these depictions. Even the Bible puts Nero in bad light. Most people know that the Latin language uses letters to represent numbers; these are called Roman numerals, such as VIII, representing 8. The same is true of Greek and Hebrew: The letters had mathematical values, so there were no separate numerals. When the name "Nero Caesar" is put into numerical notation in Hebrew, it comes out to 666. The book of Revelation identifies this as the number of an evil beast who deceives the world on behalf of the dragon, or Satan.[10] Pagans and Christians alike had reasons to despise Emperor Nero!

But he didn't start out the way he would end. The young Nero was a child of bright promise. Although his family upbringing—orchestrated by the wily and murderous Agrippina—scarred him with constant political violence, the boy himself was sweet-tempered and artistic. In particular, Nero was gifted with musical ability. He loved playing the harp, and he enjoyed the musician's persona and subculture. Later, he also made himself into a decent athlete, especially as a chariot racer. A strong case can be made that Nero would have preferred a career in the performing arts instead of the cut-and-thrust world of Roman politics.

But that was not to be. Over time, the decadence of imperial Rome warped Nero's moral vision. As is always the case, his unlimited power corrupted him. He started making bad choices, growing ever more debauched and self-indulgent. Nero ended his life as a disgusting beast of a man. Yet his early reign was marked by restraint and mercy, especially as taught to him by his tutor, the eminent philosopher Seneca.

---

10. Revelation 13:4, 11, 18.

At the age of fourteen, Nero underwent a cultural rite of passage. He set aside the magical amulet every Roman boy wore around his neck from birth, a golden locket with lucky charms inside it. Now he donned the plain white *toga virilis*, the toga of manhood. He appeared publicly in the Forum for the first time, no longer wearing the purple-striped toga of a boy, but now obviously an adult. Monetary gifts were distributed to the people in his name, but especially to the Praetorian Guard. Races and gladiator games were held in the Circus Maximus to keep the citizens happy.

To top it all off, Nero was given a magnificent title: Prince of the Youth. Since the word *princeps* was the primary designation of emperors, everyone could see that this young man was being groomed for future rule. In the eyes of the Romans, a life of promise lay ahead of the god-beloved youth. Nero's noble birth and years of training had prepared him to reign. His sole purpose was to spread Rome's message of good news to the world. Unfortunately for Nero, the content of his "gospel" stood diametrically opposed to the one Paul had received from God. These two gospels were on a direct collision course—and in the end, only one of them would endure for all time.

CODA

We consider in this conversation how Ananias's courage in the face of personal fears can serve as a model for us all. We also discuss the meaning of Christian baptism. In Saul's case, his baptism launched him into a lifetime of ministry. Before people can serve God effectively, they often need to go through a "wilderness experience." Our conversation in this coda reveals that hard times are often part of God's plan to make his followers effective for his service.

BRYAN: In the opening scene of chapter 4, Paul, or Saul, as he is still called at this point, is blind and lying on a cot in a darkened room in Damascus. In a vision, Ananias hears from God that he is to go to the house where Saul is, lay his hands on Saul, and heal him. Ananias obeys—though he is nervous to do so. I just wonder—have you ever felt scared to do God's will? And how do we as Christians overcome our fears when God is asking us to do something scary?

KATHIE: God asks us to do something scary every single day, which is to breathe! Just to live is scary. As we go through life, we're going to encounter all kinds of powers and principalities. We will be tempted all day long. We will be challenged all day long. If we get used to that and stop being surprised by it, that's half the battle. Paul talks so much about the battles we face, and how he got through them. We'll touch on it later when we talk about how he got the thorn in his flesh and all of those things, but he realized the greatest truth we can learn as believers—to trust God even when we can't see the way ahead.

BRYAN: We walk by faith, not by sight.

KATHIE: Yeah, but fear can be powerful. I think of the scripture that says, "Don't be afraid of what you're going to say, because God will be there with you. God will give you the words to say."[11] I have never, I don't think, ever in my entire life, written out a speech. And I've given hundreds and hundreds of them. I never do. I just pray, "Lord, give me utterance." Otherwise, my ego is going to be in that speech, but if I'm relying on the Holy Spirit to guide me, it's his words. Do I make mistakes? Of course I do. But the biggest mistake we can make is not to rely on the Holy Spirit but on our own might. And Paul understood better than anybody, at least in his teachings, his weakness is what made him strong because he had to rely on God. He had to rely on the Messiah, Yahweh, Yeshua. And we Gentiles who have been converted to believing in Jesus, we have got to rely on him. It's the same Savior, and the same Holy Spirit, whether in Hebrew or Greek. That's the beautiful part.

BRYAN: So then Ananias baptizes Saul, and I thought we could consider that as well. What was your baptism like? What do you think are the themes of baptism?

KATHIE: I was not baptized as an infant, as a lot of people might do for their children. The first time I was baptized was in the Jordan River during my very first trip to Israel, when I was seventeen. That was a pretty moving experience. And when I go there, I often get in the water to help our friends who are being baptized for the first time. Is there a different word in Hebrew for baptism?

BRYAN: There's not really a directly comparable Hebrew word. In Greek, it's *baptizo*. It means to dip or to immerse.

KATHIE: Yes, that's another thing I learned. You immerse yourself. And you can tell me if it's true or not in Jesus' day: You did it yourself. You laid

11. Mark 13:11, author's paraphrase.

yourself back. You weren't helped, like pastors when they dip you. No, John the Baptist didn't dip people. He was just calling them to be there. From what I understand, true baptism is when you immerse yourself. You surrender to the current, you surrender to the water, you surrender to the Holy Spirit.

BRYAN: There's some continuity but also discontinuity between the ritual washings of a Jewish mikvah, or what John the Baptist was doing, and what Christians do in baptism. After Christ rises from the dead, he sends his disciples into the world and he commands them to baptize people.

KATHIE: But does that mean you're the one that actually dips them, or does it mean they do it to themselves?

BRYAN: There is likely more involvement from the baptizer today than what would have been done before, the baptism of repentance that John was doing. Something new has happened because now you are being Spirit-baptized into the body of Christ. When Jesus says, "Go into all the world, making disciples, baptizing them in the name of the Father, Son, and Holy Spirit,"[12] he's changing it a little bit. Jesus is commanding the disciples to be baptizers because of his resurrection, and because the Holy Spirit now comes and lives in us. He makes a whole community of the Spirit. Everyone is intertwined. That didn't happen before, which is a theme of our book. Right after Christ dies, the veil is torn, and the Spirit goes out into the world. So that applies to baptism. Then after his baptism, Paul goes to the wilderness.

KATHIE: Into Arabia.

BRYAN: Yeah, into Arabia and even to Mount Sinai, you might say.

KATHIE: Which is not the Mount Sinai that we think of, though. I hear there's different candidates for it.

BRYAN: There are several mountains in Israel that people think might be the real one. We don't know for sure where Paul went, but in Galatians he makes a big deal about Mount Sinai.

KATHIE: Why would he go to Arabia?

BRYAN: Because that's the place associated with the Torah. After the road to Damascus, Paul thought, "I need a new download of revelation." Because he's converted now and realizes, "I completely missed the meaning of Torah. It was pointing to Christ, and I blew it. So I need to go back to where Torah came

12. Matthew 28:19, author's paraphrase.

from and get a new Law and be like a new Moses. I need to get a new download and reinterpret the Law properly before I can go and minister to others." Have you found God in the wilderness or even in the desert?

KATHIE: Yes, in the desert of suffering. Think about when you've been the sickest you've ever been in your life, how weak you are. Yeah, that's where God often wants to get us, so he can get our full attention. It's called rock bottom.

BRYAN: So, like a spiritual wilderness, or a place of not having resources?

KATHIE: Both. They go hand in hand. The past two years of my life have been like that. I had a terrible wilderness time of emotional heartbreak, in lots of ways, which weakens you. You just don't want to get out of bed in the morning and feel that sad anymore. And it's joyless. It's the worst thing that can happen to us. I've been in battles, spiritually. We have to remember that it's not the other person that hurt us. It's the powers and principalities that affect that person who hurt us. We have to consider the source of the goodness that comes to us, and the evil too. That's why Jesus said, "Father, forgive them, for they don't know what they are doing."[13]

BRYAN: Only God can give us that perspective.

KATHIE: No one can do it who hasn't been given over to the Holy Spirit by their own surrender. We can only serve one master. God has forgiven us, so that's what gives us mercy for other people.

BRYAN: It sounds like you have had some really hard times in your life.

KATHIE: I have. Another desert experience was going through false accusations. I was accused of being a child molester because I supposedly had sweatshops. That was one of the worst seasons of my life—feeling utter hopelessness because I couldn't get anybody to listen to the truth. People believed what they wanted to believe. "The Giffords have sweatshops!" People wanted to sell their newspapers and magazines. No one was talking about the fact that Frank and I had just built a home to take care of children with AIDS and children with crack addiction. That's not a story to them. There was this cultural thing about canceling people. Many people said, "You need to fire her!" Nobody cared about the truth. That was a wilderness experience. The very next year was Frank's infidelity, and that was crushing. But God healed our marriage. And God healed our family. Although our family never broke

---

13. Luke 23:34 NLT.

up, I was never the same person. I have scars to this day from it. Yet the Lord overcomes it. This morning I was looking at the scar from my surgery six or seven months ago when I had my hip fixed and I was thinking, "Look, I am not in pain anymore." The pain is diminished, but there's still a scar. That's the reminder of what I went through and how God helped me overcome it. He heals, but he leaves scars as reminders.

FIVE

THE PATHWAY TO THE THRONE

On the day Nero claimed the imperial throne, the commander of his royal bodyguard asked him for a password. Nero looked at him and said, "*optimam matrem*," the "best mother." Clearly, when Nero ascended to power, he thought highly of the woman who had birthed him, nurtured him, and helped him rise to the top. So who was Agrippina? How did she come to wield such great authority? And how did her ruthless scheming affect her only son? Nero can't be understood without taking a look at the complexities of his upbringing in the imperial household.

Historians call her Agrippina "the Younger" to distinguish her from her mother of the same name, Agrippina the Elder. Their lineage descended from the great Caesar Augustus, as well as from many other scions of imperial Rome. Although women couldn't serve as emperors, everyone knew Agrippina the Younger had the bluest of blood coursing through her veins. Any progeny of hers would certainly be a contender for the imperial throne someday. Nero would be, by virtue of his noble bloodline, a likely Roman emperor.

And well did his mother know it. Hungry for power from her earliest days, Agrippina wanted to rule the world through her son. But before she could bear a child with the ability to claim supreme power, the young Agrippina had to get herself in the right position. For an ancient Roman noblewoman, that meant she had to be connected to a rich, powerful man. Her husband,

Ahenobarbus, wasn't placed highly enough. Fortunately, she had another family connection at hand: her brother, Caligula, the prince who took over for the degenerate Emperor Tiberius on the isle of Capri (possibly after smothering him in his bed, though the cause of his death, or its exact perpetrator, isn't known for certain).

Though Caligula came from noble parentage like his sister, he didn't live up to expectations. His reign stands as an enduring symbol of debauchery and murder. He was a deranged sociopath and violent egomaniac.

The ancient sources say Caligula took cruel pleasure in tormenting the commoners and aristocrats alike. Just to be mean, he would retract the awnings at gladiator games at high noon, baking the crowd under the sun's heat while forcing them to watch crummy, mismatched bouts. He would make senators jog alongside his chariot and serve as waiters at his table. Other great men were branded with hot irons and sentenced to death by overwork in the mines. Caligula ordered random executions for no reason but that he had the power to do so. He would even make parents watch the slaughter of their sons, then invite the bereaved to dinner and force them to make happy chitchat over the meal. On one occasion, over several days' time, he had a man beaten to a pulp with heavy chains. After the stink of his rotting brain in his wounded head became unbearable, the depraved emperor finally ordered the victim's death. No one ever got executed by a swift coup de grâce but by slow, numerous injuries. Caligula's sadistic motto was "Strike them so they can feel themselves dying."

Agrippina, who was in her early twenties at this time, surely recognized her brother's demented personality, so she tried to navigate it as best she could. At first, she cozied up to him like a good sister, along with her two younger siblings. Caligula seemed to appreciate the support. Images of the three royal ladies, posing together as goddesses, appeared on coins minted during this time—the first Roman currency ever to depict living women by name. The emperor also honored the three sisters publicly by granting them the same privileges as the elite vestal virgins. Though many people were being murdered left and right, Caligula's brotherly favor was raising Agrippina's status to new heights.

Yet all wasn't well behind closed doors. The historian Suetonius reports Caligula lived in a state of "perpetual incest" with the three girls, sometimes copulating with them one after the other like a serial rapist. His favorite sister was the second eldest, Drusilla, with whom he started having sex while he was still a young lad. Suetonius says, "The rest of his sisters he did not love with so great affection, nor honour so highly, but often prostituted them to his favourites"—that is, he pimped them out to lusty noblemen of his court.

To make matters worse, Caligula took another lover whom he actually liked. When she bore him a daughter, he married the lady as his new queen. Such proof of fertility meant she might conceive a future emperor, replacing Agrippina's two-year-old son, Nero, as next in the royal line. In fact, Agrippina's offspring stood in mortal danger of assassination as an imperial rival. All of this mayhem explains why Agrippina began to conspire against Caligula instead of remaining loyal like she had at first.

Certain historical sources claim that, in the autumn of AD 39, Caligula got word his two sisters Livilla and Agrippina were working to kill him while they were out of town (or at least, they knew about attempts by others to try to). Caligula took swift action at the news. Lepidus (the plot's instigator, who had also been Caligula's gay lover) was immediately put to death, while Livilla and Agrippina were remanded to Rome for trial. On the journey, the soldiers forced Agrippina to carry Lepidus's cremated bones and ashes in an urn. Incriminating love letters between them were read aloud at the trial. As the guilty sisters were being exiled to a remote island, Caligula reminded them of his lethal power with the warning "I have swords as well as islands." He then dedicated three daggers—one for each of the plotters—to Mars, the god of vengeance, to give thanks for escaping his close brush with death.

Alone, bored, rejected, and utterly hopeless, Agrippina hit rock bottom on her distant island. *Will I ever escape this barren place? What will happen to my son?* Little Nero had been given to Ahenobarbus, his father, for upbringing—but that turned out just as poorly for the boy as the loss of his mother. Ahenobarbus died the next year, leaving Nero in the care of two very different aunts on his father's side. Though both women were fabulously wealthy, their personalities differed. Aunt Domitia was a penny-pincher who invested little in Nero's welfare. Apparently, Nero didn't take to her at all. Years later, as an adult, he visited her sickbed while she was suffering from constipation and ordered her to be given a deadly dose of laxative, then seized her properties while her corpse was still warm. As for the other caretaker, Aunt Lepida, Nero enjoyed her company much more. She was the prototypical "favorite aunt" who would indulge her nephew's whims, providing a stark contrast to Agrippina's authoritarian style.

After two years on the island, Agrippina suddenly found her fortunes reversed when Emperor Caligula met his deadly fate. As he was making his way with an upset stomach through a covered passage to the latrine, assassins attacked him. One account says he was stabbed in the back of the neck and the chest. Another describes a thrust through the jaw. Either way, the assault knocked him to the ground. As he lay dying, he shouted as if anyone cared, "I'm still alive!" Instead of receiving any help, the outburst earned him thirty stab wounds, some even through his genitals. Caligula was twenty-nine years old when he died. During the last four of them, he had tyrannized Rome like an insane madman.

The imperial throne now passed to a new ruler, Agrippina's uncle Claudius, whose immediate actions included the order to bring the exiled sisters back from their remote island. Agrippina returned to the capital in triumph. She received back all her properties and resumed her rightful place as a bright star in Rome's aristocratic constellation. Her uncle had just been installed as the most powerful man in the world. But even that wasn't enough for Agrippina. She intended to become not just his niece but his wife.

While Agrippina was striving and conniving for power on behalf of little Nero, what was Paul up to? After escaping Damascus in a basket, he had visited Peter and James in Jerusalem to familiarize himself with the leaders of the faith. To avoid trouble in Israel like he had aroused in Arabia, the disciples advised him to relocate to his hometown of Tarsus. While Paul was praying in the temple, a vision from Jesus confirmed this was the right plan. He immediately returned by ship to Tarsus, a wealthy city near the southern coast of what is today the nation of Turkey.

The Bible doesn't say much about what happened during the next nine years of Paul's life. Yet we do know of two important events that occurred during this span—both of which he recorded in his second letter to the

Corinthians. Each event affected him so powerfully that they transformed his calling to ministry.

First, Paul had a mystical vision that forever changed him. It was such an out-of-body experience that he had to speak as if it had occurred to someone else, though he was clearly talking about himself. The Corinthians had been questioning Paul's credibility as an apostle. Although he didn't want to boast, he felt the need to offer such an impressive story as proof of his legitimacy. Here is what happened, according to his own words:

> It is doubtless not profitable for me to boast. I will come to visions and revelations of the Lord: I know a man in Christ who fourteen years ago—whether in the body I do not know, or whether out of the body I do not know, God knows—such a one was caught up to the third heaven. And I know such a man—whether in the body or out of the body I do not know, God knows—how he was caught up into Paradise and heard inexpressible words, which it is not lawful for a man to utter. Of such a one I will boast; yet of myself I will not boast, except in my infirmities.[1]

What did Paul mean by being caught up to the "third heaven"? In ancient thought, the world above the surface of the earth had three parts. The first (lowest) was the air where clouds form and birds fly. Above this was the second heaven, the realm of the celestial bodies such as the sun, moon, and stars. The third heaven was the highest place above the visible firmament. Way up there, God had laid wooden beams across the heavenly waters for his royal house.[2] He sat upon a glorious throne with the earth as his footstool.[3] When Paul said he got called up to the third heaven, he meant he was literally summoned into the throne room of God to hear truths so profound he couldn't even express them in words.

Notice, however, that Paul didn't want to boast about this lofty summons and its inexpressible revelations. Instead, he wanted to celebrate his personal weakness. That's why he went on to describe the second aspect of his mysterious decade in Tarsus. He said,

---

1. 2 Corinthians 12:1–5.
2. Psalm 104:3.
3. Isaiah 66:1.

> Lest I should be exalted above measure by the abundance of the revelations, a thorn in the flesh was given to me, a messenger of Satan to buffet me, lest I be exalted above measure. Concerning this thing I pleaded with the Lord three times that it might depart from me. And He said to me, "My grace is sufficient for you, for My strength is made perfect in weakness." Therefore most gladly I will rather boast in my infirmities, that the power of Christ may rest upon me. Therefore I take pleasure in infirmities, in reproaches, in needs, in persecutions, in distresses, for Christ's sake. *For when I am weak, then I am strong.*[4]

Modern commentators have spent a lot of time trying to determine what this "thorn" in Paul's flesh might have been. Some say it was violent persecution or personal antagonism from an enemy who opposed him. Others claim it was a fierce temptation that Paul often fought and wanted removed. Still others argue it was a physical infirmity, perhaps epileptic fits, leprosy, or eyesight troubles. The possibilities are almost endless.

In the end, no one truly knows. Yet three things are clear: It was persistently troublesome, it felt like a satanic attack, and the weakness it caused was publicly embarrassing. The idea of a "thorn" can be understood more like a splinter, something that lodges under the skin and causes pain on a continual basis. Yet this affliction wasn't purely physical, for Paul called it a messenger (literally, an "angel") from Satan—that is, a demon. He said, "You know it was because of a bodily ailment that I preached the gospel to you at first, and though my condition was a trial to you, you did not scorn or despise me, but received me as an angel of God, as Christ Jesus."[5] In other words, while the infirmity was something that people might have despised or rejected, Paul had been warmly embraced despite his obvious, shameful condition. It weakened him so much he had to pause in Galatia and stay there to rest, leading to his evangelism of that region.

Putting all of these things together, perhaps the thorn was demonic warfare, which caused terrible shame. Paul often referred to his awareness that he was a blood-guilty persecutor of Christians, so perhaps the Accuser (which is

---

4. 2 Corinthians 12:7–10.
5. Galatians 4:13–14 ESV.

what "Satan" literally means) terrified him with traumatic memories and nightmares. Since extreme anxiety can lead to skin diseases, perhaps Paul looked like a leper when these flare-ups occurred. Although this can't be known for certain, the conjecture makes sense of the limited data. In any case, Paul's time in Tarsus was marked by an extraordinary spiritual ascent into the heavens, but also a descent into a debilitating condition that would trouble him for the rest of his life. Yet Paul was able to endure God's *thorn* because he had visited God's *throne*.

No doubt Paul and Nero had opposite ideas of what a throne was all about. Little Nero, protected by his ambitious, unscrupulous mother, received every earthly benefit. After he survived the years of her island exile, his destiny regained its former shine. Agrippina was determined to be the "best mother" she could be. If that meant allying herself with the debauched throne of Caligula, so be it. Once the crown passed to her uncle Claudius, Agrippina set her sights on his reign as a new way to advance her son's prospects. Due to her striving and conniving, Nero had every reason to think he would someday sit on the imperial throne.

Paul, on the other hand, had no such privileged status. Instead, he received something even better: a trip to the heavenly throne, where he learned things that even a princess like Agrippina couldn't begin to understand. To avoid pride—so common in the hallways of Roman power—God allowed Paul to be afflicted with an irritant that wouldn't be removed. It kept Paul continually embarrassed, humbled, and dependent on help from outside himself. Did that make Paul weak? Perhaps in a physical sense, but not when it came to divine power. Instead of the best mother, Paul had the ever-present help of his heavenly Father. That was why he could so confidently proclaim, "When I am weak, then I am strong."[6] Paul knew that nothing was impossible with the true King on his side.

6. 2 Corinthians 12:10.

CODA

Our conversation about this chapter considers how Nero's mother manipulated her son and tried to live through him—a temptation for parents of every era. We also discuss Paul's "thorn," which afflicted him yet kept him dependent on God. And we explore the nature of mystical experiences. Are they valid? Do people still have them today?

BRYAN: In chapter 5 we're seeing Nero begin to move toward the throne. And for the first time we meet Agrippina, we see who she was, and how she was a master manipulator and a conniver.

KATHIE: Oh, yeah, that's what manipulators are. She was a chess player. She was playing chess with human beings and literally knocking over kings and queens. Others were just pawns—anybody that had gotten in her way. Now, back then, a woman could not be caesar. But she could be an augusta, right?

BRYAN: That's right. She could get that title, and she did get that title—as we will discover in chapter 7. Once she married Claudius, her goal was to get Nero on the throne. Have you ever seen the phenomenon where mothers try to advance their sons? There's a fine line between supporting your child and helping him along, versus living through him. Do you see that a lot in your world?

KATHIE: Yes, all the time. I say to my friends who want their kid to do this or become that, "Scripture says that God's dreams and your child's dreams were woven together inside you, in the mother's womb."[7] Such a great work was being done in our hearts while our mothers were doing the hard work of making us in the womb. But—and this is important!—my mother never had the right to dream my dreams. She never did that. If I'm grateful for anything from my mother and father it's that they let me dream my own dreams. They knew they had a strange child. They had three kids. And I was a middle child. My brother was a brilliant writer and a brilliant student and a brilliant athlete. All those are good things, but he wasn't weird like me. My sister was a beautiful singer, and a great athlete too. Not world-class, either one of them, but very, very good. Our parents let us be ourselves.

BRYAN: But as far as living through a son, have you ever felt that with Cody? Do you ever feel that as a mom? Do you ever have to roll yourself back?

7. Psalm 139:14; Jeremiah 1:5.

Agrippina didn't roll herself back. She wanted to live through Nero. But you don't do that.

KATHIE: No. First of all, I already had my own career. It was well established long before I was pregnant with Cody. There were things I still wanted to do, dreams I wanted to fulfill. Although my parents wanted to protect me, my father used to say, "I love you too much, Kathie, to deny you the privilege of making mistakes." I was always grateful for that.

BRYAN: Yeah. That's wise. And then also in this chapter, Paul is caught up in a vision. He talks about being caught up to the third heaven. We can't even imagine that. Can we go into God's throne room like the book of Revelation talks about? What does that even mean? What do you think he saw there in God's throne room?

KATHIE: He saw the face of God. He saw the grandeur. Emperor Nero in all of his finery, and even King Solomon in all his glory, they were nothing in comparison. Paul says we cannot see or hear, nor can we ever imagine, what God has in store for those who love him and believe in him.[8] That's why we look forward to heaven. We're not going to sit on a cloud and play the lyre. We're not going to do that. I bet there will be singing, though! Oh, there'll be glorious music beyond anything I could ever write, or Beethoven could ever write.

BRYAN: Even *I'll* be able to sing! Hey, maybe you and I will sing, which you wouldn't want to have happen on earth. But maybe with a heavenly voice I could sing with you. There won't be critics in the audience.

KATHIE: Imagine how great it'll be in heaven! Barbra Streisand can move you on earth. Imagine what the choirs of the angels and the saints in heaven will be able to do! That's what Paul experienced when he was caught up to the third heaven.

BRYAN: We need to contrast it to the different kind of glory that Nero sought.

KATHIE: And all of the caesars. Didn't they all love being worshiped?

BRYAN: Absolutely. Nero's mother is trying to get him on a throne, and he wants a throne, but here's Paul, who has been to the very throne room of God. The actual throne! And in this chapter Paul talks about his thorn. He says, "When I am weak, then I am strong," which isn't what Nero thought, is it?

---

8. 1 Corinthians 2:9.

KATHIE: No. In fact, he would manipulate things to never seem weak to anybody.

BRYAN: Yeah, whatever it took to keep up appearances. But Paul admits his thorn. And we don't even know what it was. We know he calls it a messenger from Satan. And we know that it was persistent, and he prayed but it wouldn't go away. Maybe in some ways it was like you were talking about with your injury to your hip, where you had something painful and it felt like a messenger of Satan that wouldn't ever stop. But the Lord makes you strong in those weak times, doesn't he?

KATHIE: Yes. And you know what? Our impulse is to try to fight it. We do everything we can in our culture to work on our bodies, work on our face. We can get all kinds of surgeries just to avoid the inevitable. Who knows how old we are? First of all, of course, God knows, because he counts the days of our lives. But your body also knows. Your body knows how old you are, no matter how many times you carve it up, or you lipo it. Your body's kind of laughing at you, like, "I know how old you are!" Back in Cleopatra's day—and we talked about her in *Herod and Mary*—these women had their makeup. There are many mentions in the Bible of beauty products that women used, some that are still used today. It's natural to want to be, first of all, beautiful for the person you love. You want to remain attractive. You want them to not be looking at another woman. You think, "Look here! Keep looking right in these eyes!" It's natural. And men are that way too. All humans are vain by nature. And that's why I say, "Fix your eyes upon Jesus, the author and finisher of our faith, who for the glory set before him endured the cross." And that cross wasn't beauty, but shame. We have to understand the shame of it, because he was naked and he was accused of being a criminal. And he knew it was all a lie, but he endured it in order to "sit down at the right hand of the throne of God."[9]

BRYAN: And I think Paul had that same mentality of his weakness being his strength. He didn't like it, of course. It wasn't enjoyable for him. To the Corinthians, he was this foolish guy that couldn't do public speaking. And yet he said it's the foolishness of the cross that brings victory. Paul knew it was his weakness met with God's strength; therefore, God gets the glory. There's

9. Hebrews 12:2, author's paraphrase.

such a contrast between an imperial throne and the weakness of Paul. But he's looking to attain the throne room of Christ. And he does.

KATHIE: I think there's a message here that nothing has changed. Look around at the world leaders today and what they do in the name of achieving their own glory and achieving their own wealth. There's countless of them. It's that way in Syria and Nigeria, what they're doing to Christians. It's everywhere. They're all over the world, just like they always were. There have always been Neros. There have always been Caligulas. There have always been Herods.

BRYAN: Do you think many people today have been caught up in a mystical experience like Paul?

KATHIE: Maybe, but you don't have to be. You've seen God if you've seen his presence in life. You've seen his throne room through Scripture and through your mind's eye. And I've seen the places where Jesus walked. That's why I encourage people, if they can, to go to Israel, the Holy Land, to see where it happened and learn the stories. About 90 percent of what is in the Gospels about Jesus happened in Galilee. You're a full-time teacher and you're the professor, but I believe we're all teachers. It's so effective when we can teach about the things we've seen and we know firsthand!

BRYAN: The angel said, "Come and see the place where he lay."[10]

KATHIE: That's exactly right. Come see the place where he lay. See that the tomb is empty. And if you know that, you know everything.

10. Matthew 28:6 NIV.

SIX

THE BEGINNING OF MISSION

It was just another day in Tarsus . . . until the visitor showed up and changed the direction of Paul's life forever.

The day had started out normally enough. Paul, a professional tentmaker by trade—a broad term that included all kinds of canopies, awnings, and portable shelters—was going about his day-to-day routine. His family, affluent and multigenerational in Tarsus, owned a large and profitable tentmaking shop in town. Everything about the area was so conducive to the business that Cilicia, the region around Tarsus, had given its name to the fabric from which the tents were made: *cilicium*. Weavers made the cloth from the hair of local goats, rendering a jet-black material that was especially good at shedding water.

Although observant Jews didn't handle dead animals because it made them ritually impure, animal products could be purified so they'd be clean enough to use. Interestingly, some goatskins even served as the writing surface for the holy Torah. So like other Jews, Paul had learned how to balance the rules of his faith with the commercial demands of secular living.

It was while Paul was busy at his craft that a visitor's voice called out: "Shalom, brother!"

Glancing toward the door, Paul couldn't help but smile. The salutation came from his dear friend Barnabas, whose name meant "son of encouragement." Barnabas, originally from Cyprus, had introduced Paul to Peter and

James in Jerusalem. Having taken up residence in Jerusalem, Barnabas often gave charity to followers of the Way.

Paul immediately dropped his tools and rushed to embrace his visitor, giving him a friendly kiss. "What brings you to Tarsus?" he asked after greetings had been exchanged.

"Joyous news! The work of the Lord has spread to Antioch. God is doing a great thing there. Many of the brethren are embracing the Savior."

Though Paul welcomed the report, his gaze fell to the floor as a pang of guilt stabbed him. He knew all too well why missionaries had scattered from Jerusalem to Antioch: because of his own bloodthirsty persecution, especially the violent murder of Stephen.

As Paul stared at the ground, wrestling with his conflicted thoughts, he felt a hand settle on his shoulder. When he looked up, his eyes met those of his friend. "The Lord has washed you clean," Barnabas reminded him. "He has taken away your sin and is turning it into something new."

Paul nodded his assent to this precious gospel truth. His friend had lived up to his name with this needed word of encouragement. Revived in spirit, Paul asked, "Do only the Hebrews in Antioch believe?"

"No! The Greek-speaking Jews are also confessing Jesus. And some of them have even been spreading the word to . . ." Barnabas hesitated as a grin came to his face. His expression brightened as he finished his thought: ". . . to the Gentiles."

"Praise God!" Paul exclaimed. "Christ is a light to all nations!"

"Nobody understands that better than you." Barnabas's gaze grew intense and his demeanor became serious. "Paul, I have come to you for a purpose. The elders in Antioch believe it is time for you to help me bring the gospel to those outside the house of Israel. Will you help me fulfill God's worldwide mission to the Gentiles?"

Instead of answering, Paul glanced around his family's shop. It was a comfortable, productive place. Its income made life easy, allowing Paul to focus on evangelism. God had blessed his years here. The Jews of Tarsus were hearing the message of salvation through their Messiah. *You shouldn't leave*, whispered a voice in Paul's head. *Why give up all this? Your work here is enough . . . you don't need to do more. How much can God expect of you? Hasn't he asked enough from you already?*

As Paul wrestled with his thoughts, another voice broke through the confusion, causing him to recall the words of Jesus on the Damascus road: "Go, for I will send you far away to the Gentiles."[1] *How far is "far away"? Even to the ends of the earth!*

Paul untied his work apron and set it aside. Walking over to a wall, he removed a satchel from a peg. From inside a cupboard, he retrieved a loaf of bread, a cloth-wrapped cheese, and a gourd of water. After putting them into the satchel, he looked up. As his eyes met Barnabas's eyes, he said, "I'm ready. When God issues a call, you have to forget what lies behind and strain toward whatever lies ahead."[2]

"Suffering may lie ahead," Barnabas remarked.

"I know. But after it, I shall receive the prize of the upward call of God in Christ Jesus."[3]

Paul and Barnabas traveled together from Tarsus to Antioch, the third-greatest city of the empire after Rome and Alexandria. It was a sophisticated, urban metropolis with a nearby port. And since the port was only a four-day sail from Caesarea in Israel, many Jews had immigrated to Antioch and now called it home—about a tenth of the Antiochian population. Jewish travelers kept the connection to their homeland alive by traveling back and forth between Antioch and Jerusalem, exchanging news about important developments in their faith.

Another aspect of Antioch's religious culture that made it interesting to Paul was the city's population of Gentiles who worshiped the pagan gods. But due to the large Jewish presence in Antioch, a kind of hybrid worship had developed over time. Some Gentiles had rejected their multiple divinities and decided to worship the God of Israel alone. Intuitively, these former pagans had realized that the monotheism and morality of Judaism were the right way to go. The "God-fearers," as they were called, could listen to synagogue services and study Torah. They were, however, second-class citizens in the worship

1. Acts 22:21 ESV.
2. Philippians 3:13 NIV, author's paraphrase.
3. Philippians 3:14 NKJV.

of God. The path to full synagogue membership and Passover celebrations required circumcision and total conversion to Judaism.[4]

Then Paul arrived in Antioch. He had a radical new message, one that would occupy his thoughts—and stir up a great deal of trouble—for the rest of his life. Paul claimed that God's presence no longer had to be accessed in a temple made with hands, a building of stone and timber located in Israel's capital city. Instead, God could be found anywhere. He would reside within each believer who came to him through Jesus the Messiah.

Furthermore, just as the temple had been bypassed, so had some of the Torah's requirements. The essential spirit of the Torah would of course remain the same, as none of its ethics or morality had disappeared. Yet God had set aside some of the Law's more stringent requirements. Among these abolished demands were the kosher food laws. But for the male God-fearers who had set their affections on Yahweh, another abolished command mattered even more. No longer would they have to undergo a painful surgery on their penis to gain full access to God's spiritual blessings. Jesus now offered direct access to God, apart from the rite of circumcision. When Paul came to Antioch with that liberating message, many God-fearers were glad to hear it!

The Jerusalem leaders, however, grew concerned. Circumcision had been granted to the patriarch Abraham as the essential mark of God's covenant with Israel. On the eighth day after an Israelite boy's birth, a "circular cut" (which is the literal meaning of *circumcision*) was made with flint knives to remove the foreskin. Forever afterward, Israelite men would be visibly distinct from other men. God had been clear about the necessity of this rite: "And the uncircumcised male child, who is not circumcised in the flesh of his foreskin, that person shall be cut off from his people; he has broken my covenant."[5] Who was a newcomer like Paul, especially a former persecutor of the faith, to declare that this time-honored sign of the covenant was invalid?

Though this issue might seem irrelevant today, it actually puts the nature of the gospel into clear focus. Is God's salvation contingent on human actions, what Paul referred to as "works of the law"? Or is salvation so free that it comes by grace alone, without humans having to lift themselves over the bar of God's

---

4. Exodus 12:48.
5. Genesis 17:14.

nearly impossible standards? In other words, do people have to carry out difficult religious duties to receive divine mercy for their sins? Or do they need only to believe in the death and resurrection of Jesus to be saved?

The debate over Paul's "faith versus works" message came under deep scrutiny in the sixteenth century, the era of the Protestant Reformation. Figures such as Martin Luther (1483–1546) and John Calvin (1509–1564) argued that the sacraments of the Roman Catholic Church could be equated with the Jewish works of the law that Paul had so vehemently rejected. The Reformers claimed salvation came instead by faith alone (*sola fide*)—that is, by believing the gospel message, not by participating in a church hierarchy with a sacramental system of penance and rewards. Although those debates happened a long time after Paul walked the earth, they addressed the heart of the gospel. The way to salvation isn't through outward deeds—whether circumcision, sacraments, or any other human performance. Instead, faith in Jesus must blossom first in the believer's heart. Any holy works done afterward must be the resulting fruit of saving faith.

For a whole year, Paul worked alongside Barnabas in Antioch spreading the good news to the Gentiles. With so many God-fearers joining the faith while keeping their uncircumcised status, a new word emerged to describe the converts, a term never before used: "Christians."[6] Prior to this, the believers in Jesus had seen themselves as followers of a spiritual Way within Judaism. Many Jewish converts continued in this pattern. Yet now that Gentiles were visibly following Jesus, too, somebody named them after their founder, and the name stuck.

Originally, it might have been a slur, a way of associating those foolish Gentile believers with their crucified namesake. Or perhaps the citizens of Antioch viewed the new sect like a philosophy, in the same way the followers of Plato were called the Platonists. In any case, the Gentile believers were happy to be named after Christ. The term "Christian" came to be used elsewhere in the New Testament.[7] Soon, it became the most common designation for Jesus' worldwide followers.

---

6. Acts 11:26.
7. Acts 26:28; 1 Peter 4:16.

The busy evangelistic work of Paul and Barnabas came to an unexpected halt when a Spirit-filled prophet arrived in Antioch with a dire prediction: A famine was about to engulf that part of the world. Since Antioch was a wealthy city with lots of distant trade and nearby agriculture, the Christians knew they would have more margin to survive the shortfall than their friends in Jerusalem. Out of brotherly love, they decided to take up a collection for famine relief and send it down to Judea with the church's two foremost evangelists—Paul and Barnabas, who would be accompanied by a young fellow worker named Titus.

While Paul was in Jerusalem to deliver the financial aid, he explained to the apostolic leaders the gospel that he was preaching to the Gentiles. In particular, he informed them about the freedom from circumcision that the gospel entailed. He explained how Titus, who was an uncircumcised Greek, wasn't forced to accept the knife in order to stay within the Christian family. Satisfied by the explanations, the Jerusalem leaders—Peter, James, and John—gave Paul and Barnabas the "the right hand of fellowship, that we should go to the Gentiles and they to the circumcised."[8] In other words, the duties of gospel proclamation would be split. Peter and the other apostles would evangelize Jews with the message of Jesus, while Paul and his companions were tasked with bringing the message to those outside the house of Israel.

With this task so clearly assigned by the apostolic founders, the church of Antioch decided—through the leading of the Holy Spirit—to send Paul and Barnabas on an overseas mission. The itinerary took the travelers from Antioch's harbor to Barnabas's homeland, the island of Cyprus, where amazing events showed how gifted Paul was for Gentile evangelism.

The leader of the island was a Roman proconsul, a man of intelligence and spiritual interest. Unfortunately, a Jewish false prophet and magician had been whispering in the proconsul's ear, leading him astray. Because the proconsul was a genuine seeker, he gave an audience to the newly arrived missionaries so

8. Galatians 2:9.

he might hear their message. True to his zealous character, Paul boldly confronted the false prophet as a son of the devil, then struck him blind through divine judgment. This led to a great spiritual triumph: "When the proconsul saw what had happened, he believed, for he was amazed at the teaching about the Lord."[9]

From Cyprus, the missionaries sailed to the mainland of Asia Minor, where they again met with evangelistic success. But in another city named Antioch (of which there were many in the ancient world), the missionaries suddenly ran into trouble. Some Jewish traditionalists objected to the gospel's inclusion of Gentiles and freedom from law keeping. These men opposed and reviled Paul and Barnabas. Nevertheless, the two missionaries didn't back down. They explained their divine commission through the words of Isaiah 49:6, "I have set you as a light to the Gentiles, that you should be for salvation to the ends of the earth."[10] When the Gentiles learned that the one true God cared about them, they rejoiced. Whoever God had appointed to eternal life believed the good news of Jesus.

After this success, the evangelists advanced to other cities in the region of Galatia, not only proclaiming the gospel but healing a crippled man. Yet the previous hostility now turned into outright violence. Opponents from earlier stops followed Paul to the city of Lystra and stirred up the crowd against him. The very thing that had happened to Stephen now happened to Paul: The mob took him outside the city walls and stoned him, leaving him for dead. But God had other plans. After the enraged crowd dispersed, some disciples realized Paul had only been knocked out. Miraculously, while his injuries looked bad, they weren't enough to kill him. His friends helped him stand up and escape. The next day, he and Barnabas left the city where the locals wanted to kill them.

Instead of fleeing into the safety of anonymity, however, the intrepid missionaries backtracked their steps to the very cities where they had been persecuted, strengthening and encouraging their converts at every stop along their way. They reminded the new Christians that the kingdom of God could be attained only after suffering tribulations—a prediction Jesus himself had

9. Acts 13:12 NIV.
10. Acts 13:47.

given to his disciples.[11] Paul's half-healed bruises and jagged scars from his recent stoning lent great authority to his words.

Reaching the coast at last, the two friends caught a ship bound for the port of Antioch. They had completed the first stage of the task for which they had been commissioned by the Jerusalem apostles and Antiochian elders. Despite many hardships, God's grace had kept them safe and brought them home.

When the Antiochian church gathered to hear their report, the missionaries declared "all that God had done with them, and that He had opened the door of faith to the Gentiles."[12] Everyone could see the gospel was having its intended effect. People all over the world were getting to know the God of Israel. Though Paul had just finished his first missionary journey, he understood that more voyages with Barnabas would be needed soon. He had traveled to a faraway land to reach the Gentiles. But he hadn't yet reached the uttermost ends of the earth!

CODA

In this conversation, we discuss Paul's mission to take the message of the Jewish Messiah to the Gentiles across the world. We also focus on Jesus' love and care for women. Faith in Jesus isn't about rule keeping or man-made religion but about receiving God's tenderness, then sharing his love with everyone. This message is good news indeed!

BRYAN: In chapter 6 we begin with Paul. He's gone back to Tarsus and is working in the family business when Barnabas shows up.

KATHIE: Let's remind people where Tarsus was, okay?

BRYAN: Good idea. It's in what we would today call Turkey, in an area named Cilicia, where there were goats with a special fur. It was the hair of the goats that was important, more than the leather. The goat's hair was woven into an effective fabric that was waterproof, making it good for tents. Paul's family had a business that used that particular goat-hair fabric to make waterproof

11. Matthew 10:22; John 15:20.
12. Acts 14:27.

tents. So, very likely, Paul was quite wealthy. Jews could be tentmakers because they didn't have to kill the goats, just shear the wool and weave it.

KATHIE: I love how you explained to me how he could be a tentmaker. It was woven goat hair, not the skin of animals. That's important because when you've studied the Torah as much as I have, you learn that you don't touch dead animals, and you can't get leather without somebody touching a dead animal. I mean, for the Jewish priest, that's their job, to do all this slaughtering, but then they had to become ritually pure again after each time, didn't they? That's why there's all the mikvahs all over the place. They had washings to do afterward, and there was a specific way to do it. You were always having to be cleansed. It wasn't easy to be a ritually pure Jew at the time!

BRYAN: Right. And for Paul, I believe it came to him in the form of fabric, much like woolen cloth with a natural waterproofing. Paul wasn't out there herding goats or slaughtering them. He was a city guy and spent all his time in an urban context. Now, with Barnabas coming to him, for Paul to have gone on this mission meant leaving behind wealth and to leave his family. But Barnabas knew that the mission from Antioch had to go out to the Gentiles, and he knew nobody could do that better than Paul. So he goes up to Tarsus, which is not far from Antioch, and he says, "Hey, do you want to go on a mission?" And Paul says, "You betcha!"

KATHIE: He always wanted to go on a road trip, didn't he? But those roads were not good back then.

BRYAN: After Paul's conversion, and after Damascus, when he goes to Jerusalem, Jesus meets him at the temple in a vision and says, "Go, I will send you far away to the Gentiles."[13] So yeah, Paul always wanted to go on a road trip, because Jesus had put him on that mission.

KATHIE: And he always wanted to go to Rome.

BRYAN: That's coming up in chapter 7; we'll circle back to that. Paul wanted to go beyond Rome because Jesus wanted him to go to the end of the earth, and Spain was the end of the earth. So Paul is in Tarsus, and then suddenly he is called to Antioch and everything starts to happen for him. In this chapter, we also saw that Gentile believers are first called Christians at Antioch.

---

13. Acts 22:21 NIV.

KATHIE: Jews were followers of the Way. They never converted to another religion called Christianity. It's the other way around. Gentiles converted to a sect of Judaism at the time, and that's what it was. Saul became Paul, and it shows how God's calling on our lives so often changes our names. We become new creatures in Christ, meaning the sanctification part of the believer's life. And that's important because in another place you were talking about how Christianity got started. Bottom line—it started when Jesus was born and he fulfilled the Hebrew Scriptures of what was going to happen when a Messiah came. We knew where he was going to come from—it was going to be Bethlehem. It's an ancient Jewish story, Bryan. This is so critical. I have friends in my life who are devout and serious believers in Jesus as their Savior, but they don't know where they came from. It's important to embrace the Jewishness of our faith.

BRYAN: You've said it well! And I agree. Christianity is not another "religion," separate from Judaism. It's the fruit that grew out of Israel's root. The branch of David has leafed out in Jesus the Messiah. But some of those old Jewish ways of doing things had to be left behind, if you were a Gentile. That was Paul's gospel of grace. And a big one was circumcision. For a Jew, how shocking would it have been that you could come to God and be uncircumcised? As a Gentile, they were said to be equal, even without circumcision. That was just shocking to a Jewish person back in those days, wasn't it?

KATHIE: And a female Gentile was equal, too, who didn't even have a private part like that. It was amazing that she could be equal. Jesus called women the daughters of Abraham.[14] He was a radical feminist, always teaching equality.

BRYAN: So a shunned group, like women or Gentiles, *they* are allowed to come close to God through Jesus. The gospel was making people encounter God in a way that had never been done before, right? Jesus was truly the ultimate radical.

KATHIE: And he broke a lot of the Torah rules in the process, but he said the Sabbath was made for man, not the other way around.[15] He came to fulfill the Law, not to condemn people through it. That was the most radical thing

14. Luke 13:16.
15. Mark 2:27.

about him. Because the Law condemned before mercy showed up. And yet, when you read the Old Testament—and I don't even like to call it that, because it was really the old covenant, the one made with Moses—you always find blessings. I also don't like to call them the Ten Commandments because, for me, they are the Ten Blessings. "Live your life this way," God says.

BRYAN: Not the Ten Recommendations.

KATHIE: No, they aren't recommendations! But let's note that circumcision wasn't one of them, because it wasn't supposed to be permanent. That was part of the rabbinical law, the Mosaic law. It was done to set the nation apart, because the pagan world didn't partake in that operation.

BRYAN: And yet Paul circumcised Timothy because he had a Jewish mother. But he said, "You Gentiles don't have to do that."[16] Which, if you think about it, he's not a baby. If you're an adult man and you want to convert, but you have to do that, it's a high barrier to conversion.

KATHIE: I've never thought of that before. Timothy was a grown man, a young man, but still an adult. It's a much worse thing to go through as an adult.

BRYAN: Right. So imagine putting out the gospel of grace but attaching it to such a painful, scary surgery.

KATHIE: But Timothy agreed to it. He didn't have to, but he did. I've never thought about this until right now. Timothy said, "Not my will, but yours be done, Lord." And that was probably a tough one to get over. He was out of commission for a while.

BRYAN: Right! So that's why the Gentiles don't have to do that. You're not saved by works, you're saved by faith. What does that sentence mean to you? "You're not justified by works, you're justified by faith alone."

KATHIE: I have mixed emotions about it because the fruit of the Spirit is often the works of our hands and the works of our feet. The places where we go. Who we touch. What we do. Faith and works live together in such beautiful harmony. They just do. I know faith without works is dead, but works without faith is dead too. People can spend all their time doing good deeds, doing all the right things, without having true righteousness. One time the Lord spoke to me very clearly. I am always careful to say I didn't hear him audibly. He spoke to my inner spirit and my spirit heard him when he said,

---

16. Acts 16:1–3, author's paraphrase.

"Kathie, do you want to be right or do you want to be righteous?" That got me right where I live! I said, "Oh, Lord, you know I'm right in this matter. But I want to be righteous." I always try to keep that in mind every day. I tell myself, "Kathie, you have a choice here. Do you want to be right? Or is it more important that you show mercy to this person, show an understanding of where they're coming from?" And that's what Paul was doing.

BRYAN: Yes, because he cared about inner righteousness, not the outer good deeds. Unless the outer works came from the right interior spirit, they didn't matter.

KATHIE: And he was from Tarsus, so he'd been around a whole bunch more Gentiles than anybody that stayed in Jerusalem. He got down and dirty with them. He went to them and he preached to them. He had met enough of them to know that they had hearts for God. And they wanted the knowledge of God, but they didn't have a way to encounter him. Circumcision was intimidating to them. The spirit was willing, but their flesh was weak. And Paul said, "That's going to be a stumbling block to the gospel going forward."[17] The whole point of the gospel is, don't let anything in your life be a stumbling block. You just profess Jesus—born, died, raised, coming again. That's the good news.

BRYAN: "Confess with your mouth that Jesus is Lord and believe in your heart that God raised him from the dead."[18] It's not about whether you have circumcision, or, for modern people, whether you go to this church or that denomination, or do good deeds, or give to charity, or whatever. Right?

KATHIE: Right. Those are all good things but they're not *the* thing. Jesus is the thing. He alone can lead you to God. He's all you need.

---

17. Galatians 5:11, author's paraphrase.
18. Romans 10:9 ESV.

SEVEN

FAITH AND FERTILITY IN ROME

Paul felt encouraged by his recent evangelistic progress. Many of Antioch's Jews, along with some newly emerging Gentile Christians, had begun to follow Jesus. Churches had been planted in Cyprus, Pamphylia, Pisidia, and Galatia. Each place where Paul had traveled proved to be fertile soil for the seed of the gospel. But what about faraway Italy? Paul desperately wanted to get to Rome. *How can I bring the good news to the world without bringing it to that great city? Would I be the first to proclaim the gospel? Or do believers already exist there?*

Though the origins of the Roman church are shrouded in mystery, a few historical hints can be discerned. After Jesus ascended back to heaven in AD 33, some visitors from Rome (both Jews and God-fearers) heard the apostolic message announced to them.[1] The Holy Spirit translated the apostles' preaching so the travelers from Italy could understand it. Probably, these visitors went home and told their Roman friends what God was doing through Jesus. Perhaps some churches took root at that time.

1. Acts 2:10–11.

The ancient historian Suetonius made an interesting comment about an event that happened in Rome around AD 49. He said, "Since the Jews constantly made disturbances at the instigation of Chrestus, [Emperor Claudius] expelled them from Rome." Much debate has centered on who this "Chrestus" might have been. Some scholars view him as an unknown agitator who was creating trouble in the Roman synagogues. But that name wasn't common among the Jews. It was a slave name that meant "useful," which was just the kind of name a master might give to his servant. However, most Jews at that time were free and well treated by the government. They had even named one of their synagogues after Caesar Augustus. A Gentile slave named Chrestus doesn't sound like the kind of person who could put all of Roman Judaism in an uproar.

The more likely possibility is that "Chrestus" was Suetonius's misspelling of the name "Christus," a specific reference to Jesus. Although Latin speakers at that time didn't use the word *Christ*, they certainly knew the common name of Chrestus. Naturally, that was the sound they heard when people talked about the new sect. It would be easy for Suetonius to make this error. In his historical research, he had learned the Jewish community of Rome was agitated over some controversial figure. Emperor Claudius got tired of the commotion and evicted the Jews from the city. The Bible confirms this in Acts 18:2. If the emperor's decree was prompted by a Jewish dispute about Jesus (assuming that *Chrestus* was a misspelling of *Christus*), it would prove the gospel had already reached Rome by the late forties.

Many figures throughout church history have suggested the apostle Peter founded the church in Rome. Even if someone doesn't accept the teaching of the Catholic Church that Peter was the first pope, it's still likely that he established Jesus-believing communities in the capital city. Numerous traditions of the ancient church—often distinct from one another—repeat this claim, making it probable from a scholar's point of view.

Peter's own letter also suggests it. In his first biblical epistle, he wrote to the churches of Asia Minor that the church "who is in Babylon, elect together with you, greets you."[2] It's next to impossible to believe that Peter was sending a greeting from a church in the literal city of Babylon in Mesopotamia. Instead,

2. 1 Peter 5:13.

he was probably using "Babylon" as a code name for Rome, just as Scripture does elsewhere.[3] So Peter probably did work among Jews in Rome to spread the gospel of Jesus, while Paul knew different community leaders there, many of whom were Gentiles. Eventually, he mentioned some of them in his letter to Rome without making any reference to Peter.[4] Apparently, the believers in the capital city were moving in different social circles. Sometimes the Jews and Gentiles worshiped together, while other times they were more separated.

When Emperor Claudius expelled the Jews from Rome because they were embroiled in strife over "Chrestus/Christus," he probably thought the matter had been settled. Little did he know that the tiny seedling of Christianity would take root and become a mighty oak that would topple the gods of Rome. But that victory was still several centuries in the future. In AD 48, Claudius was preoccupied with a much more pressing concern: His queen, Valeria Messalina, had just betrayed him for another man. *She probably needs to die,* he thought, *but do I have what it takes to go through with it?* Claudius's foolish decisions about this matter set the trajectory that would put young Nero on the imperial throne.

By all accounts, Valeria Messalina loved sex—far too much. Even the Roman aristocrats, who were by no means prudish, thought so. The poet Juvenal claimed Messalina would often wait until Claudius was asleep, then sneak out to common brothels and put herself on display. She would stand in the street-front windows designed for customer viewing, naked and wearing a blonde wig over her dark hair. Then she would haggle with the customers before accepting them, one after the other, all the way until dawn, long after the pimp had sent his other girls home. Even then, Messalina's lust wasn't sated. She would return to the palace inflamed and unsatisfied, bringing the stink of the brothels into the imperial bedroom. Although Juvenal was known for his humorous poetry and might have exaggerated his description, still, ancient people had every reason to believe that Messalina was a nymphomaniac.

3. Revelation 17.
4. Romans 16.

And then came one of the most preposterous episodes in all of imperial history. The historian Tacitus insisted this account was recorded in his sources, even though his readers would find it unbelievable. Messalina "developed a passion for Gaius Silius, the best-looking of Rome's young men." Not content with clandestine adultery, Messalina forced Silius out of his marriage to a noblewoman, then proceeded to flaunt her affair with him like a doting girlfriend. But even that wasn't enough. Messalina "became bored and began to drift into bizarre sexual practices." Then, growing ever more outrageous, she decided to proceed with a flagrant marriage to Silius, even while she was still married to the emperor himself!

While Claudius was out of town, Messalina and Silius staged a complete Roman wedding. She "passionately desired the title 'wife' because the notion was utterly scandalous—and that, for the profligate, is the ultimate pleasure." The devious pair summoned witnesses to legitimize their marital contract, made their formal vows, sacrificed to the gods, threw a fantastic wedding banquet, kissed and snuggled, then retired to their bridal chamber like giggling honeymooners.

Meanwhile, Claudius was tipped off when his two favorite prostitutes informed him about his cuckoldry at home. He rushed back to Rome, alternating between fury at the betrayal and panic that the public might believe the wedding was real and had made Silius the legitimate emperor. While Claudius was on the way, his brazen queen threw an extravagant festival to commemorate the autumn grape harvest. Winepresses squeezed out juice, vats overflowed, choirs sang bawdy songs, frenzied women danced around in animal skins, and Messalina and Silius dressed like followers of the wine god Bacchus. Everyone was reveling in drunken debauchery.

One would think this would be too much for a dignified emperor to endure, but Claudius was under his wife's spell in a bad way. Instead of demanding her immediate death, he let things tumble toward a half-hearted trial that would probably exonerate her. When he wasn't criticizing Messalina's scandalous behavior, he would lapse into fond affection for the good times they'd shared. Although Silius had been sentenced to a quick death, Messalina's trial the next morning would probably let her off the hook. She seemed destined to survive, or even to thrive, because she had vanquished her husband in the public eye.

Certain palace officials, however, had other plans. While Messalina was drafting her defense plea in the evening, aided by her mother, Lepida (Nero's favorite aunt), a powerful bureaucrat named Narcissus arrived with devious intent. Though this man might have had Christians in his household,[5] he himself was ruthless. His alliances lay elsewhere and he feared the queen. He also knew that Emperor Claudius, at that very moment, was reclining at a banquet, mellowing out with wine and feeling sorry for the "poor woman" who had gotten herself into such a predicament. Claudius had even started reminiscing about their previous sexual escapades. Everyone could see where this was going: Messalina was going to get away with it all!

Taking matters into his own hands, Narcissus ordered his henchmen to execute the adulterous queen. Despite Messalina's pleading, the guards smashed open the doors and burst in. Everyone reviled her, even a former slave who normally wouldn't have dared to hurl such shocking insults. Messalina tried to act nobly, committing suicide by her own hand, but she fumbled with the dagger. Finally, somebody ran her through with a blade. When Claudius at his dinner table received the news, "he simply called for a cup and carried on with the routine of the banquet." In the coming days, he hardened his emotions toward Messalina, and the Senate erased her memory from public recollection—though not enough for her story to be completely forgotten today.

This sordid affair had profound implications for Nero's future. Agrippina and Messalina hated each other, for they were intense rivals. Messalina had borne Claudius two children: a daughter, Octavia, and, more dangerously, a son named Britannicus. Nero would have been a likely heir to Emperor Claudius, who was his great-uncle. But once Britannicus came along, the newcomer assumed first place in line for the throne. Although Agrippina didn't orchestrate Messalina's downfall, she benefited from it immensely because it reduced Britannicus's rank. Now the boy was the son of a disgraced queen.

When Nero's father had died a few years back, Agrippina had married again. But that fellow also passed away, leaving his vast fortune to his wife and stepson. Even better, the death freed Agrippina to marry for a third time. With Messalina out of the way, Agrippina set her sights on a twofold strategy that would cement Nero's imperial prospects in stone.

5. Romans 16:11.

First, Agrippina arranged for the daughter of Claudius and Messalina, little Octavia, to be engaged to Nero. Their wedding happened four years later, in AD 53. Though the marriage wouldn't turn out to be a happy one, it had important political ramifications. The first five Roman emperors were part of the Julio-Claudian dynasty, which united two major aristocratic families.[6] The Julians were descended from Julius Caesar and his adopted son, Caesar Augustus. The Claudians were another prominent clan, intertwined by marriage with the Julians. If a Julian boy like Nero married a Claudian like Octavia, the two sides of the imperial dynasty would be united in a single marriage. Everyone would smile on a royal couple like that!

But Agrippina went further on her son's behalf. She realized that Claudius was newly unattached and needed a noble wife. Even though Claudius was her uncle, Agrippina put herself in the running for the marriage. She brought the same appeal that the engagement of Nero and Octavia offered. Any Claudian patrician would benefit from a union with a prestigious Julian bride like Agrippina, who was Augustus's great-granddaughter. Such a marriage would unite the two houses, not in a future emperor like Nero, but right now, on the current throne.

Though the couple began having illicit relations right away, the Roman laws against incest with nieces had to be set aside before a wedding could take place. Once those legal maneuvers were complete, in AD 49 the marriage was formally consummated. Soon afterward, Claudius adopted Nero as his son. He also gave Agrippina the exalted title of "augusta"—a lofty stature normally reserved for posthumous awards and never before granted to a living woman. The title essentially meant that Agrippina was an empress, co-ruling the empire with her husband. She even began to appear on coins as Ceres, the goddess who made grain grow (the word *cereal* is derived from her name). All of this imperial glory filled Agrippina with pride. Ceres was normally depicted holding wheat stalks or a cornucopia, the signs of her fertility. *But I offer so much more*, Agrippina believed. *The fruit of my womb is destined to rule the world!*

6. For its various members, see the Family Tree at the front of this book.

While these things were happening in Rome, the apostle Paul, still living in Antioch, was beginning the practice for which he is most often remembered today: writing the epistles that would make up almost a quarter of the New Testament. His first letter, composed around AD 48, was his epistle to the Galatians. What did Paul have to say to those beloved people whom he had visited on his first missionary journey?

One of his main themes, of course, was the believer's freedom from legal works such as circumcision as a requirement for salvation. Grace saves humankind, not adherence to the rules of the Torah. Jews and Gentiles alike can come to God by faith in Jesus the Messiah.

The second half of Paul's letter moved from theological topics to describe the Christian's moral life. Divine blessing wouldn't come from the sinful lifestyles of the Romans: "sexual immorality, impurity, lustful pleasures, idolatry, sorcery, hostility, quarreling, jealousy, outbursts of anger, selfish ambition, dissension, division, envy, drunkenness, wild parties, and other sins like these."[7] Paul's list of sins perfectly described the inhabitants of the imperial palace!

In contrast to such desires, Paul reminded his Galatian readers that true fruitfulness comes from God's presence dwelling within them. "But the Holy Spirit produces this kind of fruit in our lives: love, joy, peace, patience, kindness, goodness, faithfulness, gentleness, and self-control."[8] Although Empress Agrippina, as the human embodiment of the cereal goddess, supposedly provided an abundant harvest to her people, those fruits were counterfeit. In reality, her fertility was fatal, her blessings barren. Paul wanted his Galatian converts to embrace a better way: the life-giving gospel of Israel, not the sterile gospel of Rome.

But would they do it? Or would false doctrine lead them astray? Paul found himself worried about this. *Maybe it's time,* he reasoned from his home base in Antioch, *to pay them another visit?*

---

7. Galatians 5:19–21 NLT.
8. Galatians 5:22–23 NLT.

CODA

After reflecting a little bit on Paul's desire to go to Rome, we turn our attention to the lascivious and power-hungry life of Agrippina. She serves as an example of people who use sex to get ahead in life. Kathie shares some of her experiences with that world in the entertainment business. We then talk about the contrast between Agrippina's persona as a grain goddess and the true fruitfulness that comes from the Holy Spirit.

BRYAN: In this chapter we turn our attention to Rome. Around this time of his life, when he's already done a missionary journey, Paul begins to get ants in his pants to do it again and keep going. He begins to think, "I want to go west. I want to go all the way to the west." But why? Because he knows that he can reach the ends of the earth there. If you think about the ancient world, they didn't know what was out there. To the east was the Silk Road that led to India and China. No Roman person could get to the end of that world. They knew there was a lot of land out that direction, but the west was more achievable. The Scripture reads, "My name will be great among the nations, from where the sun rises to where it sets."[9] And Paul thought, "I could get to the sunset." So he begins to look at Rome. You've been to Rome, right?

KATHIE: Oh, yeah, many times.

BRYAN: Do you like it? What's your impression of Rome?

KATHIE: Personally, I adore Italy. And next to Israel, it's my favorite place. I have three places. There's Israel, Italy, and Scotland. Anytime you want to put me on a plane, I'm there! So I love Italy. And I love the Italian culture. I love their shoes. I love their pasta. I love their caprese salad. I love everything and it's just beautiful. To me, though, Rome is not the most beautiful city, not by any means. I love Florence more than Rome as a beautiful city.

BRYAN: What about the Jewish Quarter? Have you ever been to the Great Synagogue in Rome? The beautiful white dome?

KATHIE: Yes, I did visit that. I have been to that Jewish part.

BRYAN: And also, of course, there's the Colosseum, which wasn't there in Paul's and Nero's time. It came a bit later. That's where Nero's Golden House

---

9. Malachi 1:11 NIV.

was. We'll come back to the Colosseum in another chapter. Anyway, Rome was a place where both Peter and Paul ended up.

KATHIE: Yes, they had a heart for it, didn't they? Because that was the center of power in the world at the time, and where the caesars were—unless you think about Tiberius or Caligula, who went to the isle of Capri instead. Personally, I would have lived on Capri too! Might not have done the things they did there, though.

BRYAN: So Paul wants to go to Rome, and we'll see him getting there eventually. But also in this chapter is the crazy story about Messalina.

KATHIE: I had never heard about Messalina before! She's truly a "mess." Maybe that's where the term "hot mess" came from! [*Laughs.*] It seems she had this sex addiction, which is a real thing.

BRYAN: I was going to ask you about that. Agrippina, too, is known for her infidelities and using her sexuality to get ahead in life. You probably saw that a lot in the entertainment business.

KATHIE: Oh, absolutely. Both women and men used their sexuality for advantages. That's why for years it has been called the "casting couch"—because a lot of the time that's the way you got the job. And, gosh, I can't even believe how grateful I am that the Lord saved me from all of that. I think it was the fact that I came to walk with Yeshua when I was twelve. And I left home at seventeen. I was on the cusp of becoming a young woman, obviously. Wherever you are going, don't separate your lives. Don't divide your private life from your public one. Be the same person wherever you go. Share the gospel, and God will not only give you favor, he will give you great blessing.

BRYAN: I know you feel blessed in your life.

KATHIE: Truly, what I have achieved in my career is beyond anything I could have ever dreamed of as a little girl going off into the big world. But you have to be the same person and take your stand. There was a song they wanted me to sing in Nashville that says, "I don't care what's right or wrong . . . Help me make it through the night."[10] And I thought, "I can't sing that. I won't sing that. I *do* care what's right or wrong." Why? Because I had met Yeshua personally when I was a young girl, and he had influenced and informed everything about my life.

---

10. "Help Me Make It Through the Night," by Kris Kristofferson, *Kristofferson*, Monument, 1970.

BRYAN: In this chapter, Paul is looking at Rome. And then we mentioned the sexuality of Messalina and Agrippina, so let's consider the fertility theme. Agrippina thinks she has all the blessings and abundance to offer.

KATHIE: She's the goddess Ceres. The queen of fertility.

BRYAN: Yeah, the goddess of grain, which is where we get the word *cereal.*

KATHIE: That's right. Cereal. The grain, the fertility, and food.

BRYAN: And as part of that she was the goddess of abundance. Demeter was her counterpart in Greece, and then Ceres in Rome.

KATHIE: What about Dionysus? I thought he was fertility too. Wine and fertility and all of that.

BRYAN: Yes, any agricultural deity would be somewhat about fertility, but usually the fertility deities were female, whereas Dionysus was male. He was actually the god of debauchery, the god of orgies, the god of sexual parties and drunken parties.

KATHIE: Otherwise known as the first semester of college!

BRYAN: A lot of fraternities do actually bring in Dionysus as a Greek kind of thing. They make their frat parties Greek themed. But Ceres wasn't debauched like that. It wasn't really about her sexuality. It was more her maternal, mother-goddess aspect that brought earthly abundance. You know, Mother Earth. She gives fertility, fecundity, harvest, and grain, which is, of course, the core staple that you live on. It makes your daily bread. Your food comes from her. So there's the idea of Agrippina, that she can give you the abundance.

KATHIE: And she can give you a good time too. Well, with a little help from some others, if you get Dionysus to come along.

BRYAN: I thought it was interesting that at the same time, as we highlight in our chapter, Paul writes his first letter. Of course, that's what he's famous for, writing his epistles. And his first letter was Galatians, which talks about the fruit of the Spirit. So I thought we could finish with you talking a little bit about the contrast between fruitfulness from the gods or goddesses of paganism, versus fruitfulness from the Spirit. And maybe that passage is special to you?

KATHIE: I mean, there's not a scripture that's not precious to me. They've meant different things to me at different times in my life. The thing about physical fruit is that there's a shelf life to it. But spiritual fruits are eternal. They last forever, and God's Word never returns void. Earthly fruit is like seeing a brown banana, or that pear that you forgot was in the back of your fridge, and you get it out. It once was sweet, it once had beauty to it, it once had fruitfulness and a good, fresh scent. And now it stinks.

BRYAN: So that's the fake fruitfulness of Agrippina, isn't it?

KATHIE: Yes, but the fruit of the Spirit lasts forever. Our bodies are going to wear out no matter how many times we go and get them fixed. Or how many operations we have, or how many scars we've got from surgeries and all that stuff. They are still going to wear out. And one day we will go to our Savior's arms. Scripture promises us that. But our physical, earthly bodies will die. Ashes to ashes, dust to dust. Then we will have perfect heavenly bodies.

BRYAN: Until then, we have this fruit: "Love, joy, peace, patience, kindness, goodness, faithfulness, gentleness, and self-control. There is no law against these things!"[11]

KATHIE: There is no law. And the lawless things that these wicked characters did, all that didn't just happen. They chose to do it. They committed those sins. But they had never been taught otherwise until Paul came along, and then later all the other apostles. They could have learned it. Just like the Pharisees and Sadducees could have learned it when they had Jesus in front of them. But now we do know right from wrong. Now we have the Word of God. The fruits of the earth don't last. But the fruit of the Spirit will last forever, because it comes from the Lord, so it's eternal. That's the harvest I want—the one that lasts.

11. Galatians 5:22–23 NLT.

EIGHT

A SECOND JOURNEY

Now that Paul had evangelized several cities throughout Asia Minor, and had written his Galatian converts a letter warning that no one should "bewitch" them with bad doctrine,[1] his desire grew to pay them a second visit. Every day he could see the busy traffic through Antioch's western gate. Its highway crossed the Orontes River and led up to Cilicia, his home region, with Galatia beyond that. *I must go to my people! A false gospel has crept into their churches. Lord, will you send me soon?*

Paul's eagerness to guard against theological errors—because those errors were at the heart of the gospel—grew even stronger when some troublemakers from Jerusalem brought false teachings to Antioch. These legalistic interlopers, who had learned their tricks at the feet of the Pharisees, insisted, "The Gentiles must be circumcised and keep the law of Moses."

To resolve the dispute, the church in Antioch sent Paul and Barnabas down to Jerusalem to convene a council. After a week's travel, the delegates received a warm welcome from the local elders. Extensive meetings gave everyone the chance to wrestle with the profound differences between the pro- and anti-circumcision parties.

In the end, the council affirmed that pagan converts to Christianity didn't need to be troubled by works of the law. Certainly, they didn't have to undergo circumcision. Jewish believers, of course, should still observe

1. Galatians 3:1.

their ancestral traditions. Yet salvation didn't hinge on such things. It came instead by the grace of the Lord Jesus. Only three basic requirements were asked of the Gentile Christians: (1) avoid eating foods that had been previously dedicated to idols; (2) avoid eating blood, or meat with the blood still in it; and (3) abstain from sexual immorality. The first two commands sought to avoid Gentiles giving offense to Jews with conservative scruples when they came together for table fellowship. The third command, obviously, stood as a requirement for everyone.

Elated by this ringing affirmation that Gentiles were free from law keeping, Paul and Barnabas returned to Antioch. The Jerusalem elders sent two holy prophets to accompany them: Judas (not the traitor, but a different man) and Silas. The travelers arrived in Antioch and encouraged the Christian brothers and sisters with their report. Then everyone got back to their daily lives and busy evangelism in the city.

After some days being back in Antioch, Paul found his mind turning to the Galatian churches again as well as the others he had visited. He approached Barnabas with an idea, saying, "Let's go back and visit each city where we previously preached the word of the Lord, to see how the new believers are doing."[2]

Barnabas agreed but then proposed something that Paul didn't much like. "I want to take John Mark with us. He's my cousin. Let's give him a second chance."

On their first trip, John Mark had been included at the outset. He was a young fellow with a great heritage in the faith. His godly mother owned the home with the upper room where Jesus and his disciples had eaten their Last Supper and where the Holy Spirit came down at Pentecost. Later in life, Mark was destined to write one of the four gospels in the Bible, though Paul didn't know this yet. All he remembered was when the going got tough, Mark had backed out. Instead of facing hardship, he had left the trip and gone running home to his mother in Jerusalem. It didn't help that soon afterward Paul had

2. Acts 15:36 NLT.

been stoned and left for dead. It seemed to Paul that Mark wasn't ready to count the cost of preaching the gospel, so he told Barnabas, "We shouldn't take him along. In fact, I refuse to go with him."

The dispute created enough of a rupture between the two friends that Barnabas took Mark with him by boat to Cyprus, where the first journey had started out, and Paul took Silas in the opposite direction—a land route into Galatia.

Paul and Silas traveled to Tarsus, then turned up into the treacherous mountains, navigating a narrow pass called the Cilician Gates before entering the Galatian highlands. In the city of Lystra, where Paul had been stoned, they joined up with a young convert named Timothy. Paul would eventually come to love Timothy as a son and would write two biblical letters to him. Although the missionaries happily informed the Galatians about the council's decision against law keeping, Paul also circumcised Timothy because his mother was Jewish. This showed that Paul wasn't against circumcision per se, but only against enforcing it on Gentiles as a necessary requirement.

After spending some time in Galatia, Paul, Silas, and Timothy advanced to an area they had never visited before, the land of Phrygia, where they were faced with a decision. The adjacent regions were all unevangelized, so they weren't sure which province to enter. Should they go west, into Asia? Or should they go north, into Bithynia?

One night, in the coastal city of Troas on the Aegean Sea, Paul was asleep in his bed when he was suddenly awakened. A blazing light shone around him with a male figure standing in the midst of the glow. This time it wasn't the Lord himself but a man who said he was from Macedonia—a region in the continent of Europe, just north of Greece. "Come over to Macedonia and help us!" cried the desperate-sounding man.[3] It seemed the Holy Spirit was making the decision for them by forbidding the two options they were considering and sending a vision about what to do instead. Paul now knew what his next step should be in the global advance of the gospel.

The next morning, Paul told Silas and Timothy to pack up, saying, "God has called us to preach the gospel across the sea." This is when a fourth helper joined the team: Luke, who would eventually author his own gospel, as well as

3. Acts 16:9 NLT.

the book of Acts. What an amazing foursome God was assembling to spread the word! Their momentous trip to Macedonia and Greece in AD 49 (along with any missionary work that might have been happening in Rome) became the gospel's initial foray into the European context—the land where so many dramatic events of church history would occur over the coming centuries.

After crossing the northern edge of the Aegean Sea, the missionary team arrived in the Roman outpost of Philippi. They immediately found success: a woman named Lydia, a merchant of expensive purple cloth, embraced the gospel and was baptized. Yet trouble followed soon after when Paul cast a demon out of a slave girl. Once her masters realized they could no longer benefit from her contact with the spirit world to tell fortunes, they dragged Paul and Silas before the authorities and spoke against them.[4] After a vicious mob demanded punishment, the city officials ordered the apostles stripped and severely beaten with wooden rods, and then they were thrown into prison.

But even this resulted in gospel success. A fierce earthquake struck the town, the doors of the prison immediately flew open, and the chains of every prisoner broke away from the walls. Though everyone could have escaped through the wrecked doors, they all remained in the dungeon. When the terrified jailer saw what had happened—knowing he would have been executed if any of the prisoners had escaped—he asked Paul and Silas, "Sirs, what must I do to be saved?" They answered, "Believe in the Lord Jesus and you will be saved, along with everyone in your household."[5] That night the jailer took the beaten men to his home, washed their wounds, and gave them food to eat. In return, the jailer received the Bread of Life and the washing of rebirth, along with his whole family.

The next day the city magistrates sent the missionaries out of town. After saying goodbye to Lydia and some other believers, the men continued to the next big city: Thessalonica. Here, Paul visited the Jewish synagogue for three straight Sabbaths and explained how the Hebrew Scriptures pointed to Jesus the Messiah. Although some of his listeners believed the good news, others stirred up trouble with the city fathers again. But at least it didn't result in another beating or imprisonment.

---

4. Acts 16:19. Luke does not tell us why he and Timothy were not arrested as well.
5. Acts 16:30–31 NLT.

From there Paul and Silas continued on to Berea, where the Jews gave close attention to Paul's biblical message. To their credit, the Bereans examined the Scriptures to assess the validity of what they were hearing. And to God's glory, and Paul's encouragement, many of them believed the gospel message.

Yet the Thessalonian agitators were dogging their every footstep. Arriving in Berea, they repeated the same accusations of heresy. Paul had become the lightning rod, the one whom everyone opposed. To avoid further trouble, the local believers sent him away by sea, telling him to await a rendezvous with Silas and Timothy at his next destination: Athens, the famous Greek capital and home of the world's leading philosophers.

Paul bided his time in Athens but found himself constantly infuriated by the heathen idols he saw all around him. He wanted the true gospel to take root in the city. As always, he debated with Jews and God-fearers, yet he also engaged the pagan citizenry. This brought him in contact with Athenian philosophers, which raises some important questions: How did Greek philosophy function in ancient society? And how did it relate to the new "philosophy" of Christianity?

While God's appointed foursome was busy spreading the good news in Europe, an important figure entered Nero's life: the great Roman philosopher Lucius Annaeus Seneca, normally just called Seneca. He became Nero's personal tutor in AD 49. His version of Stoic philosophy would have a profound effect, not only on the impressionable young man who was soon to be emperor, but also on the early church as the ideas of Stoicism and Christianity intermingled.

It's essential to consider how Nero was affected by ancient Greek philosophy, as well as how Paul used its ideas to proclaim the Christian faith. Seneca's writing that had the biggest impact on Nero was his treatise *On Mercy*. He wrote it the year Nero turned eighteen, intending it to serve as a manifesto for how a good emperor ought to rule. For an all-powerful person, the hardest virtue to achieve, yet the one with the most value, was mercy. An emperor could too easily be ruled by passions such as anger or malice, especially when nothing more than a word, or the snap of the fingers, could achieve the satisfaction of revenge and destroy an enemy. Emperor Caligula had lived like that, and so have many other tyrants and bullies in history.

But Seneca counseled the opposite. Nero should act like Caesar Augustus, whose later years were marked by the virtue of *clementia*—that is, clemency or mercy. This required a rational mind that controlled the passions and acted according to "universal reason." Seneca declared, "Mercy means restraining the mind from vengeance when it has the power to take it." Due to Seneca's influence, the early part of Nero's reign exhibited cooperation with the senators and avoidance of the vindictive brutality of earlier regimes. Unfortunately for Nero, he eventually let the passions creep back into his life until they took over his soul and turned him into a monster.

When Paul started engaging with the foremost intellectuals in Athens, he quickly realized his evangelistic strategy had to incorporate a new philosophical approach. Those Greek academicians wouldn't know what to make of Jewish arguments about the Torah, circumcision, or food laws—nor did they care. But they cared a lot about how the world above connected with the world down here where humans lived. What great principle could bridge the gap between the heavenly and earthly realms?

At first, the elite Athenian philosophers who listened to Paul considered him a foolish babbler. But then a few of them took an interest in his ideas and invited him up to Mars Hill, which served as a popular gathering place for the city's intellectual crowd. This rocky protuberance is still visible in Athens today below the higher crest of the Acropolis. In ancient times, it was the epicenter of Greek philosophy, the place where the world's leading thinkers debated the great ideas of their day.

A short trek up some rocky steps brought Paul to the summit of Mars Hill. As he stood before the assembled scholars, he tried his new approach of using secular thinking to explain the gospel. He quoted two philosophers (one of whom was a Stoic) to show that Greek thought had already accepted the idea of people being the children of God. If that were so, could nonliving statues carved from silver or stone give birth to humans? Of course not! Idols were dead images that couldn't procreate. They weren't gods at all. Paul explained that the true God is immaterial and alive. In the past, God overlooked the foolishness of idolaters. But now he "commands all men everywhere to repent, because He has appointed a day on which He will judge the world in righteousness by the Man whom he has ordained. He has given assurance of this to all by raising Him from the dead."[6]

At the mention of bodily resurrection, many of the scholars mocked Paul. They said, "How could this be? You have no idea what you're talking about." The Greek philosophy of those times wanted the soul to escape the prison of the flesh, not get trapped in a material existence after death. Yet Paul knew resurrection was a nonnegotiable part of the gospel. There was no way around the proclamation of the risen Christ, even if it offended Greek ears. He could only proclaim the truth and let God go to work. In the end, some Athenian men and women *did* believe the good news, while others remained stuck in their idolatrous ways.

Having explained the Lord's message as best he could—using cultural bridges that would make the gospel understandable—Paul had done his job. Those whom God had appointed for eternal life would believe. Now it was time to move on.

After collecting his things, Paul left Athens and journeyed on to a place that would deeply influence his life and ministry. He followed the rugged coastline of Greece until he came to Corinth, a notoriously immoral city with no Christian presence at all. But that was just what Paul wanted to fulfill his calling: a place to break new ground for God. The advance of the gospel was about to take one more step in its journey toward the ends of the earth.

CODA

Paul's conflict with Barnabas introduces our conversation about what to do when Christians have a falling-out. We discuss how God can bring healing even out of the worst kinds of brokenness. Then we turn to Paul's engagement with Greek philosophy. We discuss how the Christian gospel transforms both the mind and the heart.

---

6. Acts 17:30–31.

BRYAN: In this chapter Paul heads out on his second missionary journey. But before he leaves, he goes down to Jerusalem for the so-called Jerusalem Council's discussion about circumcision.

KATHIE: Yeah, that would have been a fun meeting! A meeting about the private part! Of course it was God who had established that ritual.

BRYAN: And like we said in chapter 6, circumcision wasn't placed on the Gentile believers. It was too hard for them to bear. The gospel had come by grace, not by works. If a Gentile had faith in Jesus, that was enough. They didn't have to keep the kosher laws. Paul and Barnabas were about to go out to the Gentiles with that message, but one thing that happened on their first trip was that, as they got going, John Mark didn't stay with them. He went back home. He wasn't able to stay with the team. It seems like he became afraid of persecution. So Paul says to Barnabas, "I don't want to bring John Mark with us this second time." It becomes a sharp disagreement between them, so Paul goes with Silas on his mission while Barnabas and Mark go elsewhere. That leads us to the first topic to discuss: Have you ever had a falling-out with a fellow Christian? Like Paul and Barnabas had this falling-out. What's your wisdom and guidance on something like that?

KATHIE: I've had many of them. We don't stop being individuals when we become a part of the body of Jesus. We remain very human and very individualistic, and I think that's from God. He wants us to figure things out. And he wants us to humble ourselves, like we talked about the other day. And again, I always try to say, "Do I want to be *right* or be *righteous*?" And, ultimately, it always comes down to that.

BRYAN: Can you think of any specific ruptures you've had in your relationships?

KATHIE: There was a period in my life where I had to take a yearlong break from two of my dearest friends, from both of them. A year's break because they had hurt me and a friend of mine so deeply. Basically, they were gossiping. Gossip is such an ugly thing, and I won't allow it in relationships with my friends. The Holy Spirit doesn't let me do it. It destroyed my life for a long time. It was a betrayal. They thought they were doing the right thing and trying to protect me. The older I get, it's funny, but I want people to just allow me to be me. I've done pretty well in this world. I've made some mistakes. But don't judge my judgment. And don't tell me who I can love, and who I can't. I don't like it when people try to get involved in my personal life and my attitudes. If you care about me, pray for me. Please! I don't want any more opinions. So, yeah, I've had those ruptures.

BRYAN: You've been there. And yet God brings good out of it. And he brings healing, doesn't he?

KATHIE: Total healing. At the end, when the total healing comes, you have to be very careful to never bring it up again. It's easier to forgive than it is to forget. We'll talk more in chapter 10 about the scars we have. Our scars—they're there as reminders.

BRYAN: But what's amazing about John Mark, while there was this early breach—not just with him, but the breach was with Barnabas as well as Mark—later Mark goes on to write the first gospel. The first one written in order of time is Mark's gospel in the New Testament. And he works with Peter to do that. And Paul, when he's in the Carcer, in the dungeon, he writes to Timothy, "Get Mark! Bring him to me because he is so valuable to me."[7] So clearly, they had a kind of healing, and that's who God is, isn't he? He's the God of healing broken relationships.

KATHIE: He's Jehovah-rapha—the Lord Who Heals. And healing comes in all kinds of ways. I had a miraculous healing on my pelvis, and I've had some miraculous healings in my soul, from deep soul wounds. But I don't trust the way I used to. I don't trust human beings anywhere near like I used to. Now they have to prove their faithfulness. I'm becoming more and more like my husband was. Frank said to people, "I'm not going to trust you until you prove your truth." And my father was careful with people. So I want to be wise like a serpent and innocent like a dove.[8]

BRYAN: Some people are like a German shepherd in their relationships. Maybe you tend to be more like a golden retriever.

KATHIE: No, I'm a teacup Maltipoo. Love me!

BRYAN: Yeah, we had a Chihuahua that we had to release into heaven. Little dogs are their own thing. So another question is this: In this chapter Paul comes to Athens. And Athens, of course, was the intellectual city of its time. It'd be like Harvard or Oxford today. Very intimidating. But Paul was great

---

7. 2 Timothy 4:11, author's paraphrase.
8. Matthew 10:16.

with contextualizing the gospel, even for intellectuals. So I wonder, you're a person of the heart, and maybe I'm a professor and a person of the mind. What do you think Christianity is for? Is it for the mind? Or is it for the heart? Or both? Or is one a little bit suspicious? I mean, sometimes each side suspects the other side of not getting it right. Too dry and intellectual, or too emotional and squishy. You know what I mean? Is Christianity for the mind or for the heart?

KATHIE: It's both. We're supposed to test the spirits. We're *admonished* to test the spirits. Don't just assume this is of God and that is not. Sometimes, Scripture talks about how evil can show up as an angel of light. So again, we're supposed to test the spirits, which is using our mind. But also I feel like the Lord has been teaching me for a long time—for decades, really!—"Kathie, I need you to develop a tough skin. But keep a tender heart. Don't let the stupid stuff affect you. Don't let the things people say define you. Yet don't stop loving the people that are just so hard to get along with."

BRYAN: I think that's a good way to put it. You're a person of the heart. And you love Jesus, and you want other people to love Jesus. And you're a person of tough skin, like you were saying. But this book, and also *Herod and Mary*, are showing that, you and I together, we're people of the mind as well, because we want readers to know history. We want them to understand the deep things of the Bible and of theology. Things that Paul talked about, that Jesus talked about.

KATHIE: Hearts come together with minds, right? The heart and soul and mind. Everything is bound by love. That's what the Shema says: "Love the LORD your God with all your heart, soul, mind, and strength."[9] Have no other gods before him. But to be an effective missionary, you have to bind it with love. That's the difference maker.

BRYAN: That was why Paul was such a good missionary. Maybe we take a lesson from that.

KATHIE: You and I have talked a lot about the fact that in the Western world there's such a tendency to be bound up by religion instead of freed up by relationship. And I think we do such a disservice to the Holy Spirit, such a disservice to the kingdom of God, when we lose relationships, as if certain people are untouchable or have to be shunned. I was told for a long time, "You

9. Deuteronomy 6:5; Mark 12:30, author's paraphrase.

can't be in show business! You've gotta be a missionary to Africa, or you gotta go to China." And I said, "What about the calling of God on my life, which nobody else knows?" For me, I've had that calling on my life since I was being formed in my mother's womb. How dare we, as believers, try to tell anybody else how the Holy Spirit is speaking?

BRYAN: You were called to be a missionary to Hollywood, and to entertainment people.

KATHIE: Yes. Billy Graham told me that. And Pastor Jack Hayford, when I first went out to Los Angeles. There were a few of us, maybe ten or fifteen of us, who were in the arts or in show business. We felt called to it. And when I look back now, I see how God entrusted me with the gospel. I would have been a terrible missionary in some remote hut, because I like electricity. And running water. But really, we *were* in a mission field. And I said, "If God has called me here, he will use me." I'm not like Paul in Athens, going into the lecture hall at Oxford University or something. But God has called us to go everywhere, and he has called us into the world of the intellect. And that's what Paul means when he says, "I am all things to all men, that I might win some for Christ."[10]

BRYAN: Is it scary to be a missionary like that?

KATHIE: Fear creeps in, and when fear creeps in, it's harder to hear the voice of God. There's a pounding in your head from fear. We don't want any voice to drown out the peace of God that Jesus promised us. He said, "In the world you will have trouble. But take heart! I have overcome the world."[11] And he says to not be afraid, to not be dismayed—I am with you. If we just fix our eyes on him, we can be strong. Can you imagine how Paul, every time he stood up before a group, must have wondered, "Oh, my God, I'm going to get beaten here! I hope I'm not getting beaten or stoned today."

BRYAN: Yeah, I'm sure he was intimidated. I've been to Athens where you can go up on Mars Hill to the exact same place that Paul was when he spoke to the scholars. For Paul it would have been like stepping into mockery or stepping into a place where the people are all smarter than you, and they look down on you like a fool.

---

10. 1 Corinthians 9:22, author's paraphrase.
11. John 16:33.

KATHIE: But he didn't let the fear keep him bound. Fear is insidious. It's like a whispering in your ear that grows and grows—unless we keep fixating on Jesus. Then it stops growing and fades away. God had his people in Athens. He had souls there to save. So Paul took courage and spoke the gospel to them. That's all we can do too.

NINE

NERO TAKES THE THRONE

In AD 51, the people of Rome witnessed an extraordinary spectacle they knew would forever affect their lives. Thirteen-year-old Nero was coming of age. He was becoming a grown man right before their eyes!

It was during the March festival called Liberalia that Roman boys crossed the threshold to adulthood. Since Nero was the most prominent of the rising debutants that year, his rite of passage was celebrated with public ceremonies in the Forum and sporting events in the Circus Maximus.

Nero was also now appearing in the *toga virilis*, the pure white toga worn by aristocratic men. That day, during the parade in the circus, the symbolic pageantry was taken up a notch when Nero arrived wearing the purple-and-gold toga of a conquering hero. And who else was seen that day? Nero's stepbrother, Britannicus—but he was clad in a youth's toga with obvious stripes that proved he wasn't yet an adult. Clearly, Emperor Claudius had elevated his adopted son from Agrippina over his natural-born son from Messalina. The crowd breathed a sigh of relief. They didn't really care who the next emperor would be. They just wanted the heir apparent to be obvious to everyone, so a future civil war could be avoided.

Behind the scenes Agrippina continued to advance Nero's prospects while trying to get Britannicus demoted. She replaced some pro-Britannicus public officials, especially within the Praetorian Guard, with men who would support her own bloodline instead.

She also presented to her husband a grievance about Britannicus, a petty complaint intended to put the boy in a bad light. "Hello, Britannicus," Nero had said when the two boys happened to meet in the palace, to which his stepbrother had replied, "Hello, Domitius"—the childhood name by which Nero was known before joining the family of Claudius. Whether that was just a slip of the tongue or intentional disrespect is hard to tell. In any case, Agrippina made a big deal about it to the emperor. "You see?" she screeched. "He's ignoring your adoption and calling him by his old name! He's disregarding the vote of the senators!" After blaming the snub on the insidious voices whispering in Britannicus's ear, she convinced Claudius to send away the boy's tutors, while keeping the best of them, Seneca, for Nero. Again and again, Britannicus was being marginalized in favor of Agrippina's son.

Britannicus's sister, Octavia, also served as a tool in Agrippina's schemes, but in exactly the opposite way: She was favored as Nero's future spouse. When a girl turned thirteen, it was time for her to marry. Since she was Nero's stepsister, Octavia first had to be adopted into another noble clan to sever her ties with her family of origin. Once that was taken care of, she became her ex-stepbrother's wife. The teenaged pair didn't really like each other, so this marriage was more about uniting the Julio-Claudian dynasty than any kind of actual loving relationship.

Although the people of Rome rejoiced to see a clear line of imperial succession—with a nice royal marriage to make sure it would continue—it nevertheless raised a question: When would Emperor Claudius pass off the scene? He was, after all, in his mid-sixties, an advanced age for men of those days. People began to wonder, *How is the old fella doing? And how might handsome young Nero fare as emperor?*

It's not like Claudius was popular. He had ruled harshly enough to turn the people against him. The superstitious masses began to grow even more agitated when some bad omens occurred. Earthquakes shook the city several times, causing some people to get trampled in the ensuing panic. Certain unlucky birds (so it was believed) came out of nowhere and roosted on top of the Capitoline Hill. Then a famine hit hard, reducing the city's remaining supply of grain to only fifteen days' worth. After that, the people would begin to starve, since Italy didn't produce its own bread and had to import it continuously. Crowds surrounded Claudius while he was in the Forum and pressed him with their desperate complaints. Only after his bodyguards escorted him through the turbulence did he escape. Fortunately, more grain ships arrived and alleviated the hunger. But Claudius never forgot his scary encounter with the mob.

A giant public-relations fiasco diminished Claudius's status even further. Nero had a front-row seat for the disaster, no doubt causing him to vow, "Someday, when I'm emperor, I'm going to give my people spectacles that actually work!"

The disastrous event was supposed to celebrate the opening of a drain for a mountain lake in central Italy, a massive engineering project designed to control floods and manage the marshy lands nearby. This giant public-works project, which had taken more than a decade to complete with the labor of thirty thousand workmen, had resulted in a drainage tunnel almost four miles long. To commemorate the opening of the spillway, the emperor's retinue went up to the alpine lake and staged a naval battle on the waters.

This first part of the celebration went well; in fact, it was a smashing success. Rowed warships plied the waters in actual live combat as nineteen thousand condemned criminals fought one another to the death while dodging missiles shot at them from catapults on nearby rafts. All the surrounding villages attended the event, lining the mountainsides as if in a natural theater. Claudius presided over the battle in a magnificent military cloak, while Agrippina stood at his side wearing a gown whose cloth was woven from threads of gold. The convicts fought so bravely that those who survived the carnage earned pardons for their capital offenses.

Then the moment of truth arrived. It was time to open the new drain—but due to faulty construction, no water would flow! Over the next few months the drainage tunnel had to be dug deeper. Claudius put on a second show, this time with gladiators fighting on pontoon bridges. Servants also laid out a lavish banquet near the lake's outlet. This time, when the floodgates were opened, such a huge torrent of water gushed out that it destroyed the constructions with a loud bang and threw all the diners into a panic. Agrippina used the disaster to blame the presiding bureaucrat, Narcissus, of mismanagement and embezzlement. When he barked back that she ought to shut up and know her feminine place, Agrippina realized her power wasn't as strong as she had thought. If this government functionary—formerly a slave!—could talk to her like that, maybe she needed to strengthen her standing in the palace.

A chance remark, uttered soon afterward while Claudius was inebriated, heightened Agrippina's fears and ultimately led to the emperor's downfall. "I guess it's my fate," he drunkenly moaned, "to have to bear, then punish, the flagrant crimes of my wives." Since Agrippina didn't want to go the way of Messalina, she decided to preempt any future executions that might come her way.

First, she eliminated her longtime rival, Nero's aunt Lepida, whom he liked very much. Lepida equaled Agrippina in wealth, beauty, and aristocratic lineage. To make matters worse, Lepida seemed to be gaining Nero's affection with her kindness. Lepida's "favorite aunt" routine contrasted with Agrippina's stern maternal approach of using Nero as a pawn, not loving him for who he was. The historian Tacitus remarked that while Agrippina could present Nero with an empire, she couldn't stand him *as an emperor*. But the worst of their mother-son strife still lay in the future. For now, Agrippina trumped up charges against Lepida—that she had cast evil spells on Agrippina, or let her slaves cause riots that disrupted public order—which resulted in Lepida's execution.

With yet another enemy out of the way, only one obstacle remained before Nero could be installed on the throne: Emperor Claudius himself. It was time to act. Agrippina decided to use poison but debated which one to choose. *If I use something swift, it'll be too obvious. But if I let him linger, he might have time to figure it out and return the lineage to Britannicus. Something that works fast is what I need—but also one that addles his mind!*

Agrippina summoned a woman named Locusta, an infamous mixer of poisons. "I know just what to make," the devious pharmacist assured the augusta. When the concoction was ready, Agrippina passed it to one of the court eunuchs, the imperial taster who was supposed to guard the integrity of the emperor's table but was actually in on the plot. The co-conspirator smeared it on a juicy mushroom. Soon afterward, the clueless, drunken emperor gulped it down. Death was on its way.

But then fate intervened. As Tacitus described it, "A bowel movement appeared to have come to his aid." In other words, Claudius immediately excreted the poison and seemed to have survived the toxic assault. Terrified, Agrippina realized she'd likely be caught and condemned. She ordered a palace doctor to administer a stomach-purging drug on a feather stuffed down the emperor's throat—but he should spike the medicine with a heavy dose of poison that couldn't fail to work. The doctor broke his Hippocratic oath and obeyed the augusta's command. The deadly poison did its job. Agrippina had now added regicide to her already long list of crimes.

Her next move was to stage a PR campaign before the watching aristocratic eyes. Agrippina went to Britannicus's bedroom and hugged him tight, fawning over him as if she pitied the poor boy's fate. "You look so much like your father!" she murmured through fake tears that supposedly signaled her grief. Actually, though, she was keeping Britannicus out of sight so only Nero could come forth as the new emperor, a fait accompli. At last, when the omens declared the moment was right, the palace doors burst open and Nero emerged alongside a tough fellow named Burrus, whom Agrippina had installed as her ally at the head of the Praetorian Guard. A few guardsmen looked around for Britannicus, the natural-born son of the now dead emperor. When he wasn't spotted anywhere, everyone shrugged and accepted Nero as the rightful heir to the throne.

Young Nero, just two months shy of his seventeenth birthday, was hoisted onto a litter and carried into the streets. His first stop was the guardsmen's fort, the Castra Praetoria, whose impressive walls are still visible in Rome today. "I promise to give you the same generous bonus that my father did!" he declared. The troops cheered, for Claudius had awarded a bonus at his coronation of fifteen thousand sesterces per man. Since a sesterce was a quarter of a denarius, which was the daily wage for a laborer, fifteen thousand of those coins would equate to the wages earned by a common man in 3,750 days—in other words, over a decade's worth of pay! The Praetorian Guard needed no more convincing to endorse the new emperor. Under Burrus's command, they would become one of Nero's main supports in the years ahead.

After leaving the fort, Nero proceeded to the Senate House, where he spent the rest of the day receiving honor after honor. The only title he refused was Father of the Fatherland, since he felt too young for such an accolade. Now that the Senate had so lavishly endorsed Nero's reign, and none of the provincial governors complained about the coronation, the deed was considered done. Britannicus was quickly forgotten. And Claudius was declared a god and buried with the highest honors. At last, Agrippina could relax. Her only child had claimed the throne of Rome.

As the apostle Paul approached the intimidating city of Corinth on the road from Athens, he surely felt the strain of what he was about to undertake. "I came to you in weakness with great fear and trembling," he later told his converts.[1] Since his companions weren't with him, the burden of loneliness added to the weight on his shoulders.

Corinth lay in a flat plain not far from the seacoasts on either side. Towering above the city loomed the mountain called Acrocorinth, crowned with a temple to Aphrodite, the goddess of erotic love. Her priestesses served as high-class prostitutes, more than a thousand in number. Paul could almost feel the darkness and degradation radiating from Corinth. The gods ruled this place, and not one person had yet bowed the knee to Christ. *Lord, this city is famous for its wealth and immorality. The Corinthians have everything the world has to offer. Help me turn them toward the gospel!*

God answered Paul's prayer by immediately connecting him to some new Christian friends: a husband-and-wife team named Aquila and Priscilla, two Jews who had left Rome after Claudius expelled them. Since they were tentmakers like Paul, he joined their trade and settled into a routine of work and evangelism. Paul ministered like this for the next year and half. God gave him success, and a church took root in Corinth.

In time, though, opposition galvanized against Paul's gospel work. The Lord said to him in a vision, "Do not be afraid, but speak, and do not keep silent; for I am with you, and no one will attack you to hurt you; for *I have many people in this city*."[2] When Paul continued to preach the good news, some of the local Jewish leaders dragged him before the Roman governor of the

1. 1 Corinthians 2:3 NIV.
2. Acts 18:9–10.

region, Gallio. (Interestingly, Gallio's younger brother was Seneca, the tutor of Nero.) As soon as the Jews started accusing Paul of persuading people to worship God falsely, Gallio stopped the proceedings and wouldn't continue the trial. "If it were a matter of wrongdoing or wicked crimes, O Jews, there would be reason why I should bear with you," Gallio said. "But if it is a question of words and names and your own law, look to it yourselves; for I do not want to be a judge of such matters."[3] The case was dismissed, making Paul a free man.

Eventually Paul's coworkers Silas and Timothy rejoined him in Corinth. Paul had dispatched Timothy back to Thessalonica because he was worried about the church that the missionary team had planted there. Now Timothy's report to Paul encouraged him, for the church was doing well. Paul wrote a letter to the Thessalonians (the first of two) in which he expressed gratitude for their faith, encouraged them to stand strong in trials, and reminded them Jesus would one day come back to earth to take his people to heaven (in an event sometimes referred to as the rapture).

When Paul received further news that the Thessalonians believed that Jesus had already returned and they must have missed it, he immediately sent off a second letter to assure his converts that the Lord's return still lay in the future. Until then, they should endure persecution in anticipation of glory. Paul exhorted them: "Therefore, brethren, stand fast and hold the traditions which you were taught."[4] Paul's two letters display his deep pastoral concern for the people he had converted to Christ.

After a good year and a half in Corinth, Paul finally sensed the Spirit stirring him to move on. His second missionary journey was coming to its natural end. Along with his new friends Aquila and Priscilla, the apostle walked out to Corinth's eastern seaport, got a haircut to fulfill a vow he had taken,[5] then found a ship headed toward the Holy Land. As the mooring ropes were cast off and the ship slipped from the harbor into the Aegean Sea, Paul could see the distant mound of Acrocorinth on the horizon. Though Aphrodite still had her grip on many hedonists and pleasure-seekers in Corinth, the promise of Jesus had been proven true: "I have many people in this city."[6]

---

3. Acts 18:14–15.
4. 2 Thessalonians 2:15.
5. Acts 18:18.
6. Acts 18:10.

During the journey home, Paul's ship stopped at the port of Ephesus, giving him the chance to preach to some Jews there. "Please, stay with us longer!" they begged him. Though he declined, an evangelistic spark had been lit in his heart. "I must by all means keep this coming feast in Jerusalem," he told the Ephesian believers, "but I will return again to you, God willing."[7] In the meantime, Aquila and Priscilla would remain behind in Ephesus to get the work started.

Eventually, Paul landed at Caesarea in Israel. He immediately went up to Jerusalem, kept the Passover feast, then returned to his sending church at Antioch. Although he had much work to do there, he often thought about the spiritual needs at Ephesus and Corinth. Beyond those Greek cities, the great capital in Italy also tugged at his heart.

Paul had no way of knowing what Nero was doing in Rome, nor did Nero know anything about Paul. Each man was going about his business as if the other didn't exist. Even so, their destinies would one day intersect, for the Roman Empire couldn't contain two gospels and two lords forever. Though one Lord was destined to triumph over the other, for the moment their struggle continued. Victory still lay far in the future. And as Paul was about to find out, the victory wouldn't be achieved without enduring some serious setbacks along the way.

CODA

We begin our conversation by thinking about what it means to rear children of privilege. Certainly, Kathie's kids can be described that way, requiring some special care in raising them. Then we turn to the city of Corinth, which was notorious for its sin. Kathie shares her experiences in similar contexts. We are reminded that the gospel is for everyone—whether society's elite or those struggling in its depths. Jesus is the solution for all walks of life!

BRYAN: In this chapter Nero takes the throne and we read the sad story of how he marries Octavia, the poor girl that is forced to marry him. Then Agrippina tries to murder Claudius with poison smeared on a mushroom. It's kind of famous in history that she uses a mushroom and he eats it, so he gets

7. Acts 18:21.

sick but he hangs on. Then she finishes him with more poison down his throat and he dies.

KATHIE: The poison was from Locusta, right?

BRYAN: That's right. Agrippina made sure to get the good stuff from her.

KATHIE: Yeah, she always found a way.

BRYAN: Then she takes Britannicus, which is the other boy, the prince, and she kind of hides him and hugs him and says, "I'm so sorry that you lost your father," but she's really keeping him back, out of sight, so Nero can come out and burst onto the scene.

KATHIE: Because Britannicus was Claudius's son.

BRYAN: Yes. He would have been the literal descendant of the former emperor—which is why he was a threat.

KATHIE: Was he talented at all? Was he anything?

BRYAN: Yeah, he was starting to come on the scene. And he was a little younger.

KATHIE: People really liked him, didn't they?

BRYAN: They did. More and more.

KATHIE: And he was handsome.

BRYAN: Nero is going to kill him later for all those reasons.

KATHIE: I've wanted to kill a few men for that.

BRYAN: [*Laughs.*] Well, you're not as wicked as Nero!

KATHIE: [*Also laughs.*] Some, but I'm not quite that bad.

BRYAN: So Nero takes the throne, and he's all-powerful, and he's not even quite seventeen. When that happens, it can be big trouble. Now, my question is about sons, actually all children, that have a lot of privilege. Your son had a lot of privilege in his life. Is there a kind of temptation that can, when you have that lifestyle, take over elite children?

KATHIE: I think there's a temptation for all of us from the moment we're born. I truly do. I remember saying to my kids, "Just because you guys are privileged doesn't mean you don't owe anything." There's a scripture that says, "For everyone to whom much is given, from him much will be required."[8] I used to say to them all the time, "You guys have no concept of how blessed you are." And I used to say to myself when I was growing up, "If I can't be a

---

8. Luke 12:48.

blessing, I don't want to be a burden. If I can't leave my house and go out and be a blessing, then I don't want to be a burden to anybody." Nobody needs more burdens. Everybody I know is burdened in one way or another. And I don't want to be that person who adds to their troubles. I am that person once in a while, but it's not because I want to be!

BRYAN: And your kids turned out well. I mean, they were known in Connecticut for not coming across as elitist, and they were famous for being down-to-earth even though they were prominent children. Isn't that true?

KATHIE: Totally. And I would have kicked their butts if they hadn't been! I was a maniac about manners.

BRYAN: And probably the main difference with your kids is that they didn't have all power, but an emperor like Nero did. He's a teenager, and he's all-powerful.

KATHIE: He could execute people! He could just murder them.

BRYAN: Right, and I bet you were cautious about giving your kids too much privilege. Like, you probably made them do chores or be real-world kids in some ways.

KATHIE: I tried, but with Cassidy, she's so messy. But a sweeter person you couldn't meet.

BRYAN: I agree. She's so gracious and kind. But Cody's not messy, is he? He seems more structured.

KATHIE: Cody is not messy at all. And he's clean. But as a little girl, Cass would get filthy. She would be so happy playing in the mud. But Cody hated it. It's amazing how your children can be so completely different!

BRYAN: I think our readers can probably identify with that if they have their own kids. And what a contrast there is between a Christian parent and Nero's upbringing, where Agrippina was willing to indulge her boy and do everything he wanted. But a sensible parent, not just you, but me as a parent or our readers as parents, we all need to make sure our kids have responsibilities. Let's make sure they don't think they're God's gift to the world. We must help them stay humble, even if in some ways they're very blessed.

KATHIE: Keep them humble. Right.

BRYAN: Also in this chapter we see how the apostle Paul leaves Athens, the intellectual city that we talked about, and goes to Corinth, which is like a sexual city. It's famous for that.

KATHIE: It's Vegas, baby.

BRYAN: It's Vegas, and "what happens in Vegas stays in Vegas." So let's talk a little bit about that. You've done a lot of shows in Vegas, I assume. Does it feel like Sin City?

KATHIE: No, not to me, because I was working, doing three shows a day. I always felt sad in Vegas. I felt sad for the women who had to get naked to make a living. Strippers, or showgirls, or whatever.

BRYAN: And in ancient times, the term "Corinthian girl" meant a prostitute. So that tells you about that city and the task Paul faced there—trying to plant a church in such a setting.

KATHIE: At twenty-two I moved to Vegas for a job filling in for a girl that had dropped out of a show scheduled to open up at one of the hotels. I had forty-eight hours to learn the part and be onstage—crazy, I know, but I was desperate to work, especially doing what I had longed to do my whole life. I shared a room with the two other girls—one a Baptist preacher's daughter and the other an ex–beauty queen. I would go to bed after three shows in a day, trying to get whatever sleep I could, but they would be ready to go out for their night on the town. They would be coming back early the next morning as I was getting up. I felt so sad for them. One of them knew Jesus, and one of them didn't know him at all. I just felt so broken for them partying night after night after night.

BRYAN: That really shows the kind of people the apostle Paul was trying to minister to. In that setting, there's so much brokenness, and you see that in his epistles. But he loved the Corinthians so much. And maybe he loved them especially because he saw that very same brokenness. He no doubt had a warm, caring heart, like you did for these ladies.

KATHIE: Yes, many of the ones that Jesus loved so much were the broken women. The ones who'd been used and abused. And Jesus knew they had so little choice in their life. They were used because somebody had power over them. And Jesus hated that.

BRYAN: And when he went back to heaven, he sent someone like Paul to reach the Corinthians, or someone like you to reach women in Vegas, or whoever is in our lives.

KATHIE: It makes me cry even now. Those two women, they never went out to breakfast with me because they were just going to bed, right? But it starts with having a broken heart for them. And I do think Paul had a heart for the broken. So do I, hopefully.

BRYAN: We need that as Christians, don't we?

KATHIE: If we don't have it, we aren't Christians. If we don't have a heart for people, we are not believers. Everyone will know we are Christians by our love.[9]

9. John 13:35.

TEN

KNOCKED DOWN, BUT NOT DESTROYED

One of Paul's lowest points in his life came during his third missionary journey, a five-year period of overseas ministry from AD 52 to 57. Of course, he didn't know what was in store for him when he set out. He had returned to Antioch in good spirits after his successful second trip. The ministry in Antioch had continued without interruption, but soon the urge to spread the gospel moved him onto the road again. On his third journey, Paul made his way through Galatia, then headed due west into Asia and reached the Ephesians, the people whom he had promised to revisit if God willed it. Paul rejoiced that the opportunity had now arrived.

For a while his ministry in Ephesus flourished. He preached in the synagogues for several months, but when that began to receive opposition, he withdrew and rented a public lecture hall where anyone could come and listen to him. Many Gentiles embraced his teaching. The Lord also gave Paul the ability to perform miracles, such as healings and exorcisms. Even some magicians and sorcerers repented of their occult ways and turned to Christ. Spiritual success was everywhere!

But then discouragement struck Paul hard. He couldn't shake the negative thoughts. *I'm an impostor!* he told himself in his darkest moments. *I shed the blood of innocent believers. I don't deserve to be called an apostle!* The memories of Stephen's murder, of violence and cruelty, of families torn apart by his actions, made him weep. Shame gripped his heart. Even his skin burned with physical pain.

Paul shot up in bed, startled out of his sleep by one of his guilty nightmares in his little bedroom at Ephesus. He was drenched in sweat and shaking uncontrollably. After taking a few moments to remember where he was, he stood up from his cot and walked over to a table by the window. The shutters opened at the touch of his quivering hand. Paul inhaled the cool night air, clearing his mind of satanic whispers, replacing them with the breeze of the Holy Spirit. A shaft of moonlight illumined his pens, parchments, a cup of wine, a half-eaten loaf of bread. Next to those things stood a heavy clay jar that contained the many donated coins he was collecting for the poor believers in Jerusalem. He would take the charity to them soon.

As Paul picked up the jar to inspect its contents, the heavy container slipped from his grasp. *No!* It clattered against the floor and rolled away, but miraculously, it was not broken. Even the fastener on its lid held tight. More carefully this time, Paul retrieved the jar, set it back on the table, and looked at it closely. Some fine cracks now marred the jar's glaze, and some chips had broken away from it. Yet even with these new scars, the earthen vessel stood firm. Opening it, he could see the abundance of silver coins gleaming in the moonlight—a bright love offering from faithful Christians. The vivid image stayed with Paul, prompting him to write:

> For God, who said, "Let there be light in the darkness," has made this light shine in our hearts so we could know the glory of God that is seen in the face of Jesus Christ. We now have this light shining in our hearts, but we ourselves are like *fragile clay jars containing this great treasure.* This makes it clear that our great power is from God, not from ourselves. We are pressed on every side by troubles, but we are not crushed. We are perplexed, but not driven to despair. We are hunted down, but never abandoned by God. *We get knocked down, but we are not destroyed.* Through suffering, our bodies

> continue to share in the death of Jesus so that the life of Jesus may also be seen in our bodies.[1]

Paul put the lid back on the jar and fastened it. The treasure inside was safe. Yes, the jar had been wounded. Now it bore the marks of hard use. But it would hold. God would make it hold. The treasure inside was too valuable to waste—for it had been purchased by God's Son in exchange for his own blood.

When Paul wrote to his Corinthian friends to share about his time of suffering, he had to use *we* to describe his difficult experience. Perhaps he needed to distance himself from the depth of his trauma. He wrote:

> For we do not want you to be ignorant, brethren, of our trouble which came to us in Asia: that we were burdened beyond measure, above strength, so that we despaired even of life. Yes, we had the *sentence of death in ourselves*.[2]

Poor Paul! He felt he had the weight of a death sentence on his shoulders. Satan's accusations had made him believe the full wrath of Yahweh was about to destroy him. Paul often referred to the overwhelming weight of his sin, the memory of how he was once a vicious persecutor. This ever-present "thorn" or "splinter" in his flesh pained him continuously, serving as a constant "messenger of Satan."[3]

But after Paul mentioned the "sentence of death" hanging over his head, he went on to describe the only way to overcome such deadly fears: "We should not trust in ourselves but in God who raises the dead, who delivered us from so great a death."[4] The resurrection power of Christ had overcome the grave! Sin's chains were broken; the devil had been defeated. Paul just needed to focus his mind on the great truths of the gospel. The God who had delivered him before would continue to do so, all the way to the end.

---

1. 2 Corinthians 4:6–10 NLT.
2. 2 Corinthians 1:8–9.
3. 2 Corinthians 12:7.
4. 2 Corinthians 1:9–10.

Having survived those dark days of depression, Paul wrote to the Corinthians in words that rang with praise and joy: "Blessed be the God and Father of our Lord Jesus Christ, the Father of mercies and God of all comfort, who comforts us in all our tribulation, that we may be able to comfort those who are in any trouble, with the comfort with which we ourselves are comforted by God."[5] The afflicted apostle understood that the purpose of his suffering wasn't divine punishment or vengeance. Rather, the pain was God's instrument to turn his wandering heart back to the source of true comfort. Only those who have been "knocked down" but not "destroyed"[6] can reach out to others in need, empathizing with them at the deepest level, so they, too, have the opportunity to encounter the mighty deliverance of God.

Why was Paul writing letters from Ephesus to the Corinthian church across the Aegean Sea? Wasn't he focused on the ministry in his present situation? Certainly, he was. Yet life had just struck him a double blow. To compound the spiritual discouragement he had been feeling at Ephesus, he also took a hard hit from his Corinthian converts, prompting a flurry of letters back and forth. Out of the blue, Paul learned they had cast him to the side as an embarrassing fool. His previous ministry in Corinth, when he had planted a church there for the first time, had been utterly rejected. What happened at Corinth to hurt Paul so badly?

The letter-writing chronology unfolded like this. Paul sent a total of four epistles to the Corinthians, two of which have been preserved in the New Testament, while the other two were lost in the sands of time. The first letter, one of the lost ones, attempted to address rumors of sexual immorality in the Corinthian church. A while later, Paul learned from more reports that the problems in Corinth were worse than he had thought. Divisions, elitism, and deep moral confusion plagued the church. Some Christians were even partaking in worship at pagan temples! And behind it all was a lack of spiritual love. This unfortunate discovery led Paul to write his second letter, which is known

5. 2 Corinthians 1:3–4.
6. 2 Corinthians 4:9.

today as First Corinthians. It is one of the two Corinthian epistles in the New Testament. Any reader can see that the above-named issues were the dilemmas he was trying to address.

When Timothy arrived in Ephesus with the sad news that Paul's two letters hadn't solved the problems in Corinth, Paul wasted no time. He leapt aboard a ship and sailed across the sea to handle the matter in person. Unfortunately his visit didn't go well. In fact, it was a disaster. The Corinthians doubled down on their sins, and they elevated other, more favored leaders at Paul's expense. Even though he had founded the Corinthian church—he was the first person to preach the gospel to them—they now were treating him like an embarrassment. Their other leaders were more impressive and articulate. Led by a ringleader who despised Paul, they said, "We don't need weak preachers like you anymore. Be gone! Away with you!"

Hurt to his core, Paul departed Corinth in shame, often referring to the trip as his "painful visit."[7] Once back in Ephesus, he wrote a third letter (lost today) of sharp rebuke for the Corinthians' many sins. Yet Paul believed it was for their own good. He explained: "For out of much affliction and anguish of heart I wrote to you, with many tears, not that you should be grieved, but that you might know the love which I have so abundantly for you."[8] As Paul put the finishing touches on his letter and sealed it up for delivery, his burning question was whether or not this "tough love" approach would work. He sent his disciple Titus with the letter to learn what kind of response it would receive.

In the meantime, Paul got caught up in a citywide riot at Ephesus. Luke described it in the book of Acts in a rather understated fashion: "There arose a great commotion about the Way."[9] The riot took the city by storm because big money was involved. The patron goddess of Ephesus was Artemis, whose giant temple—one of the Seven Wonders of the Ancient World—stood just outside the city. Worshipers often bought silver replicas of the idol and her temple to commemorate their visit. But with so many Ephesians turning to Christ, leaving their demonism behind, the souvenir purchases had dropped off. The silversmiths were losing a lot of business. In addition, the priests of

---

7. 2 Corinthians 2:1 NIV.
8. 2 Corinthians 2:4.
9. Acts 19:23.

the goddess feared their loss of dignity if Christianity triumphed over their religion.

Infuriated by Paul's teaching that "gods made with hands are not true gods," an angry mob began to shout, "Great is Artemis of the Ephesians!" Everyone rushed into the open-air theater at the center of town, a steep half bowl set into the mountainside (a place tourists can still visit today). For two straight hours the frenzied crowd shouted about the glory of Artemis. Although Paul wanted to preach Christ to them, his friends forbade it. They could see the people wouldn't be receptive to the gospel. They knew Paul's fiery words would put his life in peril, so they kept him out of sight.

At last the town clerk quieted the crowd and warned them Rome wouldn't look kindly on such a riotous gathering. "The courts are open," the clerk reminded the people. "Sue this fellow if you wish. In the meantime, go home." Reluctantly, the people dispersed.

After such an unsettling tumult, Paul and his fellow Christians decided the time was right for him to get out of town. His three-year ministry at Ephesus had come to a proper end. Paul decided to circle the Aegean Sea by a land route and revisit some of the churches in the north, such as Philippi and Thessalonica. He also wanted to rendezvous with Titus, who had visited Corinth by now and would have a report about whether the stern letter of rebuke had done its job.

At first, Paul couldn't find Titus and he grew concerned. His anxiety kept growing with each passing day. But at last they connected in Macedonia—and Titus had great news. The Corinthian church, including the ringleader of the opposition, had repented! They had restored Paul back into their good graces. Once again, they regarded him with warm affection. In a very real way, God had healed the troubled relationship.

Overjoyed, Paul grabbed his writing materials and began to collect his thoughts. It was time to write to the Corinthians for the fourth time. This letter that he sent ahead of his imminent visit is the one called Second Corinthians. Paul declared:

> Even if I caused you sorrow by my letter, I do not regret it. Though I did regret it—I see that my letter hurt you, but only for a little while—yet now I am happy, not because you were made sorry, but because your sorrow led

you to repentance. For you became sorrowful as God intended and so were not harmed in any way by us. *Godly sorrow brings repentance that leads to salvation and leaves no regret, but worldly sorrow brings death.*[10]

Paul knew there needed to be an important distinction between "godly sorrow" and "worldly sorrow." The former is what happens when a mature Christian leader calls out sin, then the rebuked people accept the chastisement and change their ways. They do this in response to the Holy Spirit's leading, making their sorrow "godly," or, literally, "according to God." They experience a change of mind about their sin and resolve to live in a new way. Because God is behind this, it leads to salvation without regrets.

In contrast, sorrow from the pagan world only leads to death. There is no repentance, just a doubling down into the sin, aggravating the problem all the more. The person might feel a form of sadness, but it's more like anxiety than remorse. Instead of letting that terrible feeling produce good fruit, it leads to a cycle of revenge, hatred, and ever-increasing debauchery to soothe the wounds. The only outcome of worldly sorrow is spiritual, emotional, relational, and eventually, physical death.

Emperor Nero's world ran rampant with a secular sorrow that leads to death. As Paul was writing Second Corinthians, Nero was receiving the imperial throne through bloodshed and betrayal, depravity and deceit, passion and pride. The palace atop Rome's Palatine Hill never lacked for death-dealing sorrow, even when it was cloaked by wealth, opulence, and supposed happiness.

As Nero embarked on his royal reign, would he be able to find a solution to the sorrows around him? For a while, at the start of his rule, he thought he could. His mentor, Seneca, had written a treatise about mercy that promised a wiser, nobler type of governance than previous emperors had displayed. Perhaps Nero could restore the glory days of Caesar Augustus?

Agrippina, for her part, believed her newly crowned son could anesthetize her sorrows and satisfy her heart's desires. Like an addict, she always reached

---

10. 2 Corinthians 7:8–10 NIV.

for more power, more dominance, more tools to subjugate those around her. Yet supremacy could never provide satisfaction. Then when Nero began to fall in love—not within his formal marriage but to a lowborn mistress whom he actually cared about—Agrippina sensed that her control over her son was beginning to slip away.

Godly sorrow leading to repentance would have been the right solution for the twisted house of Nero. No amount of sin is beyond the Lord's redemption. Salvation beckons to everyone, even jaded Roman aristocrats. Yet no one in the imperial palace gave an ear to the gospel, despite its being available to them.[11] Their utter refusal to change their ways led to their tragic downfall, serving as a warning to all who worship themselves instead of God.

CODA

Paul was honest about his feelings of discouragement and shame. If even such a great Christian dealt with issues like that, how much more might we deal with them today? Our conversation reflects on how to break free from guilty self-accusations. The answer is the gospel of God's grace. Christians are fragile jars made out of mere clay, yet the treasure of Jesus can be found within. When we repent and seek life change, Jesus works to seal our cracks and make his treasure shine forth.

BRYAN: Paul gets very discouraged in this chapter as he writes in Second Corinthians about hitting a low point. One of his issues is that he feels shame because he used to be a persecutor, so he's really burdened by all of that, even to the point of death, as he says.

KATHIE: Why do you think he couldn't forgive himself? He knew he was forgiven by Jesus. He knew that. It's interesting because Paul knows the gospel better than anybody. Why could he not believe it? Do you think maybe his thorn has to do with that shame?

BRYAN: Maybe it was partly that, because as he describes it, it's a messenger of Satan. Maybe he did forgive himself, but then Satan would counterattack with the whispers of "You don't measure up."

11. Philippians 4:22.

KATHIE: Putting lies in his head all the time.

BRYAN: Yeah. Just talking, talking, talking in your ears, whispering in a snaky voice, right?

KATHIE: Like a serpentine voice, definitely. So maybe that was it.

BRYAN: Do Christians deal with shame today? I mean, we do, don't we? How do we break free of that?

KATHIE: Honestly, I miss shame in our culture. But I don't want shame to define people.

BRYAN: What do you mean by that—you miss shame?

KATHIE: Nobody gets ashamed anymore. They're not ashamed of anything they've done. They're proud of it, even when it's terrible. They just aren't ashamed. They put it on display for everyone to see. I don't want my children, and especially not my grandchildren, to see so much of what's out there today. People just don't have a sense of shame anymore. Since the beginning of time, God has often used shame to bring people to their knees in repentance and then he takes away all shame after that.

BRYAN: Christians deal with shame, although they've been forgiven. Even someone like Paul was dealing with it. Maybe you have to tell yourself the gospel over and over. When Satan whispers, you shout back the truth.

KATHIE: He's the father of lies. Don't let him win over you! Don't let him speak words over you. Jesus is the only one who's over you. Only him!

BRYAN: And then Paul uses the image of "We have this treasure in jars of clay."[12] What's the meaning of "jars of clay"? Like, what do you think is the symbolism there?

KATHIE: That there is beauty in the brokenness. The beauty of God is hidden inside the destruction. I remember after Hurricane Sandy came through Greenwich, actually up the whole East Coast, our home was hit hard like so many other people's homes were—not totally destroyed, but it was going to take a lot of work to repair. The day after the storm I had everybody in our neighborhood come and stay with us because we had the most bedrooms for people to sleep in. I think every single neighbor came. Instead of leaving town, they came and stayed with us. I made my mother's special spaghetti—yeah, that's some good comfort food! And we sat around eating it together. There

---

12. 2 Corinthians 4:7 NIV.

must have been twenty of us. The next morning I walked down to the end of our property and everything was just decimated. I remember feeling brokenhearted because our old home was so beautiful and now it was in such bad shape. And I remember the Lord saying, "Kathie, you know me. I'm the creator of all things. I make all things new." So we called our property manager and said, "Come on, let's start rebuilding." We needed a builder. That's what Jesus did, and his father, Joseph. If you look up *tekton* in the Greek, it meant a builder and stonemason, not a carpenter. We've gotten it so wrong in English because later translators thought a builder must have been a carpenter, like a woodworker. But Israel didn't have much wood, so Jesus would have worked with what they had, which was stones. He would have been a stonemason.

BRYAN: And that's the idea you're thinking of for your broken home, right? You needed the work of Jesus to rebuild it. Which is the picture of a jar of clay. Because as you look at your house, once so beautiful but now all broken, inside of it is still the golden treasure. The treasure of hospitality, and friends eating together in the midst of tragedy, and a family still united. And love was still there of course.

KATHIE: Yes. And the Lord basically said to me, "Let's get to work."

BRYAN: What about you? Are you a jar of clay?

KATHIE: I'm a broken jar of clay! If you want to see all my scars, here they are! I'm all cracks and chips. I've had two cesarean section births. I have just one hip. I'm a mess!

BRYAN: So people might think, "Oh, it's a broken jar." But then if they lift your lid, what do they find inside?

KATHIE: Not much.

BRYAN: I think they find treasure, Kathie. Don't be embarrassed, because it's actually God's treasure, but I think it's in there.

KATHIE: I'm teasing with you! I'm totally aware of what a mess I am, but I am also aware of how God has healed me through the years. Every time I look at the stairs that I fell down. I crushed my pelvis. I'm just grateful to God that he healed me.

BRYAN: Praise God! And that, my friend, put a big crack in your jar when that happened, or quite a few cracks.

KATHIE: I still love antiques, though.

BRYAN: So you're an antique jar.

KATHIE: I like old things. I love this piano next to me. Frank gave it to me on our fifth anniversary, when we were first married. And it's old. Oldies but goodies. It was the last one that Steinway signed before he died. I mean, there's such a history to old things. I love that. I love the Shroud of Turin. It has been around a long time. Everything that's old has survived through hard times. Now, I do love a new baby, I'll take that any day. But other than that, I like the old stuff that has a history to it.

BRYAN: As this chapter comes to an end, we also talk about godly sorrow that leads to repentance.[13] And, of course, the Romans never did that. Nero never repented. Agrippina never repented. But Paul had repented. What does that phrase mean—"Godly sorrow leads to repentance"?

KATHIE: Do you think they were ever sorry about anything, Bryan?

BRYAN: Maybe the consequences that came to them, but I don't think they had a category for repentance.

KATHIE: What about sexual sin? They all had diseases from that.

BRYAN: I don't think they thought of it as sin.

KATHIE: No, but they were sorry that they were sick.

BRYAN: Sorry for the consequences, but I don't think they had a moral code that told them they shouldn't have done what they did, even when they abused people. The emperors thought that was okay because their divine power gave them the right to do whatever they wanted. But you have to have godly sorrow before you can have true repentance. Not just sorrow for the consequences.

KATHIE: That's exactly right. And sadly, I have too many friends who have consequences, but they don't do anything differently.

BRYAN: Maybe it takes the Holy Spirit being in us to give us that godly sorrow.

KATHIE: Totally. Everything is about the Holy Spirit. Everything.

13. 2 Corinthians 7:10.

ELEVEN

MERCY, MURDER, AND MAYHEM

Nero sought to rule like a wise and merciful emperor—at least that was his personal vision for himself at the beginning of his reign. Too quickly, however, the temptations of the gutter grabbed hold of him. Yet for a time, he tried to be a sober, measured ruler, even if he couldn't live up to his ideals for very long.

The influence of Seneca had helped cast a vision for a high-minded sort of leadership. Seneca's treatise *On Mercy*, which advised the young emperor on how to be merciful rather than harsh, helped Nero want to live up to his mentor's standards. At the funeral for Claudius, the man whom his own mother had murdered with poison, he delivered a eulogy written by Seneca that praised the dead emperor in generous terms, despite his generally bad reputation. Everyone recognized this as a gracious approach, so they respected the young emperor for the gesture, though a few old-timers criticized him for not being a good enough orator to write his own speech.

Nero also informed the Senate that his reign would be marked by shared authority, not autocratic tyranny. When serving as a judge, he wouldn't bring informers and defendants into his household so he could cut a backroom deal through bribery. Instead, legal proceedings would happen out in the open, just as they should. The senators would also retain their prerogatives of direct access to the petitions from the provinces, instead of everything being filtered through the imperial palace. Nero even promised that his fellow consul—in theory, his coruler—didn't have to swear to uphold whatever the emperor wanted. The other man could keep his independence. "My youth wasn't poisoned by civil wars and family strife," Nero told the Senate. "I bring no hatreds, no wrongs to be righted, no thirst for revenge." Although that was a bit of an exaggeration, the words comforted the ruling elites whom previous emperors had oppressed on a whim.

Beyond the sharing of power, Nero displayed some specific examples of mercy. One recipient of his forgiveness was Plautius Lateranus, a man who had participated in one of Messalina's many extramarital affairs. When Emperor Claudius had learned of it, he had demoted the man and stripped him of his properties. Now Emperor Nero gave a series of speeches extolling the virtue of mercy—speeches Seneca actually wrote and put in his pupil's mouth to demonstrate what a noble teacher he was. To prove his mercy, Nero forgave Plautius Lateranus and restored him to the Senate.

But mercy to a disgraced aristocrat and mercy toward conspirators plotting one's downfall are two different things. Nero had both of these in his life. He couldn't afford to be merciful toward the forces he sensed working against him—first and foremost, the forces within his household. Agrippina, his very own mother, was beginning to oppose him!

Their first major point of friction centered on a mistress Nero had taken, a former slave named Acte who genuinely seemed to love him. Since Nero was starved for real human affection, Acte served as a balm for deep wounds—some going as far back as his childhood. His legal wife, Octavia, held no fondness for him, since her own life had been ruined by the schemes of her husband and mother-in-law. But Acte cared for Nero. In fact, she would demonstrate her loyalty all the way to the end. This affectionate newcomer scared Agrippina, seeming to displace her own influence. "My rival, the freed slave," Agrippina would haughtily describe Acte. Or she'd say, "My daughter-in-law, the serving girl."

Those cutting words didn't help the increasing tension between mother and son. When Agrippina complained to Nero about Acte, he dug in his heels. The meaner she made her criticisms of the girl, the more she fanned the flames of Nero's resentment. Nero eventually became so angry he removed his mother from his circle of influence, deciding to put himself under Seneca's tutelage instead. Seriously frightened at the prospect of losing power, Agrippina immediately switched her tactics. "I guess I was too harsh," she cooed to Nero. "Come, use my bedroom for your liaisons with the girl, so nobody has to know." Agrippina even promised to put her vast wealth at her son's disposal as a sign of her maternal care.

Despite these wily tricks, Nero wasn't fooled. His advisers told him to be on guard against the woman who had always been so ruthless.

Nero discerned the extent of his mother's pride when he gifted her an exquisite gown whose fabric was encrusted with jewels. It was intended as a genuine gift to honor her over all other ladies. But instead of being grateful, Agrippina complained that Nero was hoarding many other expensive royal gowns, which he possessed only because she had gotten him onto the throne. Such colossal ingratitude made Nero irate. *My mother's arrogance has no limits!*

The cycle of family trauma intensified when Agrippina started complaining about her stepson, Britannicus. "He's coming of age now," she reminded Nero, "and he's the legitimate heir of Claudius, his natural-born son. You're just an interloper, brought in by adoption. You owe your position to me. Everyone knows it—that I married my uncle as a strategy, that I poisoned his mushrooms. The only moral thing I've ever done is to let Britannicus continue to live."

Agrippina was right: Everyone did know about the poisoning. It was common knowledge among the masses. Seneca had even composed a satirical account of Claudius's embarrassing death and his shameful trip to the underworld. In that humorous story, when Claudius excreted the first dose of poison, he exclaimed, "Oh dear, I think I've soiled myself!" The narrator then remarked, "Whether he did or not, I don't know, but it's certain he made a mess of everything else!"

Still, even an emperor who died in his feces carried noble blood in his veins. Nero possessed less of that blood than Britannicus, the previous emperor's direct, physical heir. Agrippina's anxiety about his claims to the imperial lineage had Nero worried. The boy was about to finish his fourteenth year, which meant it was time for him to adopt the *toga virilis*. Now that he was becoming a man, would Britannicus try to reclaim the imperial throne as the true heir of Claudius?

It was December and time to celebrate Saturnalia, the liveliest holiday of the year. During the drunken festival, Nero ordered various boys to get up and perform songs. Because people were beginning to like Britannicus, Nero ordered him to sing a hard one that should have earned him mockery, but he performed so well—even making a literary allusion to another prince who had been robbed of his rightful rule—that everyone was impressed. Everyone, that is, except Nero. He was furious. He considered music and public performance his own forte. Britannicus was turning into a serious problem!

It was time for the poisoner, Locusta, to do her thing again. Nero summoned her out of jail and ordered her to produce a deadly concoction. But when it was administered to Britannicus by his tutors, he, like his father, excreted the toxin before it could kill him.

Nero brought Locusta before him. "You fool!" he shouted, striking her with his own hand. "You gave him a laxative instead of a poison! I ought to have you executed!"

"No, lord!" she cried. "It was a weak dose so no one would blame you!"

Nero remained suspicious. "I think you're trying to cover for yourself," he accused. "Meanwhile, I'm a nervous wreck. Make me a new batch, right here in my private chambers. And make it strong."

"It'll work as fast as a sword thrust," the poisoner promised, and got to work.

After preparing a second concoction, Locusta tested it on a young goat, which lingered for five hours before it died.

"Stronger!" Nero demanded.

When the third brew was mixed into pig slop and thrown before a hog, the unfortunate creature lapped it up and fell down dead. Nero nodded his approval. "That should work. Give it to the boy!"

Aristocratic youth had filled the dining room when the poison was brought to Britannicus. Normally, assigned tasters would sample the food of nobles to uncover any attempts at foul play. Nero didn't mind sacrificing a taster for this murder, but he knew if such a man died along with Britannicus, poison would be the obvious explanation and Nero could be prosecuted. So a clever ruse was employed to cover the crime. After a steaming hot drink had been officially tasted, it was handed to the boy. When he recoiled from the heat, the taster said, "Here, let me cool it for you"—which is when he added cold water spiked with Locusta's potion. As soon as Britannicus sipped it, his body went stiff and he lost his voice and breath.

A terrified silence descended on the banquet hall. All the diners stared wide-eyed as they watched the scene unfold. The less wise among them left the room, while those with greater caution stayed put so no one could accuse them of leaving the scene of their own crime.

Only Nero remained untroubled as he reclined on his couch beside a low table. "Don't worry about Britannicus," he said mildly. "It happens to him often. He's had epilepsy since his youth. He'll recover shortly."

Nero glanced at Agrippina, discerning panic on her face. Clearly she didn't know anything about the plot. *Good,* he thought. *Now she sees two of us can play the poisoner's game.* Nero understood Agrippina was afraid because a precedent had just been set for him to murder a family member. Nothing now prevented her own assassination as well.

Nero flicked his gaze over to his wife. Octavia lay quietly on her dining couch, motionless and inexpressive. Nero smiled at that. *What a good, noble girl. She has learned to hide her emotions, even while her brother is dying before her eyes!*

And Britannicus did die, for the poison was too strong to overcome. After he was taken out of the dining room, the banquet went on as if nothing had happened. That night, during a blinding thunderstorm that some said was a sign of the gods' displeasure, Britannicus's body was cremated without ceremony and his ashes were interred. Nero later addressed the senators with some polite words of grief, and that was enough for them. Nor did the people of the streets seem to object. Rumor had it that Nero had been raping young Britannicus, so public opinion cruelly decided he was better off dead.

As for Locusta, the emperor rewarded her with a full pardon for her toxic crimes and a beautiful country estate. Nero even started sending her students to learn her dark pharmaceutical arts. One never knew when future assassins might be needed.

Once Agrippina's initial shock wore off, she jumped into action. With her position now precarious, she set about making new allies in case she would ever need their help. She put many military officers and government bureaucrats on her ample payroll. She also drew close to Octavia, who resented what Nero had just done to her brother. Wherever Agrippina could obtain more money, she grabbed it, considering it an "emergency fund" for future dangers.

Of course Nero saw what was happening. To put his mother in a state of vulnerability, he withdrew the soldiers that normally attended an augusta, especially her elite Germanic bodyguards whose loyalty was famous. Nero also forced Agrippina out of his house and made her live in her grandmother's mansion. Whenever Nero visited her, he would come surrounded by centurions who displayed his power, then give his mother a perfunctory kiss before quickly leaving. Eventually, Agrippina was accused of plotting against Nero, but because she was so wily and smooth-talking, no one could make the charges stick. Nevertheless, she remained high on Nero's watch list. Matricide had certainly entered his paranoid mind.

Around this time, Nero picked up a disgraceful habit, the kind of thing that can only be done by someone with absolute power. He started wandering the streets at night, wearing a hat, a wig, and the cheap tunic of a slave. He would carouse in taverns, get himself drunk, and bed the cheap whores in the brothels. A bunch of young cronies would attend him, whose job was to break into shops or houses, snatch any loot they could find, and beat anyone who tried to stop them. Nero often joined this burglary, sporting bruises the next day from his nocturnal misdeeds. Sometimes the violence turned deadly, with men being stabbed and their bodies thrown into sewers. The public soon figured out this was all Nero's doing, but because nothing was ever done to stop it, other gangs took advantage of the mayhem and wreaked their own havoc under Nero's name. Rome became like a captured city being pillaged by a conqueror.

One night, Nero's thugs happened upon an aristocrat named Julius Montanus, who was out walking with his wife. When Nero attacked the lady, he expected another sexual conquest, but Montanus put up an unexpectedly fierce resistance. Nero was beaten so badly he feared for his life. For many days afterward he had to stay out of sight because of his black eyes.

At first, Nero didn't seek vengeance, for he supposed his crimes had been anonymous. Then a letter arrived from the nervous Montanus, begging for forgiveness. "So he knew he was striking Nero!" the emperor exclaimed.

Montanus was immediately sentenced to death and forced to commit suicide. Since he knew whom he had attacked, Montanus had committed the capital crime of treason. Such was the destruction and trauma Nero willfully visited on the SPQR: the *senatus populusque Romanus*, the Senate and people of Rome.

In stark contrast to Nero's abuse, the apostle Paul demonstrated his love for the Romans by writing them a heartfelt letter while he was living in Corinth. He had arrived there after leaving Ephesus and circling the northern Aegean Sea. Gratified to be back in the Corinthians' good graces after his earlier "painful visit,"[1] Paul stayed with them over the winter of AD 56–57. During that time he wrote his epistle to the Romans, which many scholars consider his most important theological work. Countless theologians have plumbed its depths over the years. It became a focal point of debate during the Protestant Reformation when Paul's doctrine of justification by faith was contrasted with righteousness earned through good works. For Paul, the Christian gospel worked through God's grace alone, *sola gratia*, not through human merit.

Yet the epistle to the Romans wasn't just about heavy-duty doctrine for later churchmen to debate. It was a real letter, written to actual people for specific purposes in their lives. Paul wanted the Romans to embrace the gospel—not just as an abstract idea but as a life-changing truth that would transform them from the inside out.

And what was that core truth? Surprisingly, it wasn't justification by faith. Yes, that was *how* the gospel worked; that was its underlying mechanism. But it wasn't the gospel itself. Paul didn't go up to an unbeliever and start proclaiming justification. Instead, he gave this summary of the gospel's message: "If you declare with your mouth, 'Jesus is Lord,' and believe in your heart that God raised him from the dead, you will be saved."[2] Righteousness, being made morally right, came through faith in the risen Jesus, not by being born a Jew. That meant God's salvation was available to any faithful person, no matter his or her ethnic background. "For there is no difference between Jew and Gentile—the

1. 2 Corinthians 2:1 NIV.
2. Romans 10:9 NIV.

same Lord is Lord of all and richly blesses all who call on him, for, 'Everyone who calls on the name of the Lord will be saved.'"[3]

Paul closed his letter to the Romans with personal greetings to some people he knew in the city. Many of them were part of the common class, bearing everyday Gentile names, though some were Jews as well. He mentioned men and women as having equal worth in ministry, for the Christian movement dignified women coworkers in ways their contemporaneous culture never did.

Paul's advice to his Roman friends was practical as well as theological. He urged them to present their bodies as holy sacrifices to God, a kind of spiritual worship.[4] He also commanded them to submit to human authorities—even to wicked emperors!—because all authority comes from God.[5]

Most of all, Paul expressed his warm affection for the Romans. He told them how urgently he wanted to visit them, a goal that had so far been thwarted. But he promised that after he delivered a monetary collection to the poor believers in Jerusalem, he would come to Rome. He prayed "that I may come to you with joy by the will of God, and may be refreshed together with you."[6] After receiving the help of the Roman church, Paul intended to continue spreading the gospel all the way to Spain because for people living in the Roman Empire, long before the voyages of Christopher Columbus, Spain was considered the end of the world.

The bold plan to travel beyond the borders of Italy to spread the gospel to Spain must have excited the Roman church. They viewed themselves as people on a mission, participants in the Lord's great work across the nations. Paul cast a vision for evangelism to lost people when he wrote, "How shall they believe in him of whom they have not heard? And how shall they hear without a preacher? And how shall they preach unless they are sent? As it is written: 'How beautiful are the feet of those who preach the gospel of peace, who bring glad tidings of good things!'"[7]

Instead of prowling the streets like Nero, wreaking murder and mayhem, the beautiful feet of God's people would bring glad tidings to the world, the literal ends of the earth, and offer them the gift of peace.

---

3. Romans 10:12–13 NIV.
4. Romans 12:1.
5. Romans 13:1–7.
6. Romans 15:32.
7. Romans 10:14–15.

CODA

The focus of our conversation about this chapter begins with a consideration of mercy. It's an aspirational virtue for Christians and non-Christians alike. Similarly, everyone aspires to be brave and noble when suffering for a higher purpose. Our conversation then turns to Nero's lover Acte, a cause of family friction. Modern families are by no means immune to jealousies and rivalries. Everyone needs the guidance of God's Word to navigate the complexities of life.

BRYAN: One of our topics in this chapter has been the philosopher Seneca. He wrote about having mercy, which is such an important Christian virtue. But even some of the good voices in Nero's life said, "Hey, you should be more merciful." Really, that's such an important Christian virtue, isn't it? To be merciful.

KATHIE: It's a Jesus virtue, for sure. I think there are nonbelievers who can be very merciful and kind people. I've met them. They're good folks. And they're loving and they're generous, but they just don't know the gospel. They want to be merciful, and I respect that so much, truly.

BRYAN: Seneca was in Nero's ear trying to say, "Hey, if you're going to reign, young fella, you can do vengeance like they all did before you, or you could try this thing called mercy, which is where you have self-control instead of revenge."

KATHIE: Where do you think Seneca got it from?

BRYAN: Stoicism. The Greek philosophy of Stoicism.

KATHIE: Where did that come from?

BRYAN: Like you said, sometimes unbelievers have the right ideas. And there was a lot of overlap between Christian ethics in those days of the ancient church and Stoicism. That was the philosophy they respected the most because someone who suffers but endures it well has a higher purpose in mind.

KATHIE: Yes, suffering for a higher purpose, for God.

BRYAN: For Christians, the higher purpose is God, so they think, "I should endure persecution or even be martyred if I am called to it." And that's a very Stoic thing, really. They believed you might have to die sometimes for the greater good. And using your mind. The Stoics said, "Use your mind to discipline the body. Control the passions by controlling your thoughts."

KATHIE: "Take every thought captive."[8]

BRYAN: Right! And we talked about that a little bit, didn't we? Sometimes the non-Christian world gets it right because there are seeds of the gospel everywhere in the world. Because God's goodness is everywhere.

KATHIE: I just wish everybody knew it! I wish they would identify it as such. "Oh, that's God, that's the creator of the world doing that!" My heart is sad that I haven't been able to reach every single person with the pocket Jesus. They are little figurines that I give out to point people to Jesus.

BRYAN: That's one way to do it. We're also going to use things like this book to tell the story of Jesus. And Paul, who's telling the story of Jesus, and the story of Israel. So you're doing your best, and I'm doing my best to get God's Word out there through the written word.

KATHIE: We are, honey. We're doing our best for the Lord!

BRYAN: Another topic in this chapter was Nero's lover Acte.

KATHIE: She was a faithful woman.

BRYAN: She was a slave, a former slave, that he seemed to truly love.

KATHIE: Do you know what I bet she was? Loving to him. She was just loving and not worshipful. And nobody else ever treated him like that. Normally, when people came to him, they used him. They wanted power by bowing down to him. She came along and somehow she saw the good in him. She saw the beauty in him.

BRYAN: We need those people in our lives, don't we?

KATHIE: We need people who can see our treasure in this jar of clay.

BRYAN: The Lord uses people like that in our lives. Unfortunately, Agrippina saw Acte as a rival. But you love your daughter-in-law, Erika, and you don't see someone who comes to love your son as a rival.

KATHIE: Not a rival at all! She is such a beautiful blessing. Yes, she loves my son undeniably. She is an amazing mother and wife to him. She has been the peacemaker with some of our family stuff. We all have family stuff, right? I'm so grateful for her. And she looks like Elizabeth Taylor! She's drop-dead gorgeous.

BRYAN: Well, that's where—when you actually love your son—you want his best, even if this young lady comes in. Every mother of a son has experienced this where a young lady comes in and suddenly you're not the center of

---

8. 2 Corinthians 10:5 ESV.

the boy's affections anymore. That can be, I think, jarring for any mom who loves her son.

KATHIE: I was never the center of Cody's affection, ever!

BRYAN: I mean, he would make you a picture or pick a flower, right? He'd bring it to you, probably. He'd say, "Hey, Mom, look what I got for you."

KATHIE: [*Laughs.*] He brought it to Christine, his nanny.

BRYAN: Okay, well, you had different dynamics. But still, he's a great guy.

KATHIE: You know Cody. He's an amazing young man, and I'm teasing about his affections. He and I are just so much alike that we battled it out sometimes. He's an extraordinarily brilliant young man. And I'm grateful for him. But yeah, the daughter-in-law comes in and complements him and makes him better. And she doesn't drive a wedge between us. Ever!

BRYAN: It enhances relationships, right? What a beautiful thing.

KATHIE: It really is. And I can't imagine being an Agrippina, just aggravating all the time. "Aggravatingpina." That's what she is. I don't want anything to do with behavior like that. I want my son to adore his wife.

BRYAN: That's good. It just makes the whole world a more beautiful place. You have a healthy family dynamic and it's the opposite of Nero, really. And in this chapter we end with how Paul writes his letter to the Romans at this time. He's not in Rome yet, but he's writing to the Romans. And what a contrast between the two! You get this apostle whose heart is bursting with love. In the final chapter of Romans, he says, "Say hi to this guy and say hi to that lady and give them my love. And here's what I want to do: I want to come visit you. And here's some doctrine that will change your life." But Nero was like, "What can I take from the Romans? How can I make myself more powerful? More for me, less for you!" And Paul says, "Less of me, more for you." What a contrast, right?

KATHIE: Yes. If you're walking with Jesus, it's always that kind of a contrast.

BRYAN: Is his letter to the Romans one of your more favorite books of the Bible, or do you have others you favor?

KATHIE: I always love the one I'm reading. But people are often naturally drawn to different biblical writings. I am especially drawn to John because he was a poet.

BRYAN: Each of the four gospels has a symbol. The ancient symbol of John's gospel is an eagle, because the eagle flies high and he soars. John's gospel rises up like that. But they're all beautiful. They're all Scripture.

KATHIE: Right. They're all Scripture. They're all just followers of Jesus doing their thing. And I adore them all, I truly do. But I'm an artist, so I relate to artists.

BRYAN: You like the artistry more than the details about justification, or something like that.

KATHIE: Certain things mean a lot to me.

BRYAN: Whereas for me, I love to dig into the doctrine, but if it gets kind of touchy-feely, I'm not as likely to relate to it as well.

KATHIE: I like the touchy-feely thing. But truly, I like it all. Sometimes it's just what you need on any given day. The Lord knows what you need to feed on that day.

BRYAN: Yes! It's God's Word so it's all profitable for rebuke and training in righteousness, and for blessing us.[9] We can always count on the Bible to do its work!

9. 2 Timothy 3:16.

TWELVE

MISTRESSES, MALICE, AND MATRICIDE

Around the time Paul wrote his epistle to the Romans, two new characters entered twenty-year-old Nero's life. Though each was beloved by him, each was destined to be destroyed by his hand—or, as we shall see, by his foot.

The first newcomer was Marcus Salvius Otho. Though five years older than Nero, he became one of his best friends. Nero appreciated Otho's style and charm. The two men shared a common obsession for their personal appearances. Otho was so vain he had all his body hair plucked to give himself a smooth, effeminate look. He wore a luxuriant wig to hide his balding scalp. And he shaved his face every day, wanting no stubble at all. To keep his cheeks bright and glowing, he often applied a facial treatment of moist dough—a skin-care routine that probably drew upon the probiotic effects of sourdough yeast. One ancient report describes the fully armored Otho admiring himself in a mirror as he ordered troops into battle. Clearly, the man cared a lot about his public image!

Otho would often help his buddy Nero pursue his slightly disreputable affair with Acte. But when the second newcomer to the story arrived on the scene, everything suddenly got complicated.

Poppaea Sabina was a blue-blooded princess from Pompeii. Her beauty and vanity were famous. Historical accounts say that whenever she traveled, herds of female donkeys had to be brought along because Poppaea believed bathing in asses' milk would be good for her complexion. Her deluxe villa, preserved for centuries in hardened ashes after the eruption of Mount Vesuvius, can still be visited today with its walls and rooms intact. After divorcing her first husband, Poppaea wormed her way into Nero's inner circle with her eye on him as the ultimate marital prize. It was widely known that Nero despised Octavia. Maybe there was room for a replacement?

To carry out her coquettish scheme, Poppaea married Otho but used her new position to flirt with Nero, saying, "I know I'm supposed to be a faithful wife, but I can't resist your good looks!" The strategic flattery worked and Nero took the woman to his bed. By some accounts, the two men willingly shared her sexual favors. Other stories (perhaps also true, for the matter is complex) suggest Otho grew jealous for his wife and wouldn't let Nero's messengers fetch her for a tryst. A line was crossed when Nero himself came to Poppaea's bedroom, but Otho barred the door and made the emperor stand outside, threatening and begging until he finally gave up. That was too much for Nero's pride. He had Otho's marriage legally dissolved, then reassigned him as a governor at the edge of the world, in modern-day Portugal, where he remained until after Nero's death. The emperor in Rome now had unhindered access to the woman who had captured his interest. For the moment, she was his mistress, but marriage was a distinct possibility.

Agrippina, of course, detested Poppaea as yet another rival for her affections. But unlike Acte, Poppaea possessed high social standing, providing her with the ability to fight back. She had every reason to try to separate Nero from his mother, whose control over him seemed bizarre. Only Agrippina stood in the way of Nero's divorcing Octavia and marrying Poppaea instead.

"If you don't want me as a wife, I should just go back to Otho," Poppaea complained to Nero. "At least then I would only *hear* about how everyone mocks you as a mama's boy, instead of having to witness it firsthand!" That line of argument made a powerful impact on Nero. Yet he remained mired in passivity and indecision about how to handle his overbearing mother.

At last, something came to light that sparked enough terror in Nero to ignite him into action. The historian Tacitus recorded what happened based on the various sources he had at his disposal, all of which agreed that the basic problem was incest. Tacitus wrote that Agrippina was so driven to keep her hold on power that

> at the mid-point of the day, when Nero—even at that hour—was flushed with wine and feasting, she quite often appeared before her inebriated son all dressed up and ready for incestuous relations. People close to them began noticing the salacious kisses and the sweet talk that is usually the precursor to sexual relations.

Although Tacitus acknowledged that some people thought the desire was actually Nero's, the majority of ancient historians believed the atrocity was initiated by Agrippina. Popular opinion in the streets of Rome agreed with that view.

At this point, Seneca realized he needed to intervene. He ordered Acte, who still had Nero's ear, to tell him everyone knew about his illicit relations with his mother. "Your incest is common knowledge because Agrippina boasts of it," Acte told him. "The soldiers won't accept the sovereignty of a depraved emperor. Without their support, anyone could stage a coup against you." A shadow of dread crept into Nero's heart. Nothing terrified a sitting emperor more than insurrection. *I have to get my mother out of my life forever*, Nero realized. Then a second terrible thought followed the first: *There's only one way to make it permanent!*

Nero began to consider the best method for killing his mother. *How about poison? No . . . too similar to what happened to Britannicus. People would know. Besides, one of her servants would report it in advance. And she takes antidotes every day to guard against that sort of thing.*

A thrust from a dagger? Again, no . . . there's no way to hide it. I'd surely be blamed. And the assassin might decide not to follow through.

After grappling with the problem some more, Nero decided what he needed was a tragic accident—something instantly deadly, yet seemingly random. *Maybe I could rig the roof to fall on her?* Nero ordered his carpenters to create a mechanism to loosen the heavy panels of Agrippina's bedroom ceiling and drop them on her while she slept. But when whispers about the nefarious tampering leaked out, he ordered the project abandoned. *Still, I do like the idea of a secret accident . . .*

An admiral in the imperial navy named Anicetus suggested another "accidental" option. As Nero's childhood tutor, Anicetus had seen Agrippina up close. He hated her as much as she hated him. Nero liked the man's suggestion and agreed to try it.

The first step was to make a great show of honoring his mother, showering her with filial affection. Nero wrote her a nice letter inviting her to celebrate a festival at his seaside villa at Baiae, a beautiful resort town on the Gulf of Naples. It was the kind of grand, opulent affair Agrippina could never pass up. She said yes and began to prepare for the visit.

Upon her arrival at Baiae, Nero met her at the waterfront as she disembarked from the war galley that had been commandeered for her use. He took Agrippina by the hand, embraced her warmly, then boarded the ship with her. The crew rowed them to Bauli, a sumptuous villa not far down the coastline where the augusta would be staying. When the warship put in at the villa's dock, Nero's luxury yacht rode at anchor nearby. "It's yours to use as you wish—just another way to bless you," Nero told his mother with an oily smile.

Over the next five days, Agrippina used the yacht to attend regular feasts at Nero's villa at Baiae. He publicly honored his mother in front of the diners and chatted with her frequently, sometimes in a lighthearted way, other times in serious conversation. As the final day's banquet approached, Agrippina grew worried. A spy had informed her about some potential foul play regarding the yacht. Though Agrippina didn't want to believe it, just to be safe, that day she had herself carried in a litter from Bauli to Baiae instead of taking the ship. But when Nero was his same affectionate self at the banquet, Agrippina put her worries out of her mind.

Late that night, when the festivities had finally ended, Nero escorted his mother to the dock where the yacht stood waiting. Observers found him to be even more loving than usual. He hugged her tight, then kissed her eyes and hands. "Mother, I wish you strength and good health," he said as she boarded the luxury vessel. "I live for you. And through you, I am king."

On a calm, starlit night the elegant craft slipped away from the dock and departed for Bauli. Agrippina relaxed on a soft mattress within a sturdy framework on the main deck. She chatted with her lady-in-waiting, Acerronia Polla, who reclined beside her. "What a delight to see your son treating you so sweetly," Acerronia exclaimed. "You are surely back in his good graces!"

No sooner had the maid spoken than all hell broke loose. A trap in the overhead canopy released leaden weights onto the unsuspecting pair. Only the framework of the bedstead prevented their deaths—though the weights did strike the rudder man who was standing nearby, killing him instantly.

Despite the ladies' escape, more danger lay in store for them. The ship had been altered by adding a mechanism to break it apart, scuttling it in the open sea. When Nero's henchmen tried to make the booby trap work, it malfunctioned, creating only partial damage. While they kept striving to overturn the ship, other sailors, who weren't part of the plot, tried to save it. Eventually the yacht listed so badly to one side that the two ladies were dumped into the gulf.

"Over here!" Acerronia shouted toward the ship as she struggled in the choppy waves. "The augusta is over here!" But her plea for help brought her death instead. Believing the woman's cry had come from Agrippina, the crewmen who were in on the plot smashed Acerronia with their oars, plunging the maid into the abyss.

Terrified by what she had just seen, Agrippina sank low into the water, making no sound at all. Her shoulder had been wounded during the mayhem, and she wanted to take no more blows that would send her the way of her maid. Easing back from the turbulence, she began to swim toward the shore. But with her injured shoulder the going was difficult. *It's too far! I'll never make it!* Nevertheless, with her famous determination, she pressed on until some passing fishermen took her aboard. They released her onto dry ground, and she made her way to her villa.

Now Agrippina had to think quickly. *Tonight's weather was calm, so there was no reason for a ship to break apart. And those men clubbed Acerronia with intentional violence! This was an assassination attempt—there can be no other explanation. Now what?*

Agrippina decided to lie low and ride out the situation. First, she tended to her wound, then redressed in a clean gown as if nothing had happened. When all looked normal, she summoned a servant, Agermus, and dispatched him to Nero with the message she had survived a slight mishap at sea. "Please tell my son not to visit me," she added. "All I need to do now is rest." Agermus nodded and departed. *Very good. Perhaps that can buy me some time to think!*

Little did Agrippina know she had just sent Agermus to his death. When he arrived at Baiae to share his mistress's news, he found Nero in a state of terror. The emperor had already convinced himself the furious Agrippina would soon arrive with vengeance on her mind. She might be able to inflame the troops . . . the mob . . . the Senate . . . who knows? Somebody out there would surely want to hold the murderer responsible for his heinous crime.

Nero was desperate to bring the situation to an end. *Agrippina has to die before she can get me first! Who can do the deed?* Seneca had advised Nero that the Praetorian Guard certainly would not harm the augusta. Their commander, Burrus, agreed with that assessment. But when Agermus arrived with the message, a solution presented itself: to invent false charges that the man was up to no good. Nero quietly dropped a dagger on the floor near the messenger's foot, then triumphantly picked it up. "Look at this evidence!" he exclaimed. "Agrippina has sent this man to assassinate me. Who will put her to death for such devious plots?"

The admiral who had rigged the booby-trapped ship, Anicetus, enthusiastically volunteered. "Take only the most obedient men," Nero ordered him. "Choose soldiers who will do whatever they're told. They must act without hesitation."

While all of this was happening at Baiae, word had gotten out about Agrippina's near-lethal accident. A crowd of well-wishers had swarmed her seaside villa at Bauli. But when Anicetus's heavily armed squadron arrived, everyone scattered. He set up a perimeter around the mansion, bashed in the door, and hurled aside any slaves who got in his way. Finally, he arrived at the royal bedroom and barged in without knocking. Inside the dimly lit chamber, he found a single handmaiden attending to the augusta as she reclined on a couch.

Instant fear ran like ice through Agrippina's veins. *Anicetus! That man hates me. And look at his fierce expression. Things must have gone terribly wrong!* When the maid rose from the couch and started to flee, Agrippina cried, "What? You're abandoning me too?" After the girl was gone, a ship captain and a commander of naval marines stepped around Anicetus. They flanked him on either side with grim determination etched on their faces.

"If you have come to check on my welfare, you may take back word that I am well," Agrippina told the invaders in a haughty voice that masked her terror. "But if you have come to commit a crime, I refuse to believe my son has ordered his mother's death."

Anicetus's only reply was his cold, hard stare. The ship captain took a club from his belt, then Anicetus and the marine commander drew their swords. The captain's club struck first, smashing Agrippina on the skull. After taking a gash across her breast, Agrippina thrust her belly toward the leader of the three assassins. "Strike here, Anicetus!" she shrieked. "Strike here, for this is what bore Nero!"

In the tragic play Seneca later wrote about these events, he vividly described the death scene:

> What did it profit thee to escape the waters of the cruel sea? Thou art destined to die by the sword of thy son whose infamous crime (his) posterity will scarcely believe . . . The unnatural son is furious at his mother's escape. He grieves that she is saved from the sea, and he commits a greater crime by hastening her death. The servant sent to commit the murder lays open the breast of the mother with his sword. The unhappy woman, while dying, commands the slave to bury the fierce sword in her womb. "Here, here is the place! The sword must pierce the womb which bore such a monster!" Then, passionately weeping, she breathed her last.

Agrippina's corpse, pierced by multiple stabbings, was laid upon a dining couch for Nero's inspection as soon as he could make a visit. Many ancient sources recorded he observed her bare body and remarked, "I did not know I had such a beautiful mother." He was probably trying to pretend he had never seen her nakedness before. In any case, after nothing but the simplest of funeral rites, the body was cremated. The urn for the ashes was deposited in an open grave that was never covered with earth as long as Nero lived. Only later did the most powerful woman in Rome receive a modest tomb.

When Tacitus closed his account of Agrippina's tragic end, he recalled a childhood prophecy the magi had offered to the mother about her son. She had long expected a death like hers, for it had been predicted in the stars. The astrologers had read the heavenly omens about the destiny of little Nero. They predicted this child would reign as an emperor and would kill his mother.

"Let him kill me," the augusta had replied to the magicians, "so long as he comes to power."

Perhaps this was why Nero referred to Agrippina as "the best mother."

Nero's slaughter of his mother stands out as an atrocity in Roman history, yet it wasn't completely out of step with the times. In those days the low status of women often resulted in their subjugation and abuse. Many people think ancient Christianity was equally repressive to women, but the exact opposite was true. The early church gave women opportunities for inclusion and leadership that stood in stark contrast to the values of the surrounding society. Jesus certainly did this, and so did his followers. The apostle Paul was no exception. His treatment of women couldn't have been more antithetical to the way Nero emotionally, sexually, and physically abused the women in his life.

When considering the topic of Paul's relationships with women, it's worth asking: Was he ever married? During the time span covered by the New Testament, he had no wife. He acknowledged that James, Peter, and other apostles had wives who sometimes accompanied them in their itinerant ministries.[1] Paul claimed to possess the same right, if he had had a wife—but he did not. He wrote, "But I say to the unmarried and to the widows: It is good for them *if they remain even as I am*."[2] Clearly, Paul counted himself among the currently unmarried. Since Jewish rabbis were typically married, it's possible Paul previously had a wife who may have died. But since we never hear anything about this one way or another, we just don't know for sure.

During the years of Paul's ministry as a single, he enjoyed fruitful working relationships with women. He greeted them warmly, honored them, and commended them to others. To the Roman church, he wrote, "Greet Andronicus and Junia, my fellow Jews who have been in prison with me. They are outstanding among the apostles, and they were in Christ before I was."[3] Junia, the godly Jewish wife of Andronicus, received Paul's recognition as a standout figure among the apostles. He also wrote, "I commend to you our sister Phoebe, a deacon of the church in Cenchreae."[4] Other women co-ministers in Paul's life, or women whom he publicly addressed or honored, included Chloe,

1. 1 Corinthians 9:5.
2. 1 Corinthians 7:8.
3. Romans 16:7 NIV.
4. Romans 16:1 NIV.

Lydia, Nympha, Persis, Tryphena, Tryphosa, Damaris, Olympas, Julia, Mary, Priscilla, Lois, and Eunice.

The contrast between Paul and Nero couldn't be starker. To Nero, who had no concept of women being made in God's image, the female sex existed to be used for his pleasure or manipulated like tools for his own ends. In contrast, Paul's high regard for women can be seen in his saying, "There is neither Jew nor Greek, there is neither slave nor free, there is neither male nor female; for you are all one in Christ Jesus."[5] What a difference the gospel makes!

CODA

The terrible murder of Agrippina stands out as one of Nero's most atrocious crimes. We discuss the horror of it, reflecting on how the little decisions to do the wrong thing can culminate in big problems down the line. It's the daily moral choices that matter. Nero's matricide then leads us to discuss the stark contrast of how Jesus treated women. Kathie reflects on the Savior's love for women in a society that often disparaged them. Contrary to some modern misconceptions, the Christian faith is (and always has been) pro-woman!

BRYAN: What a wild and crazy story we have in this chapter with Nero killing his mother! Let's talk it through. He invites her to his seaside villa and builds a yacht that's going to be booby-trapped. How does someone get to the point where they have decided to kill their mother? And why go through all this trouble to do it?

KATHIE: My mother was the sweetest woman on the planet, so I can't imagine such a thing! There were times I wanted her gone, but they were very rare! Why do you think Nero wanted to kill his mother?

BRYAN: It's some kind of Oedipus complex or something like that. He's thinking, "I can't get out from under her unless she's gone. She's smothering. She's too controlling. It's either me or her." What do you think?

KATHIE: I agree. It's all of this. Logically he thinks, "I've got to break free." He was a control freak and she's a control freak too.

BRYAN: And they had an incestuous relationship with each other.

5. Galatians 3:28.

KATHIE: And they're having sex! I mean, what can't go wrong with that? She's how much older than he is?

BRYAN: Well, he's a teenager and she's probably about forty. They had some kind of really bad codependency, I think.

KATHIE: No, it's mental illness. I've got other problems but thank God I don't struggle with mental illness. I have friends who do and it breaks my heart for them. It has to be so hard.

BRYAN: Nero does eventually go crazy, and that's part of this book's story.

KATHIE: Yes, and we talked about that with Herod too. Just a little bit, by a little bit, by a little bit, and with no intervention they gradually go insane.

BRYAN: It's those small decisions we make, isn't it?

KATHIE: Oh, gosh, yes. It's so corrosive. You don't see it happening, and before you know it, you're there.

BRYAN: So what do you think, Kathie, of this plan to build an elegant yacht that was designed to collapse in the middle of the ocean?

KATHIE: He wanted it to break in half and fall on her so he could say, "Oh, my poor mother died! But it wasn't me!"

BRYAN: Because everybody knew when he poisoned people. That was sort of his deal. He had just done it to Britannicus. He killed him, and the public knew it. So you can't keep doing it without getting found out.

KATHIE: You can't give away your MO.

BRYAN: But a shipwreck can happen to the good or the bad.

KATHIE: Yeah, ship happens! Or I should say, "*Skubala* happens!" You said before *skubala* means rubbish or crap.

BRYAN: Yes, it's from Philippians 3:8, where Paul says he "counts all things as rubbish." Some Greek scholars say it was kind of a cuss word for excrement. Paul was saying, "Compared to gaining Christ, everything else is crap!"

KATHIE: Well, I think Nero was full of crap!

BRYAN: Right. Everything done by him was total fakery. Even this death of his mother. I mean, wasn't there some stagecraft in his mind? He loved to put on a show. If you're going to have your mom die, why not have her go down as it might be performed in a play—in a ship sinking into the sea? That's very dramatic.

KATHIE: Totally dramatic! All of life was a play to him, and he was always on center stage.

BRYAN: But what happens is, it doesn't work. Agrippina falls into the sea and she is able to swim toward land when some fishermen pick her up. Let's just get in her head here. She gets back to land, all wet and bedraggled, and returns to her villa. How terrified is she at this point?

KATHIE: She's probably in shock. But she's still trying to pull herself together and pretend she's going to be okay. She's a surviving actress too. She had a role to play, just like Nero thought he did. She would wake up every morning, as so many of us do, and go, "I've got a role to play today."

BRYAN: Right. "Today I'm a sister of an emperor. Today I'm a niece of an emperor. Today I'm a wife of an emperor. Today I'm a mother of an emperor." Then Nero, terrified when he hears she's still alive, is like, "Oh, great! My plan didn't work!" And the very thing he didn't want to do—because he could have just done this at the start—was to say, "Hey, soldiers, go in there and stick her. Just do it that way."

KATHIE: Agrippina is trying her best to play the role of a dignified queen, even though she's wounded. Do you think she knew they were coming? Or did she think she'd gotten away with it?

BRYAN: I think she thought she got away with it—until the admiral shows up and he's got army men with him who come at her with clubs and swords.

KATHIE: And she exposes her stomach! She bares her belly to the blade and says, "Right here! Do it right here, because this is where he came from. If you're going to kill me, you're going to kill my son too. Stab me in the place where I made Nero." Such motherly pride! This is sick *skubala*. God knits you together in your mother's womb.[6] You don't make your own babies. God makes your babies!

BRYAN: It all goes back to the prophecy at Nero's birth. You know the magi that came to visit Jesus? Different people came to Agrippina, but they were also the magi. They made a childhood prophecy over Nero by looking at the stars and saying, "Oh, he's going to reign as emperor." This is when he was a baby. "He's going to reign as emperor, but he's going to kill his mother." And Agrippina says, "Let him kill me, so long as he reigns." That's ambition for a son, isn't it? Is there a kind of tiger-mom thing here? You know how they talk about these moms that want to live through their children and get glory that way.

---

6. Psalm 139:13.

KATHIE: Yes, and that's what we talked about previously when we said you've got to let your children dream their own dreams. Children are a gift from God, and we are privileged to raise them. For the most part, they're a joy and a blessing to your life, as the Scripture says. But we don't own them. We don't own our children or our grandchildren. They were created by the Creator himself, and it's his will be done, not ours. His will.

BRYAN: Well, your view is the opposite of Agrippina's. You're the anti-Agrippina, aren't you? You see your children as a gift that God gave you. She saw herself as a goddess who had given birth to a god.

KATHIE: That's what happens when you follow either the Holy Spirit or you follow the Evil One.

BRYAN: You might remember in chapter 5 we mentioned that on the day that Nero became the emperor and took the throne, the chief of his bodyguard said, "Okay, sir, what's the new password?" So he's got to make up a password like we do when we make up passwords for our computers. And his password was *optimam matrem*, "the best mother." The thing that pops into his mind on the day that he took the throne is "I've got the best mother." I don't know if she was the best, but she got him onto the throne, didn't she?

KATHIE: What an amazing accomplishment. But what did it profit her? Or any of them? She died by his own command. Later, he dies terribly too. What does it profit them if they gained the whole world only to lose their very souls?[7]

BRYAN: So very, very true. Moving on to the end of the chapter, we focus briefly on women in Paul's life and how he contrasts with Nero, who killed his mother and was oppressive to women. With that, let's mention something that's dear to your heart—Jesus' love for women. Should a Christian be a feminist? I mean, Jesus made a new way for women, didn't he? Christianity is pro-woman, not anti-woman, isn't it?

KATHIE: Right. Not the least bit anti-woman. But you know what? I don't even like to divide the sexes. Everything about Jesus was pro-human. And whatever form you showed up in, he loved you and saw your value. And he did that in a culture that found more value in one person than the other. That's our problem too. That was Martin Luther King's whole point when he talked

7. Mark 8:36.

about not being judged by the color of your skin but the content of your character. And you know what? He was right! Jesus loves sinners equally as much as the pious followers that walked with him and supported his ministry. He did not discriminate. He was the most radical human being that ever lived because he came down to us even though he was the creator of all things and all people. "Every good and perfect gift is from above, coming down from the Father of the heavenly lights, who does not change like shifting shadows," which is said in James.[8] That's Jesus. He was the gift. He was every good and perfect thing. And all human beings are made in his image.

BRYAN: That was why Paul was able to say, "In Christ, there is no male or female."[9]

KATHIE: Yes, he was saying those things fade. Those things don't matter. Those things are not eternal. What's eternal is our souls. And God loves the soul in us, the eternal part. And he's aware of the suffering of women and how they were abused by men. He sees it, he knows it. Though the Evil One comes to kill and destroy, he can't overcome the good plans of the Messiah. Jesus has come to give life to men and women alike. He's the answer to whatever we're going through. The name of Jesus is the name above all names!

---

8. James 1:17 NIV.
9. Galatians 3:28, author's paraphrase.

THIRTEEN

MADNESS, MUSIC, AND MINISTRY

After Nero got past his initial euphoria at eliminating his dangerous mother, the magnitude of his crime hit him hard. For the next several days he wandered around his villa in a stupor. Eventually, self-preservation moved him to action. He feared that everyone hated him, that Roman society was about to cast him from their collective presence with fierce condemnation, so he wrote an urgent letter to the Senate explaining that Agrippina had sent an assassin to murder him. *Maybe that will excuse me? O gods! Help me!*

Guilt plagued Nero so intensely that he started hearing the phantom notes of a funeral trumpet echoing from his mother's grave. He also believed her ghost appeared to him with accusing words. Trying to escape his fear and shame, he moved from one countryside mansion to another. Even so, the murderer's mind was infected with dark delusions. Wherever he went, the whips and torches of the Furies, the Greek goddesses of vengeance, hounded him. Summoning some magi from the east, Nero begged them to perform their necromancy and call up Agrippina's spirit so he could apologize to her.

The guilty emperor finally worked up the courage to leave his self-imposed exile and go back to his palace in Rome. To his great relief he received a warm welcome. In fact, the citizenry hailed him like a conquering hero. Whatever their private thoughts about the matricide, no one wanted to confront him publicly or get on his bad side. Even the statues of Agrippina were pulled down and destroyed.

Nero's guilt quickly dissipated and with that release came a flood of sin. Tacitus declared he "let himself loose on all the forms of depravity which . . . respect for his mother (such as it was) had managed to check." In other words, with Agrippina's disapproving eye removed from his life, Nero could give himself over to his deepest desires.

And what were those desires? Aside from sexual lusts and a spate of violence against his political enemies, Nero began to reshape his image in ways that would gain him adulation from the masses.

For all his life Nero had been drawn to public performance—yet that sort of thing wasn't allowed for the aristocratic class, especially not an emperor. Actors, musicians, and athletes received wide acclaim but were despised as commoners, sometimes even slaves. Though the elites could *adore* them, they certainly couldn't *be* them.

Nero defied long-standing Roman tradition by turning himself into a spectacle. His unquenchable need for praise, his desperate craving for approval—intensified because of his self-loathing from the matricide—drove him to do what no other emperor had ever done: put himself on the public stage like a lowly performer. Agrippina's disapproval of such pursuits no longer mattered.

Two main areas of popular entertainment caught Nero's fancy. The first was chariot racing. Everyone in Rome, from the senators to the riffraff, loved the bloody sport. They aligned themselves with one of the four teams (Blues, Greens, Reds, or Whites) that served as political factions in the city. On race days, the Circus Maximus would hold 150,000 rowdy spectators, all laying bets on their favorite charioteers or screaming for others to hit a bone-crunching smash-up. The most successful racers became national superstars: adorned with wreaths, admired by men, adored by women. Nero wanted such avid acclaim for himself. To be heaped with praise by a massive crowd sounded like the perfect balm for his guilty soul.

Since chariot racing wasn't suitable for emperors, Nero selected a private racetrack outside the city walls and away from the public eye. Emperor Caligula had established that circus on the Vatican Field for his personal entertainment, but Nero took it over and made it his own. In the coming years he decorated it lavishly and used it often for his races. Training hard, he turned himself into a decent driver of a four-horse chariot. Once he felt confident enough in his mastery of the reins, he began to let spectators watch him race. Soon, the Circus of Nero was providing regular doses of fawning adoration as Nero won his "victories" against bogus competitors.

In addition to the racetrack, Nero's second area of public performance was the theater, where he began to sing songs and play the lyre. Such recitals—with their delicate lyrics, lilting music, coiffed hair, and gauzy robes—were considered highly effeminate. Rome's masculine aristocratic class, which had always emphasized self-discipline and warfare, viewed such behavior as far beneath their manly station. Yet Nero couldn't stay away from the adulation. He studied under the best harpists and learned to pluck a sweet string. Though his voice was weak and husky, no one dared tell him so. Instead, they applauded his every recital as if the musical god Apollo had just come down to earth. As in the circus, so in the theater, Nero received a constant stream of fawning praise that bolstered his fragile ego.

Because public musical shows were so unworthy of the upper class, Nero forced many aristocrats to join him so his shame wouldn't stand out so badly. Descendants of great families who had recently fallen on hard times were bribed to perform out of financial desperation. Highborn nobles, many of whom had never even watched the crude antics of the theater, now had to become participants themselves. Whatever skills anyone possessed had to be trained to the highest level so they could be displayed in public.

Stages were filled with the nobility of all ages—boys and girls, men and women, even the elderly. Dignified old matrons were forced to give exhibitions like showgirls. One lady in her eighties, Aelia Catella, had to dance a pantomime routine. Patricians who were too old or sick to dance were obliged to sing in choruses. The historian Dio Cassius described exhibitions that were "most disgraceful and most shocking, when men and women not only of the equestrian but even of the senatorial order appeared as performers in the orchestra, in the Circus, and in the hunting-theatre, like those who are held in lowest esteem." If any embarrassed nobles put on actors' masks to hide their shame, Nero ordered them removed to highlight their humiliation. In this way, he "exhibited the performers to a rabble whose magistrates they had been but a short time before."

To keep the flattery flowing, Nero devised a hugely wasteful yet popular scheme. His workmen created tokens in the form of little balls with words inscribed on them. Each word designated a lavish prize: gourmet foods, horses, slaves, mule teams, gold, silver, and expensive multicolored robes. When the balls were tossed into the stands, whoever managed to snatch one received the designated award. Even prizes as magnificent as ships, apartment blocks, and farmland were handed out. Though Nero appeared to be generous, fiscal conservatives recognized the giveaway as nothing but public bribery. "Sensible people," Dio Cassius declared, "were grieved . . . that he was spending so much in order that he might disgrace himself."

Did all of these actions earn Nero the love he so desperately craved? Perhaps he thought so. When he strutted onstage with the flowing locks and dainty frock of a harpist, fine-tuning his strings like an expert before giving his composition, he could forget for the moment who he really was. The fake persona of the performer—loved, admired, and applauded by all—replaced the monster who injured, betrayed, and violated the people around him. While the crowds feigned their adoration and a horde of hired fanboys clapped their hands, Nero could believe he was someone special. The good news of Rome had convinced him that fame, wealth, and extravagance would dispel the darkness within. But as Nero would eventually learn, this false gospel didn't hold the power to heal the human soul.

Having reconciled with the Corinthian believers after his "painful visit," Paul spent the winter of AD 57 in Corinth with his dear friends. But when the cold, rainy Mediterranean winter began to shift toward spring, it was time to move on. Paul earnestly wanted to bring a monetary gift to the impoverished believers in Jerusalem. Then he would head for Rome—and keep going to Spain, the "end of the earth."

Though Paul wanted to be in Jerusalem for the day of Pentecost, which normally fell in late May or early June, he felt it important to revisit the churches he had established. Backtracking by land, he circled the northern Aegean Sea and came around to Philippi. There he boarded a ship for the remainder of the journey. As he passed near Ephesus, his love for the Ephesian elders prompted him to summon them to Miletus, a nearby port. He wanted to spend a little time with them even though he knew he couldn't stay long if he was going to reach Jerusalem in time for the festival.

The godly men came and embraced him, praying for his safety. Paul explained to them that the Spirit had told him he would never see them again. Persecution, imprisonment, and afflictions lay in store for him. "However, I consider my life worth nothing to me," Paul told the elders. "My only aim is to finish the race and complete the task the Lord Jesus has given me—the task of testifying to the good news of God's grace."[1] With great weeping, they accompanied Paul to his ship and released him to his God-given mission.

A week later he reached the port of Caesarea, the main entrance into Israel. A prophet named Agabus met him there with an unexpected heaven-sent sign. Agabus took Paul's sash from his waist and bound his hands and feet with it. "So shall the Jews at Jerusalem bind the man who owns this belt, and deliver him into the hands of the Gentiles," Agabus declared. Though everyone who heard the prophecy urged Paul not to continue to Jerusalem, he was undeterred. "What do you mean by weeping and breaking my heart?" he asked. "For I am ready not only to be bound, but also to die at Jerusalem for the name of the Lord Jesus." When Paul's friends realized he couldn't be dissuaded, they said, "The will of the Lord be done."[2]

Arriving in Jerusalem, Paul received a warm welcome from James (the brother of Jesus) and all the elders. They rejoiced at Paul's report of his successful ministry among the Gentiles. Nevertheless, some local zealots were circulating bad rumors about Paul: that he taught the Jews abroad to forsake the law of Moses and to reject circumcision and other Jewish customs. James advised Paul to do a public good deed. He should purify himself and pay the expenses of some men who were keeping a vow commanded in the Torah. Animal sacrifices, which were not cheap, would need to be offered at the temple. For Paul to join these men and cover their costs would demonstrate to all the Jews that he was still a faithful Israelite.

Paul agreed to the peacekeeping strategy and did as James suggested. But trouble arose when he was spotted in the temple precincts. A shout went up

1. Acts 20:24 NIV.
2. Acts 21:11, 13–14.

from some zealous Jews: "Men of Israel, help! This is the man who teaches all men everywhere against the people, the law, and this place!"[3] The agitators even claimed Paul had brought a Gentile friend into the temple's inner courts, defiling God's holy ground. Though the claim was false, Paul took the blame anyway. The mob started beating him. Only the intervention of a Roman tribune and his soldiers saved him from their fury. The soldiers literally had to carry him out of their grasp!

As Paul was being hurried into the Antonia Fortress next to the temple, he asked the tribune if he could say something. The military commander was surprised Paul knew Greek, having assumed he was just a peasant, or maybe a foreign insurrectionist. When Paul identified himself as a Jew from the respected city of Tarsus, the tribune realized he had a man of substance in his custody, so he indicated Paul could speak. The apostle turned to the crowd, motioned for silence with his hand, and addressed his countrymen in their native Aramaic.

Paul related his personal conversion story: how he was trained as a Pharisee, was zealous for the Torah, and was a persecutor until he converted to Yeshua on the Damascus road. The people accepted all of this without a problem. But then Paul declared his direct commission from the Lord, who had said, "Depart, for I will send you far from here to the Gentiles."[4] These words stirred the mob into fury again. They couldn't grasp that God would desire to save the impure people who didn't observe the Torah. When the unruly mob began to demand Paul's immediate execution, the tribune took him inside the fortress.

The soldiers were about to flog Paul to determine why he was so controversial when they learned he was a Roman citizen, which granted him immunity from such harsh treatment. Now the tribune didn't know what to do. The next day Paul defended his beliefs before the Jewish council and various Roman officials. Meanwhile, his opponents plotted to kill him. The authorities finally decided this troublemaker had to be removed from Jerusalem, so they sent him by night under a massive armed escort to the regional capital at Caesarea. There Paul was thrown into prison to await his fate.

3. Acts 21:28.
4. Acts 22:21.

He languished in Roman custody for more than two years until a new leader named Porcius Festus came to power. Festus learned the Jerusalem agitators wanted Paul remanded to their city so they could secretly ambush him and put him to death. Such intense hostility puzzled him. *What has made the Jews so angry at this man?* It was time to find a final solution to the dilemma presented by Paul of Tarsus.

Festus summoned Paul before his tribunal in Caesarea, where the agitators from Jerusalem had come to present fierce charges against him. In reply, Paul protested his innocence. Wishing to do the Jews a favor, Festus asked Paul, "Are you willing to go up to Jerusalem and stand trial before me there on these charges?"[5] In Festus's mind, he thought, *If anyone should happen to kill him along the way, this stupid problem will be off my hands!*

Paul's reply was a firm no. "I am now standing before Caesar's court, where I ought to be tried," he declared. "I have not done any wrong to the Jews, as you yourself know very well. If, however, I am guilty of doing anything deserving death, I do not refuse to die. But if the charges brought against me by these Jews are not true, no one has the right to hand me over to them." Then Paul added the decisive words that sealed his fate: "I appeal to Caesar!"[6]

Festus's eyes widened and he arched his brows at the unexpected demand. *Aha! Now that's a good solution!* He spun around to his counselors and exchanged hurried whispers with them. After gathering their legal advice, he returned his attention to the room. Everyone at the tribunal waited to hear what Festus would say. His gaze drilled the apostle Paul. "You have appealed to Caesar?" Festus pointed his finger at the defendant and issued his verdict: "To Caesar you shall go!"[7]

The decision seemed to satisfy everyone. The Roman administrators and the Jerusalem agitators would have their greatest problem taken far away. Paul's friends would be relieved he was no longer in imminent danger. As for Paul, he would get a free trip to Rome, the very place he had longed to visit.

Yet a complication, a twist of fate, lurked unseen to everyone in the room. The Roman emperor was no longer himself. Ever since Nero murdered his

---

5. Acts 25:9 NIV.
6. Acts 25:10–11 NIV.
7. Acts 25:12.

mother, his mental health had been declining. The once-beloved emperor, the self-proclaimed "merciful" ruler who was supposed to render impartial judgments, had begun to lose his mind. Over in the capital city, Nero Caesar was slipping into madness.

CODA

Nero's longing for praise led him to the performance stage. Kathie comments on the entertainer's temptation to seek ego affirmations from the crowd. Although all of us can fall into the trap of pride, we should instead offer our abilities to God in humble service. The apostle Paul did that—and while it brought him opposition, his legacy lasted long beyond the faded glories of Rome.

BRYAN: This chapter's title, "Madness, Music, and Ministry," refers to the fact that Nero has killed his mother, which enables him to indulge himself. He goes into something that's very much part of your life, Kathie, in two ways: first is theater, performance, and music; and second, sports, because Frank was into sports. What is it like as a performer? Is the affirmation from the crowd—say, an ovation—is it addicting? Is that what Nero was after?

KATHIE: I'd like to think I was talented and Nero wasn't—though he thought he was.

BRYAN: You earned it. Besides, you didn't have the power to make them clap for you.

KATHIE: I couldn't make anybody clap, no. And I did work hard my entire life.

BRYAN: Maybe you got some bad reviews at some point.

KATHIE: Oh, yeah, I definitely did.

BRYAN: Which Nero never got, right? No one ever gave him a bad review.

KATHIE: No, he never got a bad review or they would lose their heads!

BRYAN: And, of course, you didn't think you were a goddess when you got good reviews. People told you the truth.

KATHIE: Right. Or people were jealous of me, or they were just being harsh. You have to think, "Why in the world would they say that?" Was I the greatest singer that was ever born? No. Did I pretend to be? No.

BRYAN: Who is the greatest singer?

KATHIE: In my lifetime it was Barbra Streisand. She was the aspirational singer. When she sang, I stopped in my tracks and sobbed my eyes out, thinking, "That's what I want to do."

BRYAN: What about Whitney Houston? Was she like that too?

KATHIE: She came later, and I really appreciated her. I knew Whitney. I know Barbra too.

BRYAN: When you're in that world, is the crowd addicting? Like, when you get great praise and they clap for you, do you say, "Wow, I'm full of contentment," or do you say, "Oh, I need that again! I need that again!" Like another hit of the drug.

KATHIE: You could do both. But what I loved even more than the applause was the laughter. I made people laugh. Yeah, and I adored that. Comedy. A lot of people can hit a high note. But I would always be able to pick out who I wanted to play with in the audience. I would go out and make them laugh and rub their bald head and just have fun with them. And their wives would start to scream with laughter. And that's when I said, "I got them." I don't think Nero ever got close to the crowd. He wanted it to be one-way. "I don't want to come out where you are. You should just heap me with praise." But me? I loved making people happy.

BRYAN: Maybe Nero felt some of that when he performed.

KATHIE: He didn't make anybody happy.

BRYAN: Maybe not truly happy. But he liked to think he was doing that.

KATHIE: When they left a show, and they were still alive, they were happy they hadn't gotten in trouble. I couldn't hit the highest notes in the world, and I couldn't hold the note for the longest time, but I guarantee you, very few people could make somebody laugh as much as I did.

BRYAN: Nero also realizes, "I can do this through sport too."

KATHIE: He was not a great athlete. Let's be honest.

BRYAN: No, he wasn't like Frank, who was legitimate. That was the performance of a true athlete. That wasn't you, but it was Frank. The sports world and the entertainment world are very parallel, aren't they? Because you're in front of a crowd, letting them enjoy your abilities.

KATHIE: Well, you are in front of a crowd. So few people know that Frank was born into a really, really poor family. Like, eating-dog-food poor. And you need to know that to understand the quality of the man that he became. He ate dog food and he was grateful to have it. That of course had changed by the end of his life, but his sporting ability is what got him there.

BRYAN: And then it was his broadcasting ability.

KATHIE: Of course. That too. But the beauty about Frank—well, there's so many beautiful things about Frank—but many people don't know he was a stutterer. And he was not what he considered smart. But he ended up in eight different halls of fame. And at USC he was an all-American.

BRYAN: Was he ever up for the Heisman Trophy as a college player?

KATHIE: He came in second. He should have had the Heisman.

BRYAN: So I guess to take it back to comparing it with Nero, when you want to serve God with your talents, it's totally different than when you want to become a god yourself. In the eyes of the audience, the contrast is always there. They know the difference. The Christian is just saying, "Lord, here are my loaves and fishes. Lord, you multiply these."

KATHIE: I don't have any fine food like caviar or filet mignon to give anyone, but every gift I do have is from God above, the Father of lights.[8] Sometimes you mess up. Frank fumbled the ball. I've fallen on stages. You just get up, go back out there, and finish your show.

BRYAN: Nero had some stage fright that he overcame. One time he fell out of the chariot and got back in. So maybe let's give him the credit that at least he persevered.

KATHIE: Yes, some partial credit, but he did it for himself, for the wrong reasons. So I don't know about that being worthy of credit. I'm not a Nero fan.

BRYAN: You're a Jesus fan.

KATHIE: I'm a Jesus fan! I am not a Nero fan, though I am fascinated by him. But there's nothing I like about him. There's a lot I like about Paul, just not the unibrow.

BRYAN: They also say he had bowlegs.

KATHIE: Bowlegged, yeah, not crazy about that either. He might have had nice feet.

BRYAN: We know he did. The scripture says, "How beautiful are the feet of those who bring good news."[9] Paul had beautiful feet when he brought the

8. James 1:17.
9. Isaiah 52:7; Romans 10:15, author's paraphrase.

gospel. But that didn't stop the Jews from wanting to kill him. So the final scene in our chapter is when he goes back to Jerusalem and a mob of the Jewish leaders stirs up trouble. He's arrested and they want to assassinate him. The Romans have to put him under massive armed guard to keep the mob from killing him. Why did the Jewish leaders so badly want to kill Paul?

KATHIE: The same reason they wanted to kill Jesus. They had lost power. They'd lost it and they wanted it back. And that's really it in a nutshell. Every story we write, Bryan, is about somebody that murdered people to get power. And then murdered people to keep it. All of a sudden, Paul is getting all kinds of people interested in his message. And people are coming to know Jesus.

BRYAN: Do you think underneath all this is spiritual warfare?

KATHIE: Always, because there is a constant power struggle between good and evil, Jesus and the devil. The Romans wanted to oppose Paul because he was so effective at bringing Jesus into the hearts of people. People were no longer giving money for their purposes. It's always power and money. But Jesus brings freedom.

BRYAN: Finally, when Paul says, "I appeal to Caesar!"[10] it allows us to end the chapter with these two parallel stories now headed on a collision course. Nero is doing his thing, but he doesn't know Paul. And Paul knows about Nero, but he doesn't know him directly.

KATHIE: Do you think Nero had heard about Paul?

BRYAN: Probably not about Paul just yet, but he'd heard about Christianity.

KATHIE: Oh, about Christianity, right. Because the Jews and "Chrestus" were making trouble. Claudius knew about that too.

BRYAN: Yes, but they thought Christianity was some stupid, insignificant cult. Little did they know that the Lord Jesus would triumph over them. And today their world is just crumbled ruins for tourists to visit, but Jesus is alive, and his people are living stones!

---

10. Acts 25:11.

FOURTEEN

MONSOON, MALTA, AND A MEETING

After two long years in the seaside city of Caesarea Maritima, Paul felt overjoyed to be leaving. For so long, he had yearned to make his great journey to Rome. Now, at last, that day had arrived.

Though he had been kept in the palace built by Herod the Great, Paul's imprisonment had been anything but palatial. Situated on a beautiful promontory that jutted into the sea, the palace had many luxurious rooms for its elite occupants to enjoy, along with a huge swimming pool at its center. But the palace had another function: to serve as a praetorium for military use. Paul had been imprisoned in this more austere part of the complex with only a little bit of freedom. Fortunately, his friends were given access to him so they could meet his needs.[1] Yet every day, Paul remained trapped in his little room—all while smelling salt in the air and seeing the sun set on the western horizon.

In addition to the palace, in the era before Christ's birth, King Herod had also built the magnificent harbor at Caesarea. It had two seawalls that functioned like arms to enfold ships within their embrace and guard them from Mediterranean storms. As Paul stood on the deck of a merchant ship from Adramyttium, its hold laden with trade goods, he felt like a free man, even though by law he wasn't. A centurion named Julius had been appointed to

---

1. Acts 23:35, 24:23.

guard him and some other Roman prisoners on the trip to stand before Caesar. The long journey would be arduous and oppressive, requiring about a month of sea and foot travel. Yet Paul's friends Luke and Aristarchus had come along to give him comfort.

The sun shone brightly overhead, seabirds circled against the blue sky, and a crisp breeze gave hope for a good journey. Sailors unfastened the heavy mooring ropes and heaved them onto the pier. As the cargo vessel slipped out of Caesarea's harbor and the sail caught the wind, Paul looked back to the shore. A huge building, perched atop an artificial hill, dominated the waterfront: the temple of Caesar Augustus, for whom the city was named.

When Herod had built the westward-facing city with its grand harbor, he intended it to serve as Israel's port of entry for the wealth and power of the caesars. He wanted to import Rome's glory into the Holy Land. *Little did he know how mistaken he was,* Paul thought as he turned his back on the temple and fixed his gaze upon the open sea. *The real glory is the gospel that came to Israel—and now it's on its way to Rome!*

The journey followed the coasts of Israel, Syria, and Asia Minor without any problems. Paul often found himself burrowing into his cloak when he stood on deck, for it was late September and the winds had turned noticeably colder. At Myra, the centurion transferred his prisoners onto a huge grain ship from Alexandria that was bound for Italy. This much larger vessel carried a passenger count of 276. Soon the sailing grew difficult as the winds turned adverse. Progress slowed as the Alexandrian ship struggled to make headway. Only with great effort did the captain finally reach a poor harbor on the island of Crete.

"We can't spend the winter here," he said to his crew and the centurion. "The harbor is too exposed."

Paul was standing nearby and overheard the plans, which troubled him. *The Day of Atonement has passed. It's October now. To embark on the sea is reckless!* He decided he had to speak up. "Men," he said, "I believe there is trouble ahead if we go on—shipwreck, loss of cargo, and danger to our lives as well."[2]

---

2. Acts 27:10 NLT.

Though Paul was only a prisoner, he knew he was God's instrument of the gospel. Jesus had told him, "For as you have testified for Me in Jerusalem, so you must also bear witness at Rome."[3] Paul was certain he would reach his destination, and he hoped his warning could save his fellow travelers.

Unfortunately, his advice was disregarded. The dawn of a beautiful day encouraged the captain to set sail. But no sooner had he started coasting along the Cretan shoreline than a terrible monsoon rushed down from the highlands. The fierce gales of the northeaster seized the ship and drove it away from land. With steering impossible, the sailors could only lower the sails and be driven along by winds that hurled the ship into the open sea. Without sight of sun or stars, the crew lost all awareness of their whereabouts and the ship drifted in a tempestuous ocean with no refuge in sight.

On the second day of the terrible monsoon, the terrified sailors threw much of the cargo overboard to lighten their load and protect the hull from breaking up. When the hurricane didn't abate, the next day they also discarded the ship's rigging and supplies, and its mainmast as well. Now they were just a helpless tub in a violent sea. After many days of dark, directionless drifting, Luke described the attitude of the dispirited crew: "All hope that we would be saved was finally given up."[4]

Though the starving sailors had relinquished their hope, Paul had not. He was praying deep in the hold when a brilliant light suddenly shone around him—an angel of God! "Do not be afraid, Paul," the angel said. "You must be brought before Caesar; and indeed God has granted you all those who sail with you."[5] Paul immediately approached the captain and his advisers. He urged them to take courage, for God had declared their lives would be spared, though the ship itself would be destroyed.

After two straight weeks of enduring the storm, the men sensed land was nearby. The crew took soundings and realized they were moving into shallower water. With hope rekindled, Paul urged the passengers to eat some bread for strength. He broke apart a loaf and gave thanks for it, and they began to eat. Though this wasn't exactly a Communion celebration, it followed the same pattern that Jesus had demonstrated at the Last Supper. Paul understood that

3. Acts 23:11.
4. Acts 27:20.
5. Acts 27:24.

the Bread of Life didn't provide just spiritual salvation, he gave physical help as well. To partake of Christ was to receive many kinds of blessing.

But they weren't yet safe. The fierce winds drove the ship toward the rocky coast of Malta. With a terrible scraping sound, followed by a sudden violent lurch, the keel dug into a reef and came to a halt. As the pounding waves kept up their assault, threatening to smash the hull to splinters, everyone knew it was only a matter of time before the battered ship would succumb to the relentless breakers.

The exhausted travelers, who had endured their cold, wet ordeal for so long, didn't want to die with deliverance so close. Each man leapt into the roiling surf and made it to the shore as best he could, either by swimming or clinging to bits of wreckage. Paul washed up on the beach among them, spitting out seawater and sand with his psalms as he thanked God for his salvation.

The island's people welcomed the castaways and treated them kindly, helping the bedraggled survivors to collect wood for a fire. When Paul added a tangle of brush to the flames, a poisonous viper darted from the heat and fastened onto his hand. He merely shook it off. "Aha!" the natives exclaimed. "No doubt this man is a murderer. Though he has escaped from the sea, Justice has not allowed him to live."[6] Indeed Paul was a murderer, but the price justice demanded had already been paid in full by Jesus. The dragon had been defanged; its poison had lost its power. No snake, whether earthly or satanic, could ever again claim authority over his life.

The islanders marveled at Paul's immunity to the snake's venom. "He must be a god," they decided. Then when he healed the sick father of the local chieftain, the Maltese people began flocking to him, and he cured them all.

For the next three months the castaways enjoyed the hospitality of the islanders, resting and regaining their strength. Finally another Alexandrian ship took Julius's soldiers and prisoners on board. The centurion's mission couldn't end until he delivered them all to Rome.

---

6. Acts 28:4 ESV.

The party traveled easily to Sicily, an island at the toe of Italy's boot. From there, they sailed up the boot's shin until they came to Puteoli, a little town on the Gulf of Naples. From the harbor, Nero's resort at Baiae could be seen across the bay. Since Puteoli was a major trading hub, the gospel had already reached it through the natural grapevine of seaborne commerce. Some local Christians learned of Paul's arrival and gave aid to him and his friends. They also sent a messenger up to Rome to alert the church that the respected apostle was on his way.

After a week of rest, Julius's party of soldiers and prisoners left the sea behind and traveled by foot up the ancient road called the Appian Way. At the Forum of Appius, a spot forty-three miles from the capital, a group of Roman Christians came out to welcome Paul. Some of them may have been the very people he had greeted in his epistle three years earlier. A little farther on, more Christians met Paul at a place called Three Taverns. The holy entourage accompanied him all the way into Rome, not as a despicable prisoner in chains, but as a conquering hero with a "triumphal entry" that paralleled Christ's entrance into Jerusalem. The procession entered the capital through the Capena Gate, where the enormous Circus Maximus met everyone's eyes. Once inside the city, the centurion put Paul under house arrest to await his trial before Nero.

Just like at Caesarea, the Roman imprisonment turned into another two-year waiting period. Yet Paul wasn't idle during that time. According to ancient tradition, he rented a room near the city's main Jewish neighborhood along the Tiber River. Today, Rome's greatest synagogue stands in the same area. Jewish leaders crossed the river and debated with Paul about the meaning of Israel's Scriptures. In addition, Paul used his confinement to write four of his biblical letters, known as the Prison Epistles: Ephesians, Philippians, Colossians, and Philemon. He wasn't the kind of man to waste a single second. If he couldn't exhort and encourage his converts in person, his heartfelt letters would minister to them instead.

At this point, Luke ended his historical narrative in the book of Acts. He wrote, "For two whole years Paul stayed there in his own rented house and welcomed all who came to see him. He proclaimed the kingdom of God and taught about the Lord Jesus Christ—with all boldness and without hindrance."[7] Then

7. Acts 28:30–31 NIV.

the scriptural account of Paul's ministry came to an end. After this, anything known about the apostle has to be deduced from his letters or from non-biblical writings. Based on such sources, let's see what happened to Paul when he met the emperor to whom he had appealed his legal case.

Among Nero's many selfish and repulsive acts, one offense especially disgusted the Roman populace. During a trip to the mountains, he bathed in the pristine pool that sourced the Aqua Marcia, the city's favorite aqueduct, whose waters were beloved for their sweetness and purity. When Nero became deathly ill afterward, everyone said the gods were angry at him for desecrating the sacred pool. Though Nero eventually recovered, it had raised a question: If the emperor were to die, who would be next in line for the throne?

Nero's chaste and respectable wife, Octavia, had borne him no children, because he avoided her sexually. She represented a genteel sort of propriety that repulsed him, for he preferred partners who were gross and illicit. He wanted to be rid of her. Since the citizenry loved the highborn Octavia, a paragon of Roman virtue, Nero couldn't kill her outright. Instead, he decided to divorce her for providing him with no descendants. Twelve days later, he married Poppaea Sabina, whom he had already taken as his lover. In fact, she was pregnant with his offspring. The child turned out to be a girl who died in infancy—yet the birth proved Poppaea was fertile enough to produce an heir.

Out of jealousy and fear, Poppaea, Nero's new wife, insisted he exile Octavia to a villa on a remote island lest she become a rival again. After all, her father had been the previous emperor, and his Claudian blood ran in his daughter's veins. Charges were trumped up against her: Anicetus, the admiral who had murdered Agrippina, now claimed to have had an affair with Octavia. A short time later, she received an order to commit suicide. When she refused, she was bound tightly with cords and her royal veins were sliced open. Since she bled too slowly to die, she was locked in a sauna until she expired from overheating and blood loss. After twenty-two years of constant danger, Octavia, like her parents and her brother, succumbed to the murderous intrigues of the imperial palace. She was immediately decapitated, and her severed head was shipped to Rome for Poppaea's triumphant viewing.

The ancient Jewish historian Josephus reported something else about Poppaea: She was supposedly a God-fearer—that is, a Gentile with religious interest in Israel's deity. Whenever Jewish leaders brought petitions to Rome, she encouraged Nero to answer them favorably. So it may have been at his wife's prompting that Nero summoned Paul before his tribunal to learn what this new sect of Judaism was all about.

Unfortunately, no record of their interaction has survived. Some ancient Christian texts provide vivid descriptions of a meeting between the two, but those stories probably describe a second meeting between Nero and Paul, which occurred a few years later. Clearly there must have been two encounters, because Paul recalled his "first defense" while he was languishing in the Carcer awaiting his more dangerous second trial.[8]

But at the first hearing, Paul hadn't yet been imprisoned in that terrible dungeon, nor had he written his three Pastoral Epistles: 1 Timothy, 2 Timothy, and Titus. Therefore Paul must have been released as innocent after Nero heard—and probably grew bored with—the seemingly ridiculous message about the Jewish Messiah. And so, after four years of imprisonment in two different cities with a harrowing shipwreck in between, Paul was a free man.

Now what? With his legal restrictions removed, Paul decided to continue his original mission. Ever since Jesus had commissioned him to go "far away to the Gentiles,"[9] he had been pressing toward distant lands. He had written to the Romans five years earlier expressing his desire to spread the gospel among them. Thanks to his many visitors during his house arrest, he had now fulfilled that goal. The gospel had expanded from Jerusalem all the way to Rome.

But Rome wasn't the "end of the earth"; it was the center of the ancient world. Although the proverb "All roads lead to Rome" hadn't yet been coined, the principle was well established. In the middle of the Forum—Rome's central town square—Caesar Augustus had set up the Golden Milestone, the symbolic monument from which every highway radiated and by which all their lengths were measured. Rome stood at the hub of a great wheel, the beating heart of the imperial body. In order to reach the fringe of the world with the

8. 2 Timothy 4:16.
9. Acts 22:21 ESV.

gospel, Paul would have to leave the capital and keep going west. His journey would take him to where the land came to an end and the ocean stretched to the horizon as far as the eye could see.

As Paul strolled along the sidewalk of an open plaza in Rome's bustling seaport of Ostia, downstream from the capital city along the Tiber River, he surveyed the busy men around him. A leather pouch hung from his belt, its weight heavy from the coins donated by the Roman Christians who had eagerly supported his mission to the west. The money would be more than sufficient to get him where he wanted to go.

Though slaves, sailors, and shipwrights scurried back and forth, Paul ignored them, for he needed to speak with a person of higher rank. The public square was called the Forum of Corporations. Mosaics on the pavement depicted the logos of shipping companies from all over the empire. Grain, oil, wine, even African animals for gladiator shows—all could be found in the holds of Ostia's ships. The port was the thriving nexus of vast international trade.

Paul stopped at the corporate office of merchants who imported garum, the salty, zesty fish sauce every Roman palate loved. He entered the building and approached a clerk who sat hunched over a desk, engrossed in his ledgers. Paul waited politely until the man raised his eyes. "How can I help you?" the clerk asked.

"I'd like to book passage on one of your ships."

"It's possible. We often take passengers on board. Our ships come and go from ports all over the sea—anywhere garum is made. There's a freighter leaving tomorrow for Carthago."

Paul shook his head. "Not Africa. I want to go where the best garum is from."

"Aha! Then you need to be on our ship to Tarraco. It departs the day after next. The journey should take four days. For the right price, I can book you a spot."

"I'll take it," Paul said as he reached for his belt pouch. "I am certain the Lord wants me to go to Spain."

CODA

In this conversation, we imagine the emotions that Paul must have felt during his traumatic shipwreck. It surely tested his faith in God's promises. Whenever life assaults us in some unexpected way, the faithfulness of God must be recalled. Kathie shares a story about how the Lord carried her family through a scary travel experience. The greatest comfort is knowing God is in control!

BRYAN: Chapter 14 begins with Paul's shipwreck recorded in the book of Acts. It would have been really scary, wouldn't it? To be tossed up in the ocean like that? To lose your sails and think you're going to be dead?

KATHIE: Paul knew it was going to happen. Remember, he warned everybody.

BRYAN: True. He knew the outcome. And he knew he was going to Rome, so he might have been seasick, but he wasn't scared.

KATHIE: He might have been scared for other people. Scared for who's going to be hurt, who's going to drown, who's not going to have the chance of salvation because he hadn't been able to get to them yet. There are healthy concerns, but in the bigger picture he knew where he was going. He knew he was going to Rome to die. I'm almost sure he knew that. So he said, "We're good. It's all good." I think that's kind of a pivotal idea here.

BRYAN: He had the right kind of being scared. A godly concern. Luke might have been scared. We know he was on that ship because he says "We did this" and "We did that." But he didn't have a promise to get to the end like Paul did.

KATHIE: Maybe you're right. But I'm sure Paul had shared his own destiny with him to encourage him. Paul was a great encourager of the faith. I imagine he said, "Luke, we're going to be okay. We've got work to do, so we just gotta know it's coming and take care of people and trust that we will walk with Jesus today." Doing that today is no different from a shipwreck all those millennia ago. It's still a matter of faith and trusting the Lord. Oftentimes, that's the hardest thing. I've been walking with my Savior and my Messiah since 1964. Why do I still say, "Lord, where are you?" Why do I still say at this point, "What are you doing, Lord?" He's doing whatever he's doing! You'd think by now, I'd finally say, "Well, I guess you're going about your Father's business." Just like Jesus said to his own parents when he said, "You should have known where I was."[10] But it's hard when you're in a hurricane and the boat is rising and falling and everybody's squealing and the storm clouds are dark and the rain is falling. It's hard to trust in the middle of the storm.

BRYAN: Too often we forget what you just said, which is that the Lord is faithful and has been for many years in your life.

KATHIE: Yeah, we forget his faithfulness to us. Years ago we were flying in an airplane, returning to our home in Connecticut from Florida, and there was a storm. Frank had gone to a football game, and for security reasons we were on a private plane. We even had an FBI guy traveling with us because there were always threats. Flying home, we hit something over Atlantic City called clear-air turbulence. Because I always let the kids play in the aisles, I had just said to them, "Kids, you know what? We're getting close to home." The seat belt sign wasn't even on at the time, but I said, "I just feel like you need to get in your seats, please." And though I have no idea why, I repeated, "We're getting close to home."

BRYAN: It was the Holy Spirit warning you, speaking to your spirit as a mom.

KATHIE: Yes, it must have been, because right after they were strapped in, we hit clear-air turbulence and started falling vertically a thousand feet at a time. We rolled to one side, and then the other, and then fell vertically again. I had had a glass of Diet Coke—all the crystal glass had flown up to the ceiling and shattered everywhere. We had two flight attendants—one was a guy who had worked on Air Force One for many years, the other a woman named Cheryl who was deadheading, which means she was only on the trip to get back to wherever she was supposed to be. The people who work for me were behind us screaming. And me? I am sitting there as quiet as a mouse watching Cheryl get on her knees to help Cassidy out of her seat to move her to another seat where there was no glass. I'm praying, "Jesus, keep my baby safe. Jesus, keep my baby safe." As soft as I could say it. It wasn't screaming. It wasn't panic. It was simply a prayer, "Jesus, keep my baby safe."

BRYAN: How traumatic! You can only turn to God in times like that. It's all you've got.

---

10. Luke 2:49, author's paraphrase.

KATHIE: There were two pilots in the cockpit. And since the plane was small, you could hear every word they were saying. Actually they were screaming, "Get us a different airspace! Give us an altitude! Mayday!" They were trying to get us a different escape route because if they took matters into their own hands, they could potentially run into another plane. With clear-air turbulence you get no notice. It's not on radar. It's just suddenly there. It was violent enough that every one of the compartments inside the plane opened up and dumped out. And there were several computer systems that were destroyed. It lasted for a minute and a half—the longest ninety seconds of my life! When we finally landed, the captain said, "Your chances of ever going through something like that again in your life are nil. I've been flying twenty thousand hours and I've never experienced this before." We learned later that the other gentleman, the copilot, was feeling panic as well because he wanted to get home for the birth of his first child.

BRYAN: It seems everyone on the plane experienced the same terror but with different perspectives.

KATHIE: We all wanted to live. None of us wanted to die in a plane crash. But we all dealt with the fear in a different way.

BRYAN: At least you had the faith of knowing that you were in God's hands, like Paul knew when he was on the ship. People experience things differently when they know the Savior versus when they don't.

KATHIE: Yes, but also, I was really upset with myself that I had endangered my children by putting them on that plane. You would think that on a private plane with an FBI guy, two flight attendants, and two experienced pilots you'd be good. But no. Not even there are you free of danger. I haven't thought about that in a long time. That was the most terrifying situation I've ever been in on an airplane.

BRYAN: What's the takeaway lesson from that story, which is parallel to Paul's shipwreck?

KATHIE: It's great when God gives you a word ahead of time that you're going to be okay, but he normally doesn't. And you still gotta go through the storm. Yeah, the Lord didn't tell me every time we took off in an airplane that we'd make it to the destination. But we did always pray before we took off, and we always thanked God when the wheels went down. We never took God's provision, or his protection, for granted. I still do that with my kids. When they travel, the minute they take off, they call me and I pray. And the minute they say they've landed, I pray, "Thank you, Jesus." Our days are numbered. They just are. You can take the best care of yourself, eat everything organic, do your workout, do whatever it takes, and you can still get hit by a bus tomorrow. So who do you trust? I don't trust the bus driver!

BRYAN: You trust the driver of the heavenly chariot. Only him.

KATHIE: And when he says it's time to take me home—well, that's the best day of my life.

FIFTEEN

THE END OF THE EARTH

Paul was more than ready to be on his way to fulfill his "end of the earth" mission when he embarked from Ostia with Spain as his destination. He knew the Scriptures well, proclaiming that God would be glorified across the whole earth—including its farthest western horizon. "'My name will be great among the nations, from where the sun rises *to where it sets*. In every place incense and pure offerings will be brought to me, because my name will be great among the nations,' says the LORD Almighty."[1]

Likewise, God had promised through the prophet Isaiah, "I will set a sign among them; and those among them who escape I will send to the nations: to Tarshish . . . to the coastlands afar off who have not heard My fame nor seen My glory. And they shall declare My glory among the Gentiles."[2] Where was Tarshish—and why was it considered the end of the earth, where God's fame must be heard?

Many scholars associate it with the Tartessos civilization on the Atlantic coast of Spain, which was considered the remotest extremity of the world.[3] That was why the prophet Jonah, when he was trying to escape God's oversight,

1. Malachi 1:11 NIV.
2. Isaiah 66:19.
3. Psalm 72:8–10.

booked passage on a ship bound for Tarshish.[4] Such a distant destination would take him as far away from Israel as possible. For the ancient Jews—including a biblical scholar like Paul—Spain represented the farthest western area where God's glory was supposed to be made known. *And I am his appointed messenger for that task,* Paul often reminded himself.

It is impossible to know for certain if Paul ever reached Spain or what exactly he may have accomplished there if he did. A Christian leader named Clement who lived in Rome during Paul's lifetime, and who probably knew Paul personally,[5] recorded that "after [Paul] had been seven times in chains, had been driven into exile, had been stoned, and had preached in the east and in the west, he won the genuine glory for his faith, having taught righteousness to the whole world and having reached the farthest limits of the west." For a man writing from Rome, only Hispania (Spain) could have been called "the farthest limits of the west." After Clement recorded this fact, many other Christian writers confirmed Paul's visit to Spain. In light of his strong desire to go there,[6] it seems likely he did exactly that after he was released from house arrest in AD 62.

But Paul's preaching in Spain has left no mark on history. It may be that few people—perhaps no one—believed his gospel message. This would account for the lack of any solid traditions about a church being planted in the area. Historians have no evidence of Christianity existing in Spain until some congregations are mentioned by one writer in the late second century AD.

Nevertheless, Paul wasn't the kind of person to give up when times were tough. He would finish whatever he had started. If Tarraco, the first port his ship would have reached, wasn't receptive to the gospel, he would have moved on to the next port of call. Two days of westward sailing, maybe a bit more, would have brought him within sight of the Pillars of Hercules, which today we call the Rock of Gibraltar. After passing it on his right, the relatively calm waters of the Mediterranean Sea would have given way to the much bigger swells of the Atlantic. With decent weather and the right tidal current, the ship soon would have reached Gades, one of the oldest continuously inhabited cities in all of Europe (modern Cádiz). Paul would have gone

4. Jonah 1:3.
5. Philippians 4:3.
6. Romans 15:24–28.

ashore with evangelism on his mind. But again, if he did, he seems to have had little success. Nothing in the historical record suggests that he planted a church at Gades.

But Paul was more concerned with divine obedience than earthly results. His job wasn't to hit a numerical goal but to proclaim the gospel and let the Holy Spirit do the work of salvation. "My message and my preaching were not with wise and persuasive words," Paul declared, "but with a demonstration of the Spirit's power, so that your faith might not rest on human wisdom, but on God's power."[7] Surely Paul would have struck up gospel conversations with local Gentile Spaniards. Eventually he would have told them about the saving name of Jesus. "Bah! Foolishness!" the gruff men at a seaside tavern might have responded. "What nonsense is this foreigner talking about?"

No matter, Paul reminded himself. *My task is complete. My feet have brought the good news to this distant place. The gospel has reached the ends of the earth!*

As Paul stood on the quay at Gades, gazing westward across the Atlantic Ocean, we can imagine that he felt a sense of awe at its immensity. Though the ocean seemed placid that day, he knew it could turn treacherous in an instant. No Roman vessel could ever hope to cross that vast expanse. The limits of shipbuilding and navigation made the Atlantic an impassable barrier for mariners of that age. *What is out there? Do people live on the other side who need the Word of God?*

Though Paul didn't know it at the time, it was from this very gulf that in 1492 Christopher Columbus would set sail across the Atlantic. Directly across the water, in an unbroken line of latitude, lay the mouth of the Chesapeake Bay. European colonists would one day bring the Christian message—along with much destruction—to the untamed wilderness at Jamestown in 1607. But those events happened a millennium and a half after Paul's time. God had appointed different people to carry the gospel to the New World.

As for the task that Jesus had given to Paul on the Damascus road, the faithful apostle could now say it was complete. He had persevered through pain and persecution. He had never held back from striving for the next port of call—all the way to the Atlantic coast. According to the ancient worldview, the good news had been proclaimed "in Jerusalem, and in all Judea and Samaria,

---

7. 1 Corinthians 2:4–5 NIV.

and *to the ends of the earth.*"[8] Like a good soldier in God's service, Paul had accomplished his assigned mission. From then on, he would strengthen the churches he had already planted until his commander in chief decided to bring him home.

The twisted, tormented mind of Emperor Nero craved two things: the presence of constant adoration, and the absence of any reproach. With absolute power gripped in his iron fist, he could achieve both desires—so he set about making them happen.

To gain praise, Nero sailed down the Italian coast to Neapolis (Naples), an originally Greek city famous for its artsy, Hellenistic culture. There, he sang on the theatrical stage and played his lyre as if he were the world's greatest musician. His seven-stringed harp with a sound box, called a cithara, later gave rise to the instrument known as the guitar. It didn't matter that Nero was only moderately skilled. When the Neapolitan crowds raved about his performances, he basked in the applause. He felt so needy that he convinced himself the public pretense was real praise. All the acclaim made Nero announce he would be taking an immediate tour through Greece for more recitals. Though he set out on the road, he quickly postponed the trip, claiming the citizens of Rome would be too sad to do without his presence for so long.

What about Nero's virility and sexual attractiveness? Neither his marriage with Poppaea nor his unlimited access to courtesans could sufficiently prop up his limp male ego. To reassure himself that everyone—both men and women—desired his body, Nero came up with a decadent plan. He arranged a lavish banquet on a giant raft in an artificial lake. The rowers who tugged the raft were male prostitutes. Dolphins brought in from the sea frolicked in the water, while exotic birds flitted overhead and wild animals wandered the banks.

Along one half of the shoreline, Nero stationed naked dancers and common whores in a row of huts, while on the opposite side of the water, aristocratic maidens and noble ladies were forced to serve the sexual desires of any man

8. Acts 1:8 NIV.

who approached them. While Nero and his cronies dined on the raft, reclining on cushions amid twinkling lights, the naked prostitutes gyrated to seductive music as if all they desired was a tryst with the emperor. On the other shore, where the maidens and ladies were stationed, a "slave would debauch his mistress in the presence of [her husband], and a gladiator would debauch a girl of noble family before the eyes of her father."

As night came on, the city's rabble rushed into unrestrained fornication, copulating with women far above their station in life. Once Nero was sufficiently drunk, he indulged in every kind of depravity with males and females alike. In fact, whenever he went sailing along the Tiber River, he forced respectable ladies to line the banks like prostitutes and beg him to come ashore for sex. In this way, he proved that his sexual allure was strong enough to turn all of Rome into a giant orgy.

In Nero's fragile psyche, it wasn't enough just to be approved; he also had to be free from disapproval. In other words, beyond craving affirmation, his insecurity drove him to eliminate all criticism, whether real or perceived. If harsh punishments—even murder—would silence his critics, he was more than willing to go down that road. The historian Suetonius remarked that Nero showed no "restraint in putting to death whoever he wished for whatever reason." When a comet appeared in the sky, Nero took it as an ominous sign and tried to deflect its deadly portent onto other prominent men. Many aristocrats died on trumped-up charges, though some were executed for actual conspiracies against the increasingly deranged emperor.

One of Nero's most egregious deeds at this period of his life was to order the death of his childhood tutor, Seneca. For many years, Seneca had joined Burrus, head of the Praetorian Guard, to cooperate in putting some limits on the young ruler's tendencies toward violence and pleasure-seeking. Seneca's Stoic philosophy, combined with Burrus's gruff, military-style advice, had helped to tamp down Nero's wilder urges. But when some morally depraved palace bureaucrats got in Nero's ear, chiding him for being so submissive to his childhood counselors, he began to view Seneca and Burrus as enemies.

He first took out Burrus with poison disguised as medicine for a sore throat. A few years later, Seneca's suicide at Nero's command turned into a slow, painful death. After a centurion brought the order of capital punishment, Seneca sliced open his own veins but couldn't bleed fast enough to die.

Overcome by agony, he drank poison to end his suffering, but it also failed to kill him. Finally, he submerged himself in a bathtub of hot water and expired after a long ordeal. His wife, who had nobly attempted to die with him, survived because Nero ordered her cuts bandaged, lest he look too cruel in the public eye.

In all his actions, Nero tried to gain the approval of the commoners. The rabble loved him because his lowbrow appetites and base instincts mirrored their own. As for the upper crust, with their genteel elegance and refined habits, the emperor wanted them gone. He began to say that he would gladly slaughter the entire Senate. Then he could rule as he pleased while a bureaucracy of businessmen and freed slaves ran the government. Nero wanted to destroy the checks and balances of his political framework, replacing it with autocratic rule. Even worse, some observers began to fear that Nero's desire for total annihilation went beyond the political system. Would he destroy the very fabric of Rome itself and rebuild it for his own glory?

The late summer of AD 64 brought broiling temperatures and dry winds to the narrow streets of the capital city. Nero fled to his breezy coastal villa to escape the heat while the citizens who remained trapped in their crowded tenements became increasingly lethargic and irritable as the torrid weather persisted. After so many centuries of cheap, wooden construction, Rome was a tinderbox, scorched and windblown like a parched leaf on a desert shrub. Tempers were ready to flare up, just like the city itself.

The original spark that set Rome on fire fell somewhere near the market stalls and hot-food booths that lined the archways of the Circus Maximus. What started as a simple backroom fire exploded into a citywide conflagration. The summer gusts, intensified by the growing inferno that generated its own winds, carried the sparks from shop to shop, house to house, temple to temple, and eventually, neighborhood to neighborhood. Flames spread everywhere. The cobbled streets became like beds of red-hot coals. Every building became a blast furnace. No one could stop the fire's advance. Chaos enveloped all of Rome.

In the mayhem, cries rang out everywhere: "This or that is afire!" "Where?" "How did it happen?" "Who kindled it?" "Help!" The citizens ran back and forth, some rushing inside a building to put out its fires while others exited it to escape. Men helping their friends learned their own premises were ablaze and ran home. Thieves looting their neighbors' homes crashed into the owners trying to save their possessions from the flames. Dio Cassius records:

> There was shouting and wailing without end, of children, women, men, and the aged all together, so that no one could see anything or understand what was said by reason of the smoke and the shouting; and for this reason some might be seen standing speechless, as if they were dumb. . . . Many were suffocated, many were trampled underfoot; in a word, no evil that can possibly happen to people in such a crisis failed to befall them. They could not even escape anywhere easily; and if anybody did save himself from the immediate danger, he would fall into another and perish.

As the holocaust consumed whatever lay in its path, the celebrated monuments of Rome's ancient glory fell victim to the blaze. Magnificent mansions, time-honored temples, statues of historic heroes, "and every other interesting or memorable survival from the olden days went up in flames." The bonfire raged for six straight days, died down, then flared up again for three more. The stunned populace, their faces smeared with soot, could only stare in disbelief. Rome hadn't been so thoroughly destroyed since the invading Celts had sacked the Eternal City more than 450 years earlier. But at least those pillagers had left most of the buildings intact. Now Rome was nothing but a charred ruin.

As if the natural course of the fire wasn't bad enough, Nero reportedly dispatched arsonists to ignite additional fires throughout the city. Workers with machinery also demolished some structures that stood in the way of urban planning, then set them on fire as if the flames had been the cause of their demise. If anyone tried to stop the criminals with firebrands in their hands, their reply was "Stand back! We have our orders!" Though no one declared who had issued the orders, the citizens suspected Nero. Government officials, even at the highest levels, had to step aside when the imperial thugs showed up on their properties with torches and tinder. Everyone realized Nero was using the fire to clear space for his grand vision of Rome's future—a rebuilding project in which he would set himself at the pinnacle of civic glory. In fact, the egotistical emperor was already planning to rename the city "Neropolis."

When the fire had originally broken out while Nero was relaxing at the coast, he realized that good optics would require his immediate return, so he rushed back to the blazing capital. In the days after the flames died down, his plan was to play the role of a benevolent caretaker who provided food and temporary shelters for the displaced, or a wise leader who promised to restore the city's grandeur. But while the fire still raged, Nero could only adopt the role of a fellow mourner. He had to put on a sad face and display his solidarity with the sorrowful masses.

Did Nero "fiddle while Rome burned"? Since there were no violins in those days, nobody was doing any fiddling. Many historical sources have claimed, however, that Nero climbed to the summit of the Palatine Hill, or another nearby precipice, dressed in the long, flowing robes of a Greek harpist with his instrument in hand. From the vantage point of the palace's roof, high above the red-hot carnage, he plucked his strings and sang a dirge. His chosen hymn lamented the fall of Troy, the famed city from Homer's *Iliad* whose destruction during the Trojan War had led to Rome's foundation.

As Nero sang his wistful requiem and plucked his lyre, he reveled in "the beauty of the flames" that had engulfed the metropolis below him. By laying waste to the monuments of the past, the Great Fire of Rome had opened up a new future. For Nero, this was his golden opportunity to start afresh. He could remake the city in his own image. But for the victims down in the streets who had just lost everything, the hellish inferno must have seemed like the end of the world. For them, Rome's golden gospel hadn't proven so glorious after all.

CODA

We begin this conversation by considering the global scope of the gospel. When Paul reached Spain with the message of Jesus, he had completed his God-given mission. Kathie reflects on her own rich life and the sense of completion she feels after her years in the public eye. Despite some ongoing pains and travails, Kathie reminds us to continue seeking a divine purpose until the very end. Nero made his own glory the goal of his life, but Paul's purpose was to share God's love with humanity.

BRYAN: Though we don't know for sure he made it there, in this chapter we open with imagining Paul visiting Spain. But let's consider that he maybe not only went to the Mediterranean coast of Spain, but if he really wanted to get to the end of the world, he would go out through the Strait of Gibraltar and land along the Atlantic coast. The Romans were there. They had cities. Paul could have hopped on a ship going there quite easily. He would have looked across the ocean. I know you live inland now, but you used to live on the ocean. What's it like to look at the vastness of the sea and imagine God's people somewhere else? Or all the needy people out there? Did you ever do that? Did you ever wonder if there are people on the other side who need the message of God? Like, when you think about the bigness of the world and the universal gospel, does it make you think about the lost and the hurting?

KATHIE: Well, yes, but more personal to me is when I hear a siren going off. I'm here in Tennessee. Mine is a smaller world now. And I think, "Lord, whoever is at the end of that siren, be present with them. Be present, Holy Spirit." There's nothing I can do about the millions of people that are on the other side of the sea. They're in God's hands. But I can, right now, this moment, pray for somebody who is at the end of that siren.

BRYAN: Yeah, that's good. But we could send missionaries too. You probably love the idea of missionaries going and taking the gospel to faraway lands, I'm sure.

KATHIE: Yes, as long as they aren't taking a religious dogma. I do remember so many good, godly missionaries. But so much damage was done in the name of the gospel by people that said, "You gotta do this, you gotta do that. And either you change this or that or you can't go to heaven." They didn't go to spread God's love. That's when I get angered.

BRYAN: When Paul does reach the Atlantic coast, and we picture him there, for him he has come to the end of the world that he knew. Spain was the last bit of land. They didn't have Christopher Columbus yet, so they didn't know what was over there, where we are. It was the end of the world as far as they knew. He basically had completed the task that God had called him to do, when Jesus said, "Go; I will send you far away to the Gentiles."[9] Have you ever come to that time when you sense "You know what, Lord?

9. Acts 22:21 NIV.

The task you gave me is done. I finished the main assignment. Everything now is icing on the cake."

KATHIE: I have run the race, I have kept the faith.

BRYAN: Which is what he says, right?[10] Do you sympathize with that feeling? I've won the race. I've done it. It's over.

KATHIE: The past two years of my life I think have been the most pain I have ever experienced, because of both emotional and physical pain. I've been very honest publicly about the fact that I didn't want to live in this world anymore. And I've thought, "I've done everything you've asked me to do, Lord. I raised beautiful children. I have served you, I have proclaimed you. I have not been perfect by any means, but I'm ready to go home. I can't even crawl to the bathroom door. And I don't want to live like this. If I can't be me and I can't proclaim you, then what's my purpose? I want to go home. I want to be with you." People thought I was saying I was going to kill myself. No, I was never going to kill myself! I just didn't want to live anymore. That's as close as I have gotten to the edge of the abyss.

BRYAN: Maybe it's like Paul when he's in the Carcer and he says, "I am already being poured out as a drink offering."[11] He feels like his whole body is like an empty cup. Everything that he had inside him is gone. He gave everything he had.

KATHIE: When you look back on your life and you know all the things you did wrong, you know the mistakes that you've made and you've asked for forgiveness, then all that's left is what you did for God. And I say to myself, "I wouldn't do anything differently, Lord. I got on every plane you asked me to. I shared with every single person that you asked me to. I made mistakes, but never because I was not seeking you." It was just because I was ignorant. I didn't know stuff. Walking home from where I worked out this morning on such a pretty day, I was running, or basically, I was skipping. I rejoiced, because I am out of pain. Pain paralyzes us.

BRYAN: Yeah, and Paul had that too. He said, "I have in my body the markings and the sufferings of Jesus."[12] He must have really been in pain a lot because of all the beatings and stonings and whippings. He had scars on top

---

10. 2 Timothy 4:7.
11. 2 Timothy 4:6.
12. Galatians 6:17, author's paraphrase.

of scars. But he probably had a sense of closure as he reached Spain, which he had been striving to reach. He wrote to the Romans and said, "I want you to help me to send me further."[13] And he got there, we think. And if he did, it was a sense of closure. But to your point, you were willing to go home if God called you, but he didn't. He said, "You did finish your first job, but I still have more for you to do." And it's sort of the icing on the cake. Each day is precious.

KATHIE: It is a bonus. I remember something I was told by the great actor Paul Newman many years ago. There was a fundraiser for a little dilapidated but adorable theater in Connecticut. Paul was there, but I hadn't seen him in a while, so I went into a different room. I didn't want to be one of those people who lines up just to say hello to a movie star. I thought I'd maybe have a chance to say hello later. Next thing you know, I'm in this other room and I feel this pat on my back. I turn around and it's Paul! I said, "Paul, how are you? It's been so long!" He was in his eighties then and he said, "I'm doing great. If I got a pulse, I got a purpose." Then he simply looked at me with those unbelievably beautiful blue eyes of his. I told Frank when I got home, "I'm never going to forget what Paul said—*If I have a pulse, I have a purpose*." He was there for a dilapidated old country playhouse—how much bigger is my purpose as a child of God? Every day my goal is to get up and proclaim God's goodness and his love for humankind. Every morning I'm going to take my metaphorical pulse and find my purpose.

BRYAN: And you applied that during your two years of suffering and pain.

KATHIE: Yes, although there were many days I didn't want to get up. But there were things I had to do. I had people who needed me. People that worked for me, who depended on me. "If I've got a pulse, then I've still got a purpose." I think the apostle Paul felt that way until the day he knew he was going to be beheaded—because he was a Roman citizen, so they weren't going to crucify him. In their minds, beheading was a more merciful death. Right?

BRYAN: Yeah. Much faster. No lingering pain.

KATHIE: Once you're dead, you don't need your head. Oh, that was a good rhyme!

BRYAN: And that's a great point about what Paul probably thought. He comes back from Spain to the Aegean Sea area where he had worked to

---

13. Romans 15:24, author's paraphrase.

bring all these ministries into existence, where he had planted churches, and he revisits them. He still has a purpose, even though in one sense he has finished the main task. Little did he know that he would have a major purpose of helping the Roman Christians after the Great Fire in 64. It's hard to imagine how terrible it must have been to have your whole city on fire. A whole metropolis like Rome is simply burning to the ground. And Nero, the stories say he thinks everything is a stage. Everything for him is theatrical. Everything's a show.

KATHIE: And he thinks he's the center of the show!

BRYAN: So of course, in his mind, he has to go up on his roof with his lyre and sing about the burning of Troy, which was the city that fell in the Trojan War. That's just so Nero, isn't it? Let's make this whole moment about me. Even if he didn't have an audience, he had to do it.

KATHIE: The stars were his audience. The flames were his audience. What unbelievable ego! But you've been told by millions of people how wonderful you are, how divine you are. If you've been told your whole life that you're everything, that you're a god, then you start to believe it.

BRYAN: They say maybe he started the fire, or at least he kept it going. And we'll get into that in the next chapter about how he takes the opportunity, now that everything is burned, to say, "Okay, guess what? I get to remake this city in my own image." In fact, he thinks he's going to call it Neropolis.

KATHIE: That's a bad name, compared to Rome. But here's the other thing. He was not beloved by his people at all. He was deluded at that point. He was completely deluded, like thinking that the people are with him. No, they're not. And for a guy that's been on a stage his whole life, he still didn't know how to read a room. He couldn't see they were fake clapping for him.

BRYAN: And we'll get to that too—about how even right up to his death, when they start to have an insurrection, he can't believe it. "What do you mean *insurrection*? They love me. I'm a rock star," literally. So that Great Fire serves to take Rome down to ashes, and then Nero will be the man to say, "I will remake Rome."

KATHIE: Who says, "I will bring forth beauty from ashes"? God says that.[14] But Nero said, "I will do it."

---

14. Isaiah 61:3, author's paraphrase.

BRYAN: It's Nero being an impostor. Satan also said, "I will rise up." Lucifer said, "I will ascend. I will be like the Most High. I will stand on the high places."[15]

KATHIE: With Nero up there on the high place, on the roof of his palace playing the lyre, he's like Lucifer saying, "I will ascend to be like the Most High." But he doesn't find God up there, only Satan. That's the only god he ever served. Even if he didn't know his name, that's who he was serving.

15. Isaiah 14:13–14, author's paraphrase.

SIXTEEN

INTO THE LION'S MOUTH

Having completed his assignment to take the gospel to the ends of the earth, Paul wanted to spend his final stage of life visiting the churches he had planted, strengthening the faith of the believers. He returned to the region of his fruitful ministry around the Aegean Sea. Though no historical text lays out his route during this time, he did write two biblical letters while he traveled: 1 Timothy and Titus. Using them, we can reconstruct a rough idea of his itinerary.

When Paul wrote to Titus, he noted he had left him on the island of Crete with the job of appointing elders for the local congregation.[1] Evidently, Paul had sailed in AD 63 from Spain to Crete, where he stayed for a time to make sure the church had good leadership. His advice to Titus, and also to Timothy, focused on helping these young pastors succeed in caring for their flocks, which is why 1 and 2 Timothy and Titus are known as the Pastoral Epistles.

After the congregation in Crete had been put on a good footing, Paul went to Ephesus, though he didn't see any of the elders to whom he had previously said goodbye at Miletus.[2] Perhaps these men had died or moved elsewhere in the intervening time. It's not clear how long Paul stayed at Ephesus, but

1. Titus 1:5.
2. Acts 20:25.

it was long enough to encourage Timothy and the local believers. His friend Onesiphorus served him faithfully there.[3]

Leaving Timothy behind to strengthen the Ephesian church, Paul traveled up the Aegean coast to Philippi and Thessalonica. While there he wrote 1 Timothy to encourage and advise his disciple on how to organize the church efficiently while modeling godliness before the flock.

Paul also went to Troas, then returned to Ephesus and Miletus. From there, he crossed the Aegean Sea to visit his beloved Corinthians. He probably spent the winter of 63–64 in Corinth, just like he had done in 56–57. Though this is where he'd experienced his "painful visit," Paul was thrilled to now be on such good terms with them. In fact, everything was going so well that he decided to stay for a long time.

It was early August when Paul received word of a shocking tragedy: Nearly the whole city of Rome had burned to the ground. One report claimed that, out of the city's fourteen official neighborhoods, three had been leveled to a smoking desolation, seven contained nothing but a few charred ruins, and only four peripheral neighborhoods had survived. Thousands of people had died while hundreds of thousands more were bankrupt or homeless. The soul-crushing disaster had affected everyone in the city—including the Christians.

The terrible news hit Paul hard. *I must go to them! And I must bring them a charitable offering!* For the next few weeks Paul probably collected donations from churches in the region. Though there is no historical evidence for this, it fits with his previous habits.

Paul set out on his journey to Rome in the fall, but after arriving in Nicopolis—directly across the Ionian Sea from the heel of Italy's boot—he could travel no farther due to winter storms. He would have to finish the journey in the spring. He wrote to Titus, "Do your best to meet me at Nicopolis, for I have decided to stay there for the winter."[4] Though some scholars believe Paul was arrested again and brought back to Rome as a criminal, more likely his return to Rome stemmed from pastoral concern for the suffering believers there. He obviously wasn't a prisoner at this time but had the freedom to decide

3. 2 Timothy 1:16–18.
4. Titus 3:12 NLT.

where he would stay. Eventually, Titus did reach Paul and accompanied him to Rome, though he later departed for ministry in Dalmatia.[5]

In the spring of 65, Paul and his companions crossed the Ionian Sea and arrived three days later at Brundisium (Brindisi), an Italian port at the southern end of the Appian Way. From there they would walk to Rome, a journey that took about three weeks. Having walked the same road five years earlier, then as a prisoner being marched to his trial, Paul must have remembered the chains on his wrists that identified him as suffering for the name of the Lord. This time, although he was a free man, there was no welcoming crowd of Christians escorting him triumphantly into the city. The Roman believers were currently struggling to survive—as the charred ruins on either side of the highway made clear.

At the gate where the Appian Way entered Rome, the scorched hulk of the Circus Maximus testified to the fire's devastating effects. But beyond the blackness of Rome's physical structures, something deeper and more insidious had taken hold. A dark spirit had swept through the streets and started to oppress the church. It seemed Nero's egomania was reaching new heights. When the citizenry blamed him for the destruction, the paranoid emperor found a scapegoat: the hated followers of Jesus. Imperial power had just turned its deadly gaze on the Christians. Though Paul didn't know it when he arrived at the city gates, the age of Roman persecution and martyrdom had just begun.

In the year 65, Nero wanted to play. Five years earlier, back in 60, he had established the Five Year Games, a Roman festival of chariot racing, gymnastics, and musical competitions on the pattern of Greek contests like the Olympics. Now that the next round of games had come due, Nero had no intention of letting the devastation wrought by the Great Fire stand in his way. To hold the games on schedule would prove that he could make Rome rise from the ashes like a phoenix.

Of course, he intended to claim the victor's crown in the poetic and musical parts of the competition—even though he said he would win only by the

5. 2 Timothy 4:10.

impartial decision of the judges. In reality the whole thing was fixed. The judges knew exactly what they had to do. Likewise, the crowd understood they had to stay awake for the emperor's boring performances, clap for him in regular rhythms, and show no disapproval whatsoever. The local spectators from Rome, who were used to such manufactured adoration, played their role perfectly. After Nero recited a single poem, they would beg him: "Give us your whole repertoire!"

As always when it came to recitals, Nero was willing to oblige. He returned to the stage in a harpist's gown. After pompously tuning his lyre, he began to sing. He followed all the conventional rules of a musician: not sitting down when he grew weary, or wiping sweat from his brow with anything but the sleeve of his robe, or letting a runny nose or moist lips be seen on his face. His performance dragged on and on. "Finally, bending his knee and with a respectful wave of his hand to the crowd, he awaited the verdict of the judges with feigned anxiety." To no one's surprise, he won the day.

Throughout the performance the commoners of the city had thundered their applause—but not the visitors from distant provinces who had come to town for the event. As theater traditionalists, they were unused to such flattery and considered it degrading, so they refused to play along. Soldiers stationed in the stands abused them for not clapping constantly or in the proper rhythms. Spies in the audience took note of who was present or not; who seemed to be bored or disinterested for even a moment; or, worst of all, who might dare to offer any signs of disapproval. A certain nobleman dozed off during the lengthy performance and was berated by one of Nero's lackeys. After the event, only the pleas of many aristocrats spared the man from capital punishment. The sleepy offender was Vespasian, who was destined to claim the throne soon after Nero. He would establish a new imperial dynasty and reign prosperously for a decade, but his disrespect at the theater almost cost him that glorious future.

Late one night Nero returned home after attending the chariot races at the festival. Perhaps he was drunk, or his favorite team had lost, or he had learned about some public disapproval of his recitals. In any case, Nero was in a foul mood when he entered his bedroom suite at the imperial palace. He spotted his wife asleep in an adjacent room. *Maybe sex with Poppaea would make me feel better!*

But after rousing his wife, he found her disinterested. She was pregnant and in no mood for amorous relations. When Nero pressed the matter, a rowdy argument erupted. The two spouses shouted at each other with spiraling escalation. "It's the middle of the night!" Poppaea screamed. "You came home too late from the races!"

Something inside Nero snapped. *Who is she to tell an emperor what to do? I am descended from the gods!* A fire took hold of him, a burning rage he couldn't control. Poppaea's impudent face infuriated him. *How dare she criticize me? All of Rome loves me! Yet this dog of a woman tries to shame me?*

He stormed over to his rebellious wife, his fist upraised. Though she shielded herself, the blow smashed her hard and knocked her to the floor. As Nero looked down at her, a voice inside his head shrieked: *She isn't worthy to bear your son!* He raised his foot, paused for a moment, then stomped on his pregnant wife's belly.

Immediately, blood was everywhere. With a shuddery gasp, she passed out. Later that night, she went into labor. The birth was breach and she couldn't deliver. Before the sun had risen over Rome, the gods had claimed Poppaea Sabina's soul.

The weight of public condemnation sat on Nero's shoulders like a millstone. First, he had killed his stepbrother, Britannicus. The son of Claudius, Britannicus had been popular and nobly born, so the public had disapproved of that murder.

Then he killed his mother. Everyone knew about that. It was a heinous crime.

Next, he executed his young wife. The citizens had adored Octavia.

And now he had killed his wife again . . . while she was pregnant!

Such bloodshed! The people must despise me!

Nero's awareness of the public's abhorrence of these events might have been endurable if it had existed in isolation. Many elite Romans indulged in dynastic murders, so it was somewhat normal for the ruling class. But these household killings sat against a backdrop that had universalized the people's mistrust of their emperor. The Great Fire, the death toll of which everyone blamed on Nero, had amplified their disrespect into outright disgust. It was one thing to kill a nagging wife or a political enemy. It was quite another to slaughter thousands of innocent Romans in a fiery genocide. No amount of civic rebuilding or placating the gods could return the emperor to the public's goodwill. Since the suspicion of arson clung to him so closely, it was time to name a scapegoat. Nero decided the hated Christians would make a perfect sacrificial lamb for his face-saving plan.

He rounded up as many believers as he could find, men and women who were, according to Tacitus, "widely loathed for their vices." This new cult, so the public believed, indulged in cannibalism and incest—that is, they ate human flesh and drank blood in their secret rituals, and they emphasized love between brothers and sisters. They also stubbornly persisted in their "atheistic" beliefs by rejecting the gods who made society function in an orderly way. Their founder, accurately named by Tacitus as "Christus," had been put to death under Pontius Pilate. For a while, the judicial execution had squelched what Tacitus considered a destructive sect. But then it broke out once more, "not just in Judaea, the starting point of that curse, but in Rome as well, where all that is abominable and shameful in the world flows together and gains popularity." Something had to be done about this crazed superstition!

Outside the city, on a flat area at the foot of the Vatican Hill, Nero's private racing circus had escaped the flames. He decided to put on a lavish party to celebrate the execution of the Christians "with the utmost refinements of cruelty." The believers could easily be blamed for starting the Great Fire since the neighborhood where they were concentrated—the region where Paul had been evangelizing while under house arrest—had somehow avoided being burned. Nero could claim that they must have protected their own homes while setting others ablaze. Yet most people knew these common folk weren't actually arsonists. Their real crime was "hatred of the human race." The Christians refused to carouse with the heathen or pay homage to the gods.

Nero commanded the criminals to be wrapped in fur garments, as if they were timid animals like deer or antelopes. Then he turned them loose on the sand of the racetrack and set fierce dogs onto them. The muscular Italian war dogs were trained to kill. Everyone laughed as the frantic "prey" darted back and forth until the pack took them down and tore them limb from limb. Mockery accompanied their agony as they died.

When night began to fall and visibility dimmed, Nero illumined his racetrack and gardens with a new kind of lantern. He wrapped other Christians in flammable tunics smeared with pitch, then crucified them on high poles. When a torch was set to the victims, the dancing flames of their tunics mingled with their anguished writhing as they burned—a fitting punishment for their supposed crime. While their pitiful cries echoed across the circus, Nero rode among them in a chariot like a merry sportsman enjoying a pleasant evening at the races. But even the hard-hearted Romans recoiled at the emperor's sadism. Tacitus remarked, "Guilty though these people were and deserving exemplary punishment, pity for them began to well up because it was felt they were being exterminated not for the public good, but to gratify one man's cruelty."

Almost certainly, one of Nero's victims that day was unknown to the crowd but famous among the Christians: the apostle Peter. Many reliable church traditions—some early enough to have been based on eyewitness accounts—claimed Peter died by crucifixion in Rome.[6] Jesus had alluded to the kind of death Peter would die when he said, "When you are old, you will *stretch out your hands*, and another *will gird you* and carry you where you do not wish."[7] The expression "stretch out the hands" was a common term for crucifixion, and Peter's "girding" may have referred to the flammable tunic in which he was wrapped. The gospel writer added the remark, "Jesus said this to indicate the kind of death by which Peter would glorify God."[8]

After Peter was martyred, the believers buried him in a simple grave adjacent to the circus. The ruins of Nero's racetrack now lie beneath the floor of Saint Peter's Basilica in the Vatican City. The basilica's famous dome stands over its altar, and the altar stands over the subterranean grave of Peter. Out in front of the basilica, an Egyptian obelisk imported by Emperor Caligula rises from the middle of Saint Peter's Square. It once decorated the circus's spine, the

6. An ancient text also notes that Peter was crucified upside down, which may indeed be true. The Romans often crucified their victims in grotesque positions. But until the late fourth century, there was no mention of Peter's supposed reason for his upside-down posture: that he requested it because he felt unworthy to be crucified like his Lord. That is probably a pious legend, since Rome's cruel soldiers wouldn't have accommodated the personal requests of the condemned.
7. John 21:18.
8. John 21:19 NIV.

low wall in the middle of the racetrack around which the chariots ran. Peter could probably see the obelisk while he burned to death on a Roman cross. Today, that granite spire reminds its viewers of Christian faithfulness under persecution when a madman turned his evil eye upon God's people.

It was around the time of Peter's death in AD 65 that the apostle Paul arrived in Rome. He quickly discovered that a spirit of anti-Christian hatred had taken over the city. At some point, he, too, found himself arrested by Nero's henchmen. In the summer of AD 66, they threw him into the dark dungeon called the Carcer. During his earlier imprisonment under house arrest, he had escaped the emperor, whom he depicted as a fierce lion. At that time, "the Lord stood at my side and gave me strength, so that through me *the message might be fully proclaimed and all the Gentiles might hear it.* And I was delivered from the lion's mouth."[9]

Now that Paul had finished his worldwide mission all the way to Spain, he no longer expected his deliverance to come in an earthly way. Instead, his hope was fixed on the world above. "The Lord will rescue me from every evil attack," he declared, "and will bring me safely to his heavenly kingdom."[10] Although Paul had avoided the lion's jaws during his first imprisonment, he understood a release wouldn't happen this time. His only way out was upward.

Yet that didn't bother Paul. His eyes were focused on "Jesus Christ, raised from the dead, descended from David. This is my gospel, for which I am suffering even to the point of being chained like a criminal. But God's word is not chained." Paul could endure his harsh imprisonment because he believed he would attain "the salvation that is in Christ Jesus, with eternal glory."[11] Though he eagerly desired to receive that glory, he knew before he could attain it, the bloodthirsty lion would have to eat its fill.

---

9. 2 Timothy 4:17 NIV.
10. 2 Timothy 4:18 NIV.
11. 2 Timothy 2:8–10 NIV.

CODA

We open our conversation by talking about the value of mentors, like the way Paul mentored Timothy and Titus. Kathie mentions some important role models in her professional life, and she discusses how she tried to pass on her personal wisdom to her kids. We then reflect on Nero's persecution of the Roman Christians, when the apostle Peter was killed. Nevertheless, the true gospel went forward like it always does, even in the face of opposition.

BRYAN: In this chapter Paul has been to Spain but there really wasn't much success. We don't really have any records of it, so it's just speculation, but ultimately God didn't have that work for him.

KATHIE: And yet he believed with all his heart he was supposed to go there.

BRYAN: Maybe there was an unseen work known only to God. History doesn't record everything that happens. And maybe there were some people, not mentioned in any books, but when we get to heaven, the guy will say, "Hey, I'm the first Spanish Christian!" We just don't know about it from any written records. We propose that maybe he first started in Tarraco, which is called Tarragona today. It's near Barcelona. That would be easy to get to from Rome because it's inside the Mediterranean Sea. So maybe he landed there. But then if we imagine that he wanted to get to the end of the world, he would sail out through the Strait of Gibraltar and come to Cádiz, which is on the Atlantic coast. We propose that in the chapter because it would allow him to look out and say, "I've reached the end."

KATHIE: There's nothing beyond it that seems to have been important. Little did he know, right?

BRYAN: Right! Christopher Columbus sailed from near that harbor about fourteen hundred years later. Paul didn't know there were Indians over there that needed the gospel, or any of that. But he comes back to the Aegean Sea. That leads to our first question, because this is when he writes the Pastoral Epistles, First Timothy, Second Timothy, and Titus, where he's mentoring them. Mentors are so important, and he was a good mentor to Timothy and Titus. Have you had mentors? Or have you mentored people? How does that work for you?

KATHIE: You know, I've been a mentor more than I've had one. I don't know how to say this without it sounding like "Aren't I great?" but the truth is I was a trailblazer. I did some things that nobody had ever done before—in television, for sure. People often tell me, "I'm in this business because of you." You pay a big price for it, but it's thrilling to know that God has used you.

BRYAN: Was Anita Bryant a mentor to you?

KATHIE: She was a teacher. She taught me. I probably watched her perform a thousand times, and she was great. And I learned how to get standing ovations from that woman, so I'm grateful to her for teaching me skills and techniques. But I also learned what kind of human being I did not want to be in show business.

BRYAN: Did you have other mentors?

KATHIE: It was my daddy's birthday the other day. He would have turned 101 years old. I got on the phone with my brother and my sister and we talked about him. Now, that was my mentor. And my mom would say, "Hold your head up high." My mom taught me how to make my spaghetti sauce and cook all sorts of things and to be a lady.

BRYAN: What about a spiritual mentor who led you in the faith, like Pastor Jack Hayford? Who are some of your spiritual mentors?

KATHIE: Billy Graham was my greatest.

BRYAN: That's not a bad one to have!

KATHIE: Billy was my greatest, and Pastor Jack I adored.

BRYAN: What about your kids? Did you try to pass on a spiritual life to your kids?

KATHIE: Yes, but they didn't want it from me. My son always told me, "Mom, I don't want your faith. I want my own faith." And you know where he got it? He went with us to Oxford and walked those magnificent grounds that you've walked as well. And he walked where C. S. Lewis walked, and J. R. R. Tolkien.

BRYAN: I'm sure he went into the Eagle and Child pub. They call it "the Bird and the Baby."

KATHIE: Yes! The Bird and the Baby. And when he was about twelve or so, I took them there and we sat in that little nook where they'd go, every Tuesday, those guys. Every Tuesday, Lewis and Tolkien would have lunch together. And I would cry. Cody said, "What are you crying about, Mom?" I said that these two incredible men were once sitting where we sat, talking about their books. Cody said, "Mom, that's how I came to faith." He said he would read about what they would talk about and write about. It was Narnia and Tolkien.

BRYAN: And that shows you the power of books. Paul discipled Timothy even from prison, by writing Second Timothy to him. So discipling can happen through the written word.

KATHIE: And we're doing that—or, at least, we're trying to.

BRYAN: We also see in this chapter where Nero gets angry. We talked about this a little bit before, but this is the place where it happens, where he gets angry with Poppaea and they have a spat. We don't know exactly what caused it, but something happened in the night when he came back late from the races. And he ends up kicking her to death, along with her baby.

KATHIE: Did the crowd ever forgive him for that? Were they aware of the circumstances?

BRYAN: I mean, it was known that he had done that, but he already did it to Octavia by ordering her to commit suicide. And he did it to Britannicus with poison.

KATHIE: And he had killed his mother by that time. He was very good at one thing, and that was killing people!

BRYAN: Unfortunately, sometimes it's kill or be killed, right? But that was domestic violence, which, of course, is still an issue in our world today, isn't it?

KATHIE: Sadly, yes, it's totally still an issue because in many parts of our world women are not treated the same as men. The more I learn about Nero in this book, the more I despise him. What a narcissistic jerk! Compared to Herod, he was terrible. There are things about Herod that I really respect.

BRYAN: Herod tried to follow the biblical God, but he didn't do it right.

KATHIE: He was a mess too. But at least Herod was a truly gifted man. Nero was a phony. He was a poser. Herod was a builder, and a true artistic genius. To this day, wherever I go, if I see beauty—even if I don't even know what the man or woman who made it was like—I respect what they did. I try to bring beauty into this world. The arts are so important. But Nero corrupted the arts. He was just very hard to like.

BRYAN: And to that point, this chapter ends with the famous "Nero's torches" scene. This is where he finally turns his attention to Christians, and so persecution begins. Before, you had some hostility to Christians, but now you have governmental intervention. It wasn't across the whole empire, but it did happen in Rome. And he sets these Christians on fire by crucifying them in some kind of wrapping that was impregnated with flammable substances, and they burned for his parties like torches. He also sets dogs to attack other Christians that he dresses up in furs like helpless animals. It's all just so hard to think about.

KATHIE: You know what that is? That's just sick *skubala*! That's narcissism and sadism, when you enjoy the pain that you inflict on another human being. I will never understand that. He did it publicly, in a garden. It was meant to be entertainment.

BRYAN: And everybody laughed because the source that tells us about this, which is Tacitus, says that they were all mocking them. Human lives were just a game to them—people getting torn apart by fangs. That suffering is hard to imagine. Even some of the Romans started to have pity.

KATHIE: Herod tortured people, but it was to get information for crimes.

BRYAN: Perhaps judicial torture is different than torture as public entertainment.

KATHIE: I think there's a huge difference. I mean, the whole thing where you put pain on display for people to be entertained is sickening to me. I can't watch anything like that. Horror movies and gore—I can't watch any of it. It physically sickens me. It's dark stuff.

BRYAN: And Peter, he was probably part of Nero's torches event.

KATHIE: He would have been a famous Christian by then, right?

BRYAN: Yeah, I think he would have been famous enough to have been known by name, and certainly he was known to be a leader. And a great disciple of the Lord, who truly understood who his Savior was.

KATHIE: Did you ever go up to Caesarea Philippi in Israel?

BRYAN: Sure. It's where they have the "gates of hell."

KATHIE: Yes! The gates of hell are there because it was an actual place. It was the shrine to the god Pan. They had a cave to the underworld. And when Jesus said to his followers, "Who do people say I am?" they answered, "Some say you're Elijah come back. Some say John the Baptist." And he said, "Well, who do you say I am?"[12]

BRYAN: And Peter replied, "You are the Christ, the Son of the living God."[13]

KATHIE: "You are the Messiah," not Christ.

12. Matthew 16:13–15, author's paraphrase.

13. Matthew 16:16.

BRYAN: It says "Christ" in the Bible, but he would have been speaking Aramaic originally, so yes, he said "Messiah" at the time.

KATHIE: They both mean "anointed one." He was the one prophesied forever in the Torah and everywhere else.

BRYAN: Jesus says, "Flesh and blood did not reveal that to you," but Peter got it by divine revelation.[14]

KATHIE: And the gates of hades will not win. Jesus points to the gates, to the cave, which was right there. He says the gates of hell will not prevail.

BRYAN: Yes, Jesus says, "You are Peter, and on this rock I will build My church, and the gates of hades shall not prevail against it."[15] The gates of hell certainly have not prevailed against God's church! All that to say, we love Peter and we respect him.

KATHIE: Oh, I love Peter. He was feisty and real. And he was flawed, like I am.

BRYAN: Jesus says to him, "At the end of your life, you're going to stretch out your arms and you will be led where you do not want to go."[16] And, sure enough, he was crucified. Some say it was upside down, and that he was probably set on fire, if he was part of this thing that Nero was doing.

KATHIE: So do we know that he died in Rome?

BRYAN: Almost certainly. Those traditions are extremely strong. And even in one of his epistles he says he's writing from Babylon, which was a code word for Rome. Then he was likely buried right next to the Circus of Nero on the Vatican Hill, which is why the Vatican is where his church is today: Saint Peter's Basilica.

KATHIE: It's so fascinating. Every time I go to Rome, I'm fascinated by it, but I also struggle with it too.

BRYAN: A lot of evangelical believers feel that way.

KATHIE: Yes, I'd say I'm an evangelical Christian. And I'm a Messianic Jew. Sometimes I like to think that I descended from Esther, because she was gorgeous.

BRYAN: Maybe there's a little Rahab in there somewhere too.

KATHIE: Well, okay then, I was a hooker?

---

14. Matthew 16:17.
15. Matthew 16:18.
16. John 21:18, author's paraphrase.

BRYAN: No, more like how she was with the spies. Maybe you've got her . . .

KATHIE: I have her chutzpah!

BRYAN: And also maybe some Jael, the woman who used the tent spike and took out the bad guy. None of the soldiers could capture him, so she said, "Here's my chance." Boom! Right through his temple.[17]

KATHIE: Oh, yeah! The Canaanite general that came and tried to hide in her tent. I'm remembering now. It's not the best-known story, but it's a good one! I love it when a woman takes the opportunity and goes for it. I think it's awesome. She becomes the warrior, like Deborah too.

BRYAN: Yes, Deborah, who led men in battle. It just goes to show that God uses anyone for his purposes. Peter and Paul were flawed, and these women were flawed, but God used them all.

KATHIE: If he can use me, he can use anyone!

BRYAN: God will always find a way to use someone who wants to serve him. All we have to do is be on the lookout for what he is up to—then obey.

17. Judges 4:21, author's paraphrase.

SEVENTEEN

THE GOLDEN HOUSE AND THE DARK DUNGEON

After the Great Fire of 64, a profound change came over Nero. Though he had always been prideful and eager for flattery, when public opinion turned against him after the fire, his need for approval raised his egomania to new heights. No longer did he just want the people's acclaim and admiration. Now he wanted their *worship*. He had come to believe he was the incarnation of a heavenly god. Nero considered himself a divine being who walked the earth among mortal men.

His twin pastimes made it clear which god he was most associated with. First, as a chariot driver, Nero personified the god of the sun: Helios in Greek, or Sol in Latin. The Circus Maximus belonged to this god, who was depicted as driving his heavenly chariot through the sky from dawn to dusk each day. Egyptian obelisks, which were dedicated to the sun god, often decorated circuses. Even Nero's birth had signaled his solar destiny. Before he was laid on the ground at his father's feet, his true father, the sun, had caressed him with its rays. Nero viewed himself as the light of the world, spreading warmth, illumination, and fruitfulness across the empire. As a shining charioteer, he embodied the spirit of Sol.

Nero's second pastime of music and poetry also signaled his divine status.

In every part of the empire, statues and images of Apollo depicted this blond, muscular god with a lyre in his hand. Since Apollo was a harpist and singer, he patronized the performing arts. He was also a solar deity, closely connected to—in fact, equated with—the sun god. As Zeus's son, Apollo had been sent into the world to bring enlightenment, music, healing, and prophecy to the human race. His appearance was radiant and glorious. He was the epitome of handsomeness, with a beautiful face and a perfect physique. In other words, Apollo/Sol represented everything Nero wanted to be. As the emperor turned more deranged and self-obsessed, he came to believe the divine and human realms had merged in his own exalted person. He was the ultimate narcissist who considered himself superior to all other people. The father of the gods had appointed him for the salvation of humankind.

It wasn't only Nero's two public pastimes that displayed his divine solar identity. After the Great Fire cleared much ground in Rome, he erected a gleaming statue of himself as the sun god, called the Colossus of Nero. It stood eighteen times life size. The former pedestal of the giant statue can still be seen outside Rome's main amphitheater, which is known today as the Colosseum because of the idol that once adjoined it.

But Nero's self-glorification didn't stop there. Sprouting like a yellow rose from the cinders of the city, he built a vast new complex for himself called the Golden House. It was an entire estate brought inside the civic boundaries of Rome, creating a "countryside in the city," as one ancient critic called it. The citizens could see that their emperor reigned over a perfectly manicured world, a sort of theme park of imperial grandeur. Indeed, the Golden House formed the ultimate stage on which Nero could enact his heavenly identity. With such a splendid house, he proved a man of destiny like himself could be exalted to divine heights.

As the glorious new lord of the universe, Nero achieved peace through a treaty with a neighboring empire. Three eastern kings (who were also astronomers called magi) brought gifts to pay homage to their rightful ruler. With the sunrise shining behind him, Nero crowned one of them, Tiridates, who was sitting at his feet, as a vassal king in a grand ceremony. For this special occasion not only the stage but the entire theater was covered with gold paint. All the furniture was gilded as well, so the whole place shone with a luminous brilliance. Everyone attended a "costly banquet" after which Nero sang, played the lyre, and drove his chariot while clad in the helmet and uniform of a racer. Forever afterward, this spectacular coronation holiday was known as "the Golden Day."

The Roman Christians who observed these events and monuments couldn't help but see how their emperor was usurping the names and attributes of their Lord, who had conquered death by coming out of his tomb at sunrise. The Roman week included Saturn's Day, the Sun's Day, and the Moon's Day—Saturday, Sunday, and Monday—and the Christians knew it was no coincidence their Savior had risen from his grave on the Day of the Sun. The solar orb was a special symbol of Jesus Christ. Just as it "perished" every night but never failed to rise again at dawn, so Jesus had triumphed over the gloom of death to enlighten all of humankind. "I am the light of the world," he had told his disciples. "He who follows Me shall not walk in darkness, but have the light of life."[1]

The solar imagery for Jesus went deeper in Scripture than just the New Testament references to his resurrection or ministry of illumination. The Old Testament prophet Malachi had predicted, "The Sun of Righteousness shall arise with healing in His wings."[2] King David made a prophetic reference to his royal descendant when he wrote, "The heavens declare the glory of God; the skies proclaim the work of his hands . . . In the heavens God has pitched a tent for the sun. It is like a bridegroom coming out of his chamber, like a champion rejoicing to run his course. It rises at one end of the heavens and makes its circuit to the other; nothing is deprived of its warmth."[3]

Jesus' glorious resurrection and ascent into heaven caused the early believers to hail him as their Lord. Every other king remained in his grave when he died. Even the great King David hadn't ascended into the heavens. Only Jesus could be called "Lord and Christ"—the Messiah or anointed King.[4] He was "the Root and the Offspring of David, and the bright Morning Star."[5] Jesus alone ruled the world. He alone could award crowns of honor or invite his victorious followers to approach his throne. And he alone deserved to be worshiped, which meant Nero as the sun god and the Roman Christians were at war. Their great battle could have only one victor left standing in the end.

---

1. John 8:12.
2. Malachi 4:2.
3. Psalm 19:1, 4–6 NIV.
4. Acts 2:29–36.
5. Revelation 22:16 NIV.

In the dark and smelly confines of Rome's most fearsome dungeon, we can imagine the apostle Paul thanking God for the gift Onesiphorus had brought to him. He lit the oil lamp, then dipped his reed pen in an inkwell and prepared to write on a blank sheet of parchment. Through the dark hours of the night he had been praying for Timothy, his spiritual son. Although Timothy was now in Ephesus, Paul wanted him to come to Rome. Not only would he bring some needed supplies—a cloak for the nighttime chill, several biblical scrolls, and more writing paper—his presence would be an even greater comfort. "Do your best to come to me quickly," he urged his beloved disciple.[6]

Unlike his first Roman imprisonment, the hardships of which had been relatively mild, this time the Carcer had been taking a toll on Paul's worn-out body. He didn't expect to escape alive from this horrible place. Like an Old Testament wine sacrifice poured out before God until the cup was empty, Paul could feel his life draining away. "I am already being poured out as a drink offering, and the time of my departure is at hand. I have fought the good fight, I have finished the race, I have kept the faith. Finally, there is laid up for me the crown of righteousness, which the Lord, the righteous Judge, will give to me on that Day."[7] Never mind Nero's crowns of perishable gold—Paul wanted the true King's rewards that would last forever.

Though the elderly apostle knew the day of his crowning was near, young Timothy still had a long way to go on his spiritual journey. In the darkness before dawn, Paul scratched out his final words to his protégé by the flickering flame of the lamp. He prayed the gospel would be received with full acceptance and get passed to many others. Eager to leave a multigenerational legacy, he wrote, "You therefore, my son, be strong in the grace that is in Christ Jesus. And the things that you have heard from me among many witnesses, commit these to faithful men who will be able to teach others also." Like a good soldier, Timothy should seek to please his Commander. Like a good athlete, he should play by the rules. Despite being locked in the Carcer, Paul had heard all about

6. 2 Timothy 4:9 NIV.
7. 2 Timothy 4:6–8.

Nero's rigged competitions. With a subtle dig at the cheating emperor, he reminded Timothy, "If anyone competes in athletics, he is not crowned unless he competes according to the rules."[8]

Though Timothy had been blessed with excellent role models, would he stand firm when put to the test? As Paul reflected on his gnarled fingers, his scarred arms, and his aching body, he asked God to strengthen his son in the faith for whatever might lie ahead, even if it involved suffering like he himself had experienced. He reminded Timothy that "everyone who wants to live a godly life in Christ Jesus will be persecuted . . . But as for you, continue in what you have learned and have become convinced of, because you know those from whom you learned it."[9]

How could Paul expect such endurance from someone he loved so much? Because he knew the prize would be worth whatever it cost. Earthly kings allowed their vassals to sit beside them on their thrones—but to sit next to Christ the King was the greatest privilege of all. Paul recalled how he had encouraged the believers at Ephesus, where Timothy was now ministering, with the words "God raised us up with Christ and seated us with him in the heavenly realms."[10] To encourage Timothy with the same hope, the words of a Christian hymn came to Paul's mind. He jotted down this "trustworthy saying" in the middle of his epistle:

> If we died with him, we will also live with him;
> If we endure, we will also reign with him.
> If we disown him, he will also disown us;
> If we are faithless, he remains faithful,
> for he cannot disown himself.[11]

In the years ahead, Timothy would need to remember these words. His endurance would lead to an eternal reign with Christ. If Timothy found himself tempted to abandon his beliefs, he could know Christ would remain

---

8. 2 Timothy 2:1–2, 5.
9. 2 Timothy 3:12, 14 NIV.
10. Ephesians 2:6 NIV.
11. 2 Timothy 2:11–13 NIV.

faithful, for that was his divine character. *Oh Lord, may Timothy stand strong and bring many others to your gospel!*

Once Paul had finished writing his epistle, he added some final greetings and a benediction, then rolled up the parchment sheet and put it inside a waxed leather case. When Onesiphorus visited the Carcer again, he took the letter into his care and promised to send it via a messenger very soon. It was July, so the letter should reach Ephesus in time for Timothy to depart that city and reach Rome before winter. For many days Paul prayed it would be so. What a comfort it would be to see Timothy face-to-face!

The Lord had other plans, however. On a hot day in early August, while Paul languished on his mat in a sweat-soaked tunic, the latch on the Carcer's door jangled and three soldiers entered the prison. "Get up, Christian!" one of them commanded, giving Paul a kick in the ribs before he could even begin to comply.

Paul arose and followed the soldiers outside, squinting in the bright glare of the Forum. "Where are you taking me?" he dared to ask.

Though one of the soldiers cuffed him on the back of the head, another had enough kindness left in him to give an answer. "First, you're getting a bath, because you're filthy and you stink," he said. "After that, you're going straight to Nero. And may your God help you, because his gods certainly won't!"

CODA

We reflect in this chapter's conversation on how the Bible presents Jesus as shining like the sun, radiant and victorious over darkness. It's a beautiful picture of the eternal resurrection that all of his followers will experience. Even though Paul was imprisoned in a dark dungeon for a time, he wasn't discouraged, for he kept his focus on his heavenly destiny. All followers of Jesus know they will one day meet their glorious Savior face-to-face!

BRYAN: Chapter 17, "The Golden House and the Dark Dungeon," presents a contrast between Nero and his mansions and Paul in the Carcer. Nero begins to take on a sun-god persona. After the Great Fire he builds a huge private paradise for himself in Rome called the Golden House. Though it's not there anymore, a few ruins were recently found.

KATHIE: That had never been done before, had it?

BRYAN: Not on that scale. Some people had private gardens by their houses, but this was excessive. He also built a giant statue called the Colossus.

KATHIE: And that's completely gone, or is there anything left?

BRYAN: There are some blocks of the pedestal where it stood, right next to the Colosseum. That's actually how the Colosseum, originally called the Flavian Amphitheatre, got its nickname. The Colossus was eighteen times as big as Nero was, and it had spiky rays coming out of its head, like the Statue of Liberty does. It was Nero saying, "I'm Apollo. I'm the sun god."

KATHIE: He claimed to be the s-u-n, but Jesus is the S-o-n.

BRYAN: Jesus is the s-u-n too. There's a lot of solar imagery for him in both testaments. He's the Sun of Righteousness rising with healing in his wings.[12]

KATHIE: I always think of him as the Son of God.

BRYAN: Do you ever think of him as the Sun of God?

KATHIE: No, but that's good to think about.

BRYAN: In the morning, the sun rises and sends away the darkness. The charioteer rejoices to run his course across the sky.[13] When we see that shining ball in the sky, in a way it is like Jesus' holy chariot running in glory across the sky. I'm not saying we worship the actual sun, not the actual ball of burning hydrogen and helium. It's a picture, an image.

KATHIE: You know what? I'm thinking about that, and I like it. We're raised to think in certain ways, and so "Son of God" always meant to me "the Son of the Father" in the Trinity.

BRYAN: I just wrote a book on the Trinity, so I agree. But you can also think about the sun, like the way the sun goes under the earth. Jesus says, "I will give you the sign of Jonah. I will be in the heart of the earth for three days."[14] But it can't hold him there. He's going to escape, just like Jonah was in the abyss and the monster got him. By the way, it was actually a serpent—Jonah wasn't captured by a whale. The word is *ketos* in Greek, and it meant a sea monster. He was captured by Leviathan.

KATHIE: Leviathan?

BRYAN: Right. Leviathan, the sea serpent that the Lord slays with his

12. Malachi 4:2.
13. Psalm 19:5–6.
14. Matthew 12:39–40, author's paraphrase.

sword.[15] For a time, the serpent takes Jesus beneath the earth, until Jesus triumphs over him. And then, like the sun, he comes bursting forth from below. So it's metaphorical. Again, we're not talking about worshiping the sun itself. We're worshiping Jesus, not a ball of fiery gas.

KATHIE: I just learned something new!

BRYAN: We just need to picture it, right? It's an imaginative thing. We've all been touched by the beauty of a sunrise.

KATHIE: Oh, and also a sunset.

BRYAN: Yeah, except with a sunset, in some ways, to me it's a sad thing. I mean, it's beautiful, but at the end of a great day you realize it's gone. There's that sense of sadness and loss. It has come to an end.

KATHIE: I have great memories of sunsets because every night of Frank's and my life together we would toast the sunset. We would sit on our porch by the sea and thank the Lord for the day. And when our babies were born, they'd have their little sippy cups and they would do it too. When Frank passed, and our children moved away to school, I couldn't do it anymore. It was too painful for me. So there's that sense of loss.

BRYAN: But the beautiful thing about our faith is that Frank isn't under the earth, and he's not in the grave. He's with the actual Son of God who is risen like the sun. And just as you are certain that the sun will surely come back again, so you also know that you'll see your beloved husband again, because he is alive in Jesus.

KATHIE: And my mother and my father.

BRYAN: For believers, you don't have to lose them. You just have to endure a nighttime for a while. Then there's going to be an alarm clock that is going to wake us up, and it's going to be the trumpet of Christ! That's why the Scripture says, "Awake, O sleeper, and arise from the dead, and Christ will shine on you."[16] Jesus is risen, like the bright Morning Star.[17]

KATHIE: I get up so early every day I often see the dawn coming through my window. And I pray, "Help me stay on the path of the righteous." "The path of the righteous is like the morning sun, shining ever brighter till the full

---

15. Isaiah 27:1.
16. Ephesians 5:14 ESV.
17. Revelation 22:16.

light of day."[18] I say that every morning, and "Lord, I want to be on the path of the righteous today." I'm not always, but I don't want to get off it. I know that. So I pray, "Lord, help me to stay on it."

BRYAN: Sometimes I do that too. I wake up, and a lot of times I pause. I have a small rug next to my bed that I think of as my prayer rug. I quote Isaiah where it says, "Arise, shine, for your light has come! And the glory of the LORD is risen upon you. For behold, darkness shall cover the earth, and deep darkness the people, but the LORD will rise over you, and His glory will be seen upon you."[19]

KATHIE: Do you get down on that rug?

BRYAN: I do, very often. It's my prayer rug I found in Turkey. It's not a Muslim prayer rug, it's a Christian prayer rug. It's a Hereke silk rug, the kind that used to be in the Ottoman palaces. So, for both of us, the sunrise is a beautiful reminder of the Lord.

KATHIE: Truly.

BRYAN: Also in chapter 17 we look at Paul in contrast to Nero—who's building himself statues and palaces and estates that get bigger and bigger all the time.

KATHIE: Just like his ego!

BRYAN: Everything's made of gold, and his dining room drops perfume and roses on the diners. He also has a dome that can turn like a planetarium. The slaves turn it as if everything literally revolves around him. Actually he thinks the whole universe does.

KATHIE: He just murdered people so he could take their money and build that kind of stuff.

BRYAN: To get that much gold you have to work people to death in the mines. You don't think of them as your employees; you just work them until they die, then you get the next one. The gold came from death, as it does today, sometimes, in Africa.

KATHIE: What does it profit?

BRYAN: Exactly. But Paul would say, "Here's what it profits," because he knew where he was going, even though he's in the opposite of a golden house. He's in a dungeon, in the Carcer, the Mamertine Prison.

---

18. Proverbs 4:18 NIV.
19. Isaiah 60:1–2.

KATHIE: That's where I've been to visit. You go down underneath a church and it's still there. They have his chains, they say.

BRYAN: Yes, and springs of water. They say Peter baptized some soldiers there, because he was supposedly there too.

KATHIE: Peter was there too?

BRYAN: Maybe at a different time. Or it might just be ancient traditions.

KATHIE: Do you think they ever met in Rome?

BRYAN: The tradition is that they crisscrossed each other on the way to their martyrdoms, on June 29, and they stopped to kiss each other. So they get twinned, as they say. Peter and Paul are two best buds, though we don't have good evidence for that.

KATHIE: So did they meet in Rome?

BRYAN: Maybe not, because in Paul's letter to the Romans he sends a lot of greetings, but he doesn't greet Peter. Some scholars think that the falling-out they had in Galatians unfortunately lasted for a while.

KATHIE: Or was Peter dead already? Maybe he didn't greet him because Peter had died.

BRYAN: Yes, I think it was probably about a year after Peter died that Paul died. We don't know for sure. But Paul is writing to Timothy, and he says, "I have fought the good fight. I have finished the race. I have kept the faith."[20] So we have to ask ourselves how we can also say that at the end of our lives. How do you break the tape at the finish line with that sense of accomplishment?

KATHIE: I do look back with a sense of accomplishment. Have I been perfect? Absolutely not! But did I ever give up? I wanted to. At times—especially the last couple of years—I've wanted to. Between some emotional stuff in my life, and some family stuff. But I can't. My Lord says for me to keep running the race. So I have. Until the very last day, we all have a race still left to run.

BRYAN: And when we get to the finish line, he is there to give us the prize of the upward call of God in Christ Jesus.[21] Paul knew that really well. His dungeon wasn't a prison to him, it was the porch of the golden house that awaited him—which is true for all of us if we know Jesus.

---

20. 2 Timothy 4:7.
21. Philippians 4:13.

EIGHTEEN

THE CROWN OF LIFE

Holy Scripture doesn't record anything about Paul's final trial before Nero. But a second-century text called the *Acts of Paul* provides a vivid description of what happened at the trial. How accurate is it? In truth, the tale is mostly folklore. Nevertheless, it is worth exploring because even if the events didn't happen exactly as described, the story's literary themes explain what the early Christians believed about Paul's conflict with Nero. What are those themes?

Ultimately, the conflict was viewed not as a war of words between an apostle and a politician but as a cosmic struggle for lordship between the divine Christ and the satanically empowered Nero. Two great kings were striving for dominion in a spiritual battle for supremacy. The eternal souls of human beings hung in the balance of this conflict. Those who bowed the knee to Jesus would reign victoriously, while those who pledged themselves to Nero would be met with ruin. Christ the King would certainly win this war, even if Nero managed to slay Paul along the way.

The climactic sequence in the *Acts of Paul* begins with the apostle evangelizing freely in Rome before he was cast into the Carcer. Nero's beloved cupbearer, Patroclus, desires to hear the apostolic preaching, but he cannot reach Paul because of the crowd. So he sits in a high window where he can hear the good word. Just like another young man, in the book of Acts,[1] Patroclus

1. Acts 20:9.

grows sleepy—due to the devil's malevolent influence—and falls to his death on the pavement below.

The sad news is immediately reported to Nero, but unknown to the emperor, Paul brings Patroclus inside and prays over him with all the Christians. "Now, brothers, let your faith be revealed," he says. "Come, all of you—let us cry out to our Lord Jesus Christ, asking that this boy might live so we can continue without further disturbance."[2] Sure enough, the Lord resurrects Patroclus!

Meanwhile, Nero is grieving the loss of his cupbearer in the imperial palace. After his bath he orders someone else to serve as the steward of his wine but the servants tell him, "Caesar, Patroclus is alive and standing by the dinner table."

Nero goes to the dining room. Seeing his cupbearer, he says, "Patroclus! Are you alive?"

"I am alive, Caesar."

"Who made you alive?"

"It was Jesus Christ, the king of the ages."

How can this be? With growing concern, Nero asks, "Is he going to be the king forever and destroy all other kingdoms?"

"Yes, indeed!" says Patroclus. "He overthrows every kingdom under heaven, and he alone will exist forever, and no kingdom shall escape him."

Infuriated by this prophecy of his own destruction, Nero punches Patroclus in the face. "Are you also fighting as a soldier of that king?"

Patroclus boldly answers, "Yes, my lord Caesar—for he has raised me from the dead."

To make matters worse, three of Nero's advisers jump into the conversation and declare they, too, are soldiers of the eternal king. Nero immediately throws the four traitors into a dungeon and tortures them—the people he used to love so much. Then he issues an order to arrest all other "soldiers of Christ" in Rome and put them to death.

The net of imperial persecution sweeps Paul into its web. Because the other believers give honor to Paul, the emperor discerns he is a leader of Christ's rebel

---

2. The quotations and substance of this story are taken from Bryan Litfin, *Early Christian Martyr Stories* (Baker Academic, 2014), 37–43.

army. Nero has Paul brought before him in chains and says, "Man of the great king, now my prisoner, what made you think you could sneak into the Roman Empire and enlist soldiers in my territory?"

Accepting Nero's military metaphor, and filled with the Holy Spirit, Paul replies, "Caesar, we seek soldiers not just in your territory but in the whole world! For this is our commandment, that no one should be excluded who wishes to enlist in the service of my king." Urging Nero to become the Lord's soldier, since his wealth and splendid things can't save him, Paul tells him that only by surrendering to Jesus and seeking his mercy can he be saved from the final judgment of the world, which is coming soon.[3]

Fully enraged, Nero orders all the captured Christians to be burned with fire—all but Paul. Because he is a Roman citizen, Paul isn't subject to death by crucifixion and burning. His fate will be decapitation, a swifter and less painful death. But despite the capital sentence, Paul keeps on preaching, especially to a prefect named Longus and a centurion named Cestus. Amazed by Paul's courage, Longus and Cestus ask him, "Where did you get this king whom you believe in without changing your mind, even to the point of death?"

Paul answers with a gospel proclamation that includes a stern warning. He calls on the two men to repent of their errors and be saved from Christ's fiery judgment. "We serve in the army of a king who is from heaven, not from earth as you seem to think." He alone is the "living God." Then Paul adds, "Blessed is the one who will believe in the king and live forever when he comes with fire to cleanse the earth."

"We need you to help us!" the men exclaim. "If you do, we'll set you free!"

"I'm no deserter from Christ," Paul replies.

Rather than being afraid, Paul is rejoicing that he will be able to go with his Lord and enter into the glory of the heavenly Father. Paul tells Longus and Cestus that after he has died, they should go to his grave, where Luke and Titus will minister to them. Then, having evangelized to the very end of his life, Paul, the faithful apostle, submits himself to martyrdom.

Although these events probably didn't take place exactly as described—it's Christian folklore, after all—the themes in the *Acts of Paul* perfectly display how the early believers viewed their struggle against pagan Rome. When Nero

---

3. Acts 10:42, 17:31; 2 Timothy 4:1.

made himself into the embodiment of the sun god, the ancient Christians countered that the Sun of Righteousness actually ruled the world. The Roman acclamation "Caesar is lord!" stood in direct contrast to Paul's message: "If you declare with your mouth, 'Jesus is Lord,' and believe in your heart that God raised him from the dead, you will be saved."[4] Heaven and earth could have only one Lord. The Christians knew who it was. All other impostors would perish.

After Paul's real-life trial before Nero (the details of which we don't know much about), the condemned apostle was thrown back into the Carcer to await his execution by beheading. Then what did Nero do? Surprisingly, he went to war.

But it wasn't a traditional war with swords and armor. Nero wasn't man enough for that. Instead, he conjured up a new model of warfare: a glorious road show of musical performance, theater, and chariot riding to show the world what a winner he was. He decided to go to Greece, the original homeland of competitive athletic contests, of which the Olympic games were the most famous. But instead of attending only the games that were scheduled for that year on a four-year cycle, Nero ordered all of them to be held concurrently, so he could take the crown in each one. Breaking with centuries-old tradition, he added competitions in the performing arts to accompany the athletic games. That way, all his skills could be put on display before the Greeks.

The grand tour of the games took the format of an imperial victory parade. Like a triumphant army general, Nero rode in a magnificent chariot—though when he lost control of the horses and fell out of the cockpit during one race, the judges pretended it didn't happen and awarded him the prize anyway. Instead of brawny soldiers, Nero's entourage consisted of applauding fanboys who carried harps and string pluckers as their weapons and wore stage masks and high-heeled shoes as their uniforms. When Nero acted onstage, he played both male and female roles—but whenever the role was feminine, the mask portrayed the face of his recently murdered wife. This allowed Nero to resurrect Poppaea from her grave and make her a participant in the spectacle.

---

4. Romans 10:9 NIV.

Extreme stage fright plagued the emperor before each performance, as if the outcome were actually in doubt. He urged the judges to award the prizes fairly, and they assured him they would—then they always found him to be the most deserving contestant. He would feign humility as he received award after award. Instead of the golden crown of an emperor, Nero craved the olive wreath of an Olympic victor.

As Nero's grief for Poppaea grew more intense, he did something strange while in Greece. Previously, he had taken a concubine to his bed, a woman who looked remarkably like his deceased wife. Now Nero found a slave boy named Sporus to play the role. After having him castrated to retain his prepubescent feminine traits, Nero officially married him. A fashionable lady was appointed to maintain Sporus's cross-dressing wardrobe of gowns and makeup. He was called "lady," "queen," and "mistress"—for he was truly considered the emperor's wife. Nero often kissed the boy amorously in public. Through a mockery of marriage, the deranged emperor showed he could play any role he wanted. He wore personalities like garments that he could put on and take off. According to his whims, he alternated between being a husband, wife, poet, athlete, musician, king—and, behind it all, an immortal god.

Nero's pseudomilitary campaign through Greece wasn't just about displaying his victories and claiming prizes. He actually ravaged the land like a foreign conqueror. Greedy for Greek wealth, he trumped up charges against local gentlemen and confiscated their long-held family properties. Many prominent landowners were killed and their children banished while Nero raked in the profits of his treachery. Greek temples were raided and their treasuries ransacked. Countless statues were stolen so they could decorate the Golden House back in Rome.

Upon his return home after a year and a half abroad, Nero staged his entrance into Rome like the parades of previous conquerors. He wore a purple cloak adorned with golden stars, held a laurel branch in his hand, and bore the Olympic wreath on his brow. Other crowns and awards were put on display like the spoils of war claimed in a foreign campaign. Ribbons and candies were tossed in the air, the streets were sprinkled with perfume, and songbirds were released in his train. Nero even rode in the same chariot Caesar Augustus had used for his triumphal processions. The route went from the Circus Maximus to the Forum, then to the Capitol, and finally to the Temple of Apollo atop the Palatine Hill. As Nero rode along, the crowd shouted, "Hail, Olympian victor! Augustus! Augustus! Hail to Nero, our Hercules! Hail to Nero, our Apollo! O, Divine Voice! Blessed are they that hear thee!"

At last, Nero entered his private quarters in the imperial palace. All of his awards lay strewn upon his beds and couches. The trophies of his victory met his eye at every turn—1,808 in all. He had to smile at this, for it proved the extent of his greatness. Like the solar chariot racing across the sky, Apollo's earthly incarnation had gone abroad and returned to the place where he began. Tomorrow, he believed, the dawning of his glorious brilliance would enlighten Rome once again.

After Nero left Rome in the fall of 66 for his victory tour of Greece, the apostle Paul didn't have to wait long in the Carcer. The day decreed for his execution came quickly. Although the *Acts of Paul* tells the story in its typical folkloric fashion, some of its details can be corroborated by archaeology. The anonymous author relates:

> Paul turned to face the east. Lifting up his hands to heaven, he prayed for a long time. After he had communed prayerfully with the fathers in Hebrew, he offered his neck without another word. And as the executioner struck off his head, milk spurted onto the soldier's tunic. When the soldiers and all the bystanders saw it, they marveled and glorified God, who had given Paul such honor. Then they departed to give an account of these events to Caesar.

The meaning of this "milk" has been debated by scholars. It might symbolize the holy teaching offered by Paul.[5] Or it could have been an actual eyewitness remembrance of body fluids but with a spiritual interpretation.

5. 1 Corinthians 3:2; Hebrews 5:12; 1 Peter 2:2.

The location of Paul's beheading and burial was recorded in the ancient sources to be a certain spot on the highway outside Rome called the Ostian Way, which paralleled the Tiber River on its way out to the sea. Within one hundred years of his death, the local believers erected a victory monument to mark the grave, which they called a "trophy." Such trophies were common on ancient battlefields when the victorious soldiers piled up the enemy's weapons and armor as a sign of their defeat. Paul knew his death would be followed by victorious resurrection. While imprisoned, he had written, "I want to know Christ—yes, to know the power of his resurrection and participation in his sufferings, becoming like him in his death."[6] As a martyr killed for the name of his Lord, Paul's deepest desire had now been achieved—and, through it, the gospel had advanced into all the world.

Although the physical structure of the Pauline trophy has disappeared into the sands of time, many historians and archaeologists believe its location is still known. Around the time that Emperor Constantine came to power, a chapel was erected over the trophy. Later, it was expanded into a very large church whose triumphal arch proclaimed the building to be "sanctified by the body of Paul, teacher of the world." That great basilica lasted for almost a millennium and a half, from the 380s until 1823, when an accidental fire burned it down.

Yet the fire revealed a hidden sarcophagus underneath the altar. An ancient marble slab was also discovered, inscribed with the words "To Paul, apostle and martyr." Today, the rebuilt church is called the Basilica of Saint Paul Outside the Walls. In June 2009, Pope Benedict XVI announced that carbon-14 testing on bone fragments from the sarcophagus dated them to the first or second century AD. Amazingly, these might be the actual bones of Paul! The beautiful church gives him well-deserved honor. Of course, the apostle himself didn't care about his *grave*—he cared about his *gospel*.

The gospel that Paul preached is often referred to as the Pauline gospel, which at its core is the message centered on the victory of the risen Messiah. The Lord Jesus Christ had triumphed over humankind's threefold enemy, offering deliverance from the three D's: *disobedience*, *death*, and the *devil*. Ever since Adam *disobeyed* God in the garden of Eden, humans have been doing the same and incurring God's rightful judgment for their sins. The result of

6. Philippians 3:10 NIV.

sin can only be *death*, not only physically, but spiritually and eternally. The wicked agent of human sin is the *devil*, who tempts people to disobey God and delights in their destruction. The devil and his demons aren't imaginary. They truly exist, presenting a real threat to the human race.

After meeting the Savior on the road to Damascus, Paul spent his life proclaiming to Jews and Gentiles alike that the three D's had lost their power. "Thanks be to God!" he exclaimed to the Corinthians. "He gives us the victory through our Lord Jesus Christ!"[7] Paul explained that because of Christ's finished work—his incarnation, death, resurrection, and ascension—the saying had become true: "Death is swallowed up in victory." The believer in Jesus can rejoice with a shout of triumph: "O Death, where is your sting? O Hades, where is your victory?"[8] Fear has given way to exultation. Sin has given way to forgiveness. The Enemy lies crushed upon the ground. Disobedience, death, the devil and his demons—all of these dreadful dangers have been despoiled and defeated.

That was Paul's gospel message—but actually, it's *God's message* to the world. He first declared it through the land and people of Israel. Then he expanded it to the ends of the earth through missionaries like the apostle Paul. Although Nero thought he had defeated the gospel when he sentenced Paul to death, in reality the deranged emperor had just decreed his own destruction.

CODA

The main theme of this chapter's conversation is the opposition of two kings who each claimed lordship over the earth. This was ultimately a battle not between Nero and Paul but between Satan and Jesus, the true King of kings. The weapons in Christ's battle are prayer, love, and self-sacrifice. We end our conversation by discussing the nature of the Christian gospel, which centers on the victory of the risen Lord. It's a message that invites everyone into its embrace!

BRYAN: In this chapter we use the ancient book called the *Acts of Paul* to imagine one of the two trials between Nero and Paul. What we see is that

7. 1 Corinthians 15:57 NIV.
8. 1 Corinthians 15:54–55.

there's really two kingdoms in conflict—which is how the ancient Christians saw it. The subtitle of our book is *How the Gospel of Grace Defeated the Ruler of Rome,* so let's talk a little bit about how our book is about two kingdoms and the colossal spiritual world war. We know who wins, don't we?

KATHIE: Yes, because one of them is temporary, and one of them is eternal. Ashes to ashes, dust to dust. As physical human beings, we are all going to die, but our soul is eternal. That's the biggest difference. Jesus lived his life in service, but Nero and Herod and all the others lived their lives being served, just taking, taking, taking.

BRYAN: Jesus said, "The Son of Man did not come to be served, but to serve."[9]

KATHIE: And he would get down on the ground and wash people's feet.

BRYAN: Which for a rabbi would have been astonishing, right?

KATHIE: Yes, for a rabbi to do that is unheard of. Jesus did everything that astonished people. That's why they followed him like they did. They were thinking, "Who is this man who would do that? Nobody's ever done this before. Nobody's ever spoken like this." That's what I love so much about Jesus. He loved in a way that nobody had ever been loved before, especially women.

BRYAN: But isn't there also a sense in which that's not who he is now? Because he has finished that humble time of being incarnated on earth, and now he has ascended on high. He sits at the right hand of God, which is what Stephen saw, right?[10] And he's coming back as a rider on a white horse. So in terms of someone like Nero, he isn't going to meet Jesus as the foot washer. Nero is going to meet Jesus as the one with the sword coming out of his mouth.[11] And while Nero had a good horse, it's nothing compared to the rider on the white horse, right? I mean, that's the true conquering king.

KATHIE: Which is beautiful and good. That's who Jesus is, and I love both. My faith is in both, because they're both him. Just beautiful pictures of who he is, what he was, and what he will forever be.

BRYAN: He wasn't brand-new when he came to earth. He didn't start when he came into the womb of the Virgin Mary.

---

9. Mark 10:45.
10. Acts 7:55–56.
11. Revelation 19:21.

KATHIE: Oh, gosh, no. He was there before. Who was in the burning bush? That was the angel of the Lord. Or he was the fire that led the Israelites in the wilderness. It was all Jesus. Or who was the guy, Melchik . . . ?

BRYAN: The high priest Melchizedek?

KATHIE: Yeah. Melchizedek! That was Jesus.

BRYAN: Many scholars would say that, or he's a prefigurement, or maybe it *was* Jesus himself. He had no mother or father,[12] so that might mean he's eternal. But what we know is the kingdom of Nero is not going to win. And that's true today, too, with the powerful kingdoms of the world. We can look at communist China or we can look at Soviet Russia or modern-day Russia. We can look at wicked kingdoms and regimes in Iran. They're all going to perish. We can look at wicked forces that are in America—the principalities and powers at the head of sex trafficking or at the head of horrible pornography or the sex industry. Cartels, everything. Organized crime.

KATHIE: Instead of hating these people, I just wish they knew that God loved them. Because people that know God loves them don't do those things. They don't know it, and that's why we exist as proclaimers of Messiah. Proclaimers of the good news. Just tell people that God loves them. They've never heard it before.

BRYAN: And, in some ways, we're soldiers of Christ's kingdom. We're proclaimers. But like Paul says in Second Timothy, "I have a Commander and I want to make my Commander happy."[13] So the Bible uses soldier lingo or military jargon to conquer the evil that Nero represents. You can't defeat Nero without being a brave soldier. In some ways you have to fight against evil, right? You can't just kiss evil away. Sometimes you have to fight evil. Isn't that true?

KATHIE: Oh, yeah. Unfortunately, we have to be warriors. I think I'm a warrior toward evil spirits. I war against the powers and principalities every day. But I don't want to be a warrior against people, because "Love your neighbors."[14] Where do I draw the line? There are people that hate me, but I don't want to hate them. So I war against what is controlling them, and that is powers and principalities. And I think if they knew Jesus personally, they wouldn't be that way. That's why I say it's not about religion. It's about

12. Hebrews 7:3.
13. 2 Timothy 2:3–4, author's paraphrase.
14. Mark 12:31.

a relationship. If they knew him personally, and felt how much he loved them in spite of themselves, they would cease their evil ways. Because then the Holy Spirit takes over and you cease your evil ways. Love cannot live where hate does.

BRYAN: Right, but sometimes the evildoers triumph. And they did, temporarily, with Paul. They walked him out of the city on the Ostian Way. Today you can go to Saint Paul Outside the Walls, a beautiful church that marks the spot. Paul would have walked out there but of course back then there was no church. And they cut off his head. One account says milk spurted out of him. We're not exactly sure what that means.

KATHIE: What is it in the Greek? Does it say that?

BRYAN: Just the normal word for milk. It's in the martyrdom account in the *Acts of Paul.* Some relate it to when Paul says, "I fed you with milk and not with solid food."[15] The "milk of the Word" being a symbol of teaching. Like Paul has spiritual babies and he's making spiritual progeny because he converts people.

KATHIE: Could he have had real milk come out?

BRYAN: I don't know. Maybe some kind of body fluid that the Christian watchers interpreted that way.

KATHIE: Jesus had blood and water come out of his side. I guess not actual milk. But I'm wondering about it. I'd love to know the Greek meaning of the word *milk* there.

BRYAN: I translated that martyrdom story in my book on early Christian martyrs, so I know—it's *gala*, the standard word for human or animal milk. I think it would mean any kind of milk product or a symbol of nurturing. Like in Scripture, it's the symbol of teaching. Peter says to "desire the pure milk of the word."[16] And Paul says, "As a nursing mother cares for her children,"[17] so there's a mother image that is mixed in there. But in any case, Paul dies by decapitation.

KATHIE: Yeah, and he wasn't tortured. Everybody else was tortured.

BRYAN: Because he was a Roman citizen, it was quick. He had the privilege to not be thrown to the beasts or something like that.

---

15. 1 Corinthians 3:2.
16. 1 Peter 2:2; Hebrews 5:12.
17. 1 Thessalonians 2:7 NIV.

KATHIE: But any kind of decapitation would be terrible, regardless.

BRYAN: Maybe you could say he died happy because he died for the gospel. If you had to articulate it, what would you say that Paul died for? What is the gospel truth that Paul proclaimed?

KATHIE: Jesus is the way, the truth, and the life. No man comes unto the Father except through him.[18] Paul died for that. He had murdered people out of the zeal that he had. We've talked about that. For a false gospel. But then he proclaimed the true gospel.

BRYAN: And if you could put it in a few words, how would you describe the gospel of Jesus Christ? Like your mentor Billy Graham would do.

KATHIE: I think I just said it. He's the way, the truth, and the life. No one comes to God except through him. People think that shows such terrible intolerance. No, it's the best news in the whole world! The one who's going to be there at the gate, be there at the entrance to heaven—he died for you!

BRYAN: And he rose again, or he couldn't be there.

KATHIE: He rose from the dead to prove that we can too. He sacrificed his whole life for you. That guy's the one you can trust! Everybody else has a tomb. Everybody else has a place where they all died. But Jesus is alive. And whoever puts their faith in him and him alone enjoys eternal life in heaven with him, and the Father and the Holy Spirit.

BRYAN: As we said in the last chapter, you'll be with Frank again.

KATHIE: I'll be with my mother and my father and my husband and my puppy. Our pets go to heaven, too, I believe. And Regis Philbin—I led him to Jesus. Every one of them will be there.

BRYAN: I want to watch your show with Regis in heaven! I'm sure it will be a hit. I believe there's going to be a thousand-year reign of Christ on earth, so it doesn't even have to be up in heaven. It can be in the millennium.

KATHIE: And when that happens, Regis and I will be a hit again.

BRYAN: You will be a hit because somebody's got to entertain us! I mean, people can't just work all the time. We'll need a break, even from good labor that we enjoy.

KATHIE: We're not going to be sitting on a cloud playing a lyre. I do know that. Or even being on a show playing a lyre! Whatever heaven is, I just know

---

18. John 14:6.

it's going to be better than what we have here. It'll be perfect. And we'll be without sin. But best of all, we'll be with our Savior.

BRYAN: And that's the gospel Paul died for. He was willing to die so people could hear it to the ends of the earth. We say in this chapter that Jesus defeated the three D's: disobedience, death, and the devil. So our own sin is defeated. Death is defeated by new life. The devil and his demons—defeated and gone. And that's what will make heaven so perfect.

KATHIE: The ultimate triumph.

NINETEEN

THE TRUE HOUSE OF GOD

When Nero returned from his Greece tour in February of 68, he rode a chariot through Rome's streets like a conquering hero. Everyone hailed him as the world's greatest artist and king. But the glorious acclaim was not to last. Within four months of the parade, Nero would be dead.

Rebellion was in the air. As events in the distant reaches of the Roman Empire spiraled out of Nero's control, his delusions of grandeur made him indecisive and weak. He failed to protect himself because he couldn't believe anyone would want to harm him. So entrenched was his fantasy of universal adoration that when one of his ships sank with many valuables aboard, he assured his friends, in all seriousness, that the fish who loved him would surely return the items. After so many years of convincing himself he was loved—and staging countless events to reinforce it—Nero had lost the ability to recognize it as a giant charade. He truly believed he was idolized, when, in fact, he was despised.

Why? The noblemen detested Nero because he had murdered or pillaged them too often and had shamed their social class with his lowbrow thespian antics. The Praetorian Guard scorned him for his lack of military prowess, so vital for a true Roman emperor. Even the commoners were ready for a change at the top. Though they had blamed Nero for the Great Fire, their support had returned when his civic renewal actually made Rome better.

Instead of crowded tenements that abutted one another, he had required that freestanding buildings be made of fireproof stone, with open plazas and wide avenues between them. Yet his Golden House was obviously selfish and wasteful, and his Greek tour had made the Romans realize they could live without their emperor and do just fine. Though the commoners weren't calling for his head, if the aristocrats and soldiers decided to take it, the people would just shrug and accept the next man up. Nero was in far more danger than he realized—and psychologically, he was doing everything he could *not* to realize it.

The public disdain for Nero simmered quietly in the political stewpot until the lid blew off in March of 68 and insurrection came bubbling into the open. It started in the western provinces with a nobleman named Galba as Nero's intended replacement. But after a loss in battle put Galba on the run, he fled to a remote town in Spain and prepared for Nero's henchmen to arrive and demand his suicide. Yet no one ever showed up—for back in Rome, Nero couldn't muster the will to defend himself.

Observers were shocked by Nero's cavalier attitude toward the rebellion. It was as if his mind couldn't accept it was true. Gloom and doom sometimes plagued him, but other times he went on as if nothing were the matter. He shamed himself by keeping his same daily routines and failing to prepare his armies. For example, he kept going to the gymnasium to compete in wrestling matches, and he told the Praetorians he could communicate with them only by writing lest his singing voice be damaged. Nero was more upset by the rebels' criticism of his lyre playing than their troop movements against him. When desperate war planning finally required his attention, he gave it a little time, then spent the rest of the day lecturing about the new technology of a musical pipe organ. He even summoned senators to his chambers by night as if to address an emergency—then announced to them he had found a way to get better musical tones from the organ.

Eventually Nero learned that the entire province of Spain had rebelled against him. At first he collapsed in despair and could not speak. Then he tore his clothes and beat his head with his fists. When his childhood nursemaid reminded him that other emperors had courageously endured such setbacks, he wailed that "his sufferings were unheard of, unprecedented, and worse than all others." Even so, he carried on with his lavish banquets full of debauchery and obscene songs. He also kept attending the theater. After one actor gave a particularly good performance, Nero accused him of taking advantage of the moment when the city's "best" actor was otherwise occupied.

The rebellion brought out Nero's most vicious instincts. He toyed with solutions such as slaughtering all provincial citizens and laying waste to their lands; murdering the entire Senate at a poisoned banquet; or setting fire to Rome once again—this time with wild animals let loose in the streets. Of course, he didn't dare do any of those things, so he remained stuck in his paralysis. Then he concocted the idea of a military expedition to meet the rebels head-on. But instead of fighting them, he would appear before them without weapons and tearfully plead for the return of their love. When they complied—as he imagined they surely would—he would sing a victory ode. "I need to go compose it right now!" he told his drunken friends.

Before long Nero learned more provincial legions had turned against him. He flew into a rage and overturned his lunch table, smashing his favorite goblets decorated with scenes from Homer's epic poems. Things looked dire for the emperor, so he called for Locusta, the poisoner, and obtained a suicide potion from her. He kept it in a golden box in case he should need it. Realizing it was time to relocate, he begged the tribunes and centurions of the Praetorian Guard to accompany him on a sea journey with the imperial navy, but they evaded him. "Is it really so hard to die?" someone asked—and, with that, Nero knew he had to flee the city the next morning.

Nero woke up at midnight to find his servants and bodyguards had abandoned him. After checking the nearby chambers for allies and finding none, he returned to his bedroom to discover that his luxurious bedclothes, and even his golden box of poison, had been stolen. Terrified at being alone, he cried, "Am I a man without either friends or enemies?"

He rushed outside to throw himself into the Tiber but decided to escape into the countryside instead. Only four companions accompanied him—his boywife, Sporus, and three ex-slaves, one of whom owned a villa a few miles outside the walls. Nero, barefoot and wearing a night tunic, hastily mounted an old nag. He covered himself with a cloak, pulled the hood over his head, and hid his face behind a kerchief. As an earthquake shook the ground and a thunderbolt flashed around him, he galloped away.

The five riders fled Rome on a main highway, then arrived at the overgrown side path to the villa. After turning their horses loose, they proceeded on foot, but Nero couldn't walk on the prickly ground. The others laid down their cloaks to protect his bare soles as they scrambled through briars and thickets along the path, finally arriving at the back wall of the locked villa.

"Crawl down and hide in that sandpit so you won't be seen," one of the fugitives advised.

Shaking his head, Nero said, "I will not go underground while I'm still alive."

Instead, sitting alone, he plucked thorns from his torn cloak while his companions dug an opening into the villa's cellar. Realizing he was thirsty, he drank from a puddle, declaring, "This is Nero's cocktail!" alluding to a mixed drink he had once devised. But then he grew quiet, fearful of discovery. Every rustling in the bushes or chirping bird made him think his pursuers had arrived. Fearful and paranoid, Nero waited until dawn.

Once the hole had been opened in the wall, the five men crawled into the villa's cellar. Finding themselves in a tiny room that served as slaves' quarters, Nero lay down on a cot with a dirty mattress and smelly blanket. His friends found some stale bread for him, but he refused to eat it. At last, faced with dire realities, they began to give him some hard advice. "Your end has come," they said. "It is time to put yourself beyond the reach of further abuse."

Grimly, Nero nodded. "Dig a trench for my grave. Collect marble fragments to decorate it. Gather water to wash my body and firewood for my pyre." While these things were being done, Nero wept and lamented, "By Jove! What an artist is perishing in me!" To the very end he believed he was a magnificent performer whose lost artistry would be a terrible blow for the world.

A runner arrived with a message. Snatching it, Nero learned that the citizens of Rome were rejoicing and the Senate had decreed an ancient punishment for him: to be stripped naked in public, fastened to a stake, and beaten to death with rods. Terrified, he drew two daggers and tested their points. He couldn't believe it had all come down to this. "My life is shameful—unbecoming to Nero!" he cried. "In times like this, one should be decisive. Rouse yourself!" Yet he didn't have the courage to do the deed. He ordered Sporus to start weeping for his "husband," and he commanded the other men to set an example by killing themselves first—though they politely declined.

Outside, horses galloped up to the villa and came to a stop. As the riders dismounted, they shouted, "Capture him alive!" Nero quoted a line from Homer's *Iliad*—"The thunder of swift-footed horses echoes around my ears!"—then drove a dagger into his neck with the help of one of his companions. Agonized, he fell to the ground as a centurion burst into the room. Though the man tried to prevent the emperor's death, he could not.

"Too . . . late," Nero sputtered as blood choked his airway. His final words were "This is faith!"—but the ruler of Rome had put his faith in the wrong place. His eyes bulged in their sockets, his lifeblood stopped oozing from his torn throat, and he died a horror to behold.

In the coming days, Galba, the insurrectionist, emerged from his Spanish exile and became the next emperor. He ordered Nero's corpse to be cremated and gave him a decent funeral. Nero's beloved Acte, who had somehow escaped his murderous hand, made sure his ashes were interred in his family tomb. On earth, a beautiful monument marked the spot. But beneath the earth, Nero had just learned he was no god after all.

For a year after Nero's death, a chaotic civil war fractured the Roman Empire and three men claimed the throne in quick succession. In the end, Vespasian triumphed and set up a new clan on the imperial throne: the Flavians. Nero's misrule had brought the exalted Julio-Claudian dynasty to an ignoble and ruinous end.

Vespasian was no aristocratic descendant of the gods but a pragmatic soldier who had risen through the ranks of the army. His last task as a military man was to put down the Jewish rebellion. He swiftly subdued Galilee and Judea. But before he could capture the well-fortified city of Jerusalem, the fight for the imperial throne demanded his presence in Rome. He left his son Titus to finish the job of invading Jerusalem, razing it to the ground, slaughtering its inhabitants, and destroying its temple forever.

Of course, the Roman destruction of the Jewish temple was no unforeseen accident. God had allowed the calamity for a greater purpose. For eighty years since the temple was first built by King Herod, it had been the glory of Jerusalem. Now it was gone—and that was a good thing. A final story will help explain why the temple's destruction was a divine blessing.

Imagine two people, an old man and an even older woman, standing atop the craggy summit of Golgotha, the hill of crucifixion outside Jerusalem. He is her adopted son; she is his adopted mother. They are gazing at a hole in the ground, a place for the upright stake of a cross. Their names are John and Mary.

"Do you remember what he told us that day?" John asked.

Mary didn't answer right away. She was aged and frail, more than ninety years old. Deep lines on her face commemorated a lifetime of memories—some of them wondrous, others torturous, yet God had been present in all of them.

"Of course," she said at last, then quoted the words of Jesus upon the cross: "'Woman, behold your son! Son, behold your mother!'[1] Then you took me into your home."

"It has been an honor," John said with a smile.

The two visitors from Ephesus fell silent as they surveyed the ruin that Jerusalem had become. In the distance the high hill of the Temple Mount sent up columns of dark smoke. It wasn't the smoke of conquest—that had happened several months ago, and the bulk of Titus's army had since withdrawn. The killing had been horrific. Those who survived the massacre had been enslaved and trafficked around the world.

Today, some of those newly enslaved citizens of Jerusalem were burning the debris that had once belonged to the glorious temple. Its brilliant white stones had fallen to the ground. Not one of them was left on top of another. The golden trim had been looted by the marauding soldiers. Rubble had been dumped into the streets below, and anything flammable had been gathered into piles for incineration. The Temple Mount had become a desecrated garbage heap. Instead of the sweet smell of incense, or the meaty aroma of sacrifices, the black billows of burning rubbish rose into the sky.

John's gaze fell to the ground. "I can't look anymore. It makes me too sad."

Mary put her hand on his shoulder. When he raised his eyes, she pointed to a place nearby, only a stone's throw away. It had once been a quarry pit. After

---

1. John 19:26–27.

the valuable rock had been dug out, the quarry was abandoned, and the locals had used the excavations as tombs. Soil had gathered on the floor of the pit, turning the area into a garden cemetery. "Remember the words of the angel," Mary said softly. "'He is not here; he has risen!'"[2]

The old apostle nodded solemnly. "Yes, Mother, I know. Even so, I mourn. Peter is gone now. So is James. And Paul. All the disciples who saw the Savior have departed. You and I are the only ones left. Sometimes that makes me feel alone."

Mary gestured to the smoking Temple Mount. "In former days, God had to be found up there." She moved her hand to John's chest and tapped his heart with her knobby finger. "Now this is the temple of God. The Spirit of Jesus dwells in you and me, and in all who love my son. He dwells in everyone who will come after us, like a mighty caravan of heroes, until the day of his appearing."

John's mood brightened at this reminder. The beloved disciple put his arm around his mother's shoulder and drew her close. Raising his other arm, he lifted his palm toward the sky in victorious acclamation. "The Lamb of God is coming soon!"

Mary replied in the ancient Hebrew tongue, "Amen! Come, Lord Jesus!"[3]

CODA

In our final conversation, we reflect on the differences between Nero's and Paul's deaths. One was shameful and cowardly, the other brave and confident. One of their lives had been full of satanic lies, the other grounded in God's truth. And one life had ultimately led to destruction, the other to eternal joy. Then we end this book where we began: by imagining Mary on the hill of Jesus' crucifixion (which is also where we ended our previous book, *Herod and Mary*). We rejoice to think that while the temple made with human hands is gone, the presence of God still dwells among his people—within Kathie, Bryan, and all who call upon the name of the Lord!

---

2. Luke 24:6 NIV.
3. Revelation 22:20.

BRYAN: Our final chapter is "The True House of God." We have Nero's death—not an act of bravery but a suicide—and the opposite, Paul's martyrdom, confident in God, courageously walking toward the sword. Nero is ashamed. He flees the city in terror. He sees the empire turning against him, and then the people around him turn against him. And he takes this boy with him, who he's made to look like his wife.

KATHIE: Oh, gosh. I hated all that about this boy who looked like Poppaea.

BRYAN: Nero thought, "If I turn him into a girl, with castration and makeup and gowns, he actually *would* look like Poppaea." So Nero goes around kissing him and actually marries the boy with a formal wedding.

KATHIE: And what did the people think of him doing that? They knew he was not a woman.

BRYAN: Yeah, that's true, but you already had eunuchs and emasculated men around. The shameful thing was Nero actually marries him. Other than that you were allowed to have emasculated males around you, if you wanted.

KATHIE: It shows that Satan is the father of lies.[4]

BRYAN: He loves to twist reality. If God makes them male and female in the garden,[5] then a twisted person will want to invert that most basic and fundamental unit of human existence. So Nero flees Rome and goes to a villa. They can't get in, so his helpers dig a hole through the wall. They are down in the basement, it's the slave quarters, and it's dirty. Nero tries to act like he's going to have a noble death, but he's lost it, and then he hears—

KATHIE: How old was he at that point? You said in his thirties, like, young, right?

BRYAN: Yes, he's young. He was thirty years old at the time of his death. And he's still trying to do his stagecraft. So when he hears the horses of the people that are going to arrest him, he quotes from Homer's *Iliad*, a poetic line like he is living out a tragedy, then he takes a knife and sticks it in his throat. But it's not working, and he's in agony, and his blood is oozing out as he's dying. The soldier comes close because he's going to try to keep him alive so they can punish him worse. And Nero says, "Too late!" And then his final

4. John 8:44.
5. Genesis 1:27.

words are "This is faith." Can you believe that was what his final words were? "This is faith." What could that have meant?

KATHIE: Who knows what people say or the things they do when they're facing eternity? But the only thing Nero had faith in was himself.

BRYAN: Maybe he was trying to say, "This is a noble death. This is the true faith that I have in my immortality. Look at me. Even at the end, I'm doing something great." Maybe that was it?

KATHIE: I just know it's all about ego. Everything he did was about ego. And, like you said, stagecraft. Trying to put on a show. Leave everyone with a great final line.

BRYAN: And then the final scene in the chapter—ending not with Nero sticking a knife in himself and being ashamed but with something beautiful—is where we see John and Mary. It's similar to where we ended *Herod and Mary*, our previous book, with Mary in Jerusalem. Now we imagine a scene when she's old. And of course, if it happened, Mary would have been very old because this would be AD 70. She was born in the BC period so she would be ninetyish. But it's possible. We can imagine it. And maybe she came to Jerusalem or was going to die in Jerusalem. And John would be with her because he took care of her. And we know he lived a long time past AD 70, so he was still alive.

KATHIE: At Patmos?

BRYAN: Yes, Patmos and Ephesus, and he was going to live about thirty more years after that. Maybe they came together to Golgotha and looked at the burned temple. Imagine being there when Titus had just destroyed it. Imagine if you were looking through the eyes of Mary, or through the eyes of John. If you could stand on Golgotha, from there you could see the burnt temple. You can't see it today because of the city buildings that are in the way. But back then you could have seen the temple from Golgotha, and it would be a smoking ruin. Titus destroyed Herod's amazing temple, the one we wrote about in our first book. Is that a tragedy to see the Jewish temple going up in flames?

KATHIE: I don't know if it's a tragedy. "All things work together for the good of those who love God, to those who are the called according to His purpose."[6] So there's a reason for things. Jews don't even have a word for

---

6. Romans 8:28.

coincidence in their language, because it doesn't exist for them, only divine providence. God is sovereign in all things, or he's not God at all. So, as I said, there must be a purpose here. I hate to see beauty destroyed. And Herod did make it beautiful, didn't he? It was meant for God. That's the difference between a giant statue, a colossus, and the temple.

BRYAN: And we know it's okay to make a beautiful temple because Solomon's temple was beautiful, and God showed him what to do with that. God told him to make that lavish temple. In that sense, making a beautiful temple isn't a bad thing. So for Herod to do it as well isn't a bad thing, per se. Maybe it was self-glorifying, but it also glorified God.

KATHIE: And let's remember that he was trying to please the Jews. He was trying to keep them happy. He had a big job to do. He had to keep the Romans at bay and keep the Jews from rising up and killing him.

BRYAN: He made Jerusalem beautiful and decorated that for the Jews. And he made Caesarea and decorated that for the Romans.

KATHIE: And he even called it Caesarea, for Caesar Augustus.

BRYAN: But now the Jewish temple is burned. So it's gone, and Herod is long gone, and the temple is destroyed.

KATHIE: Yet all things work together for good. The destruction of the temple was part of God's plan.

BRYAN: That's the theme of our book, isn't it? We picture and imagine and write a story about how Mary comforts John, and she says, "John, my adoptive son, it doesn't have to be sad. Where is the shekinah now? Where is God's presence now? It's here"—and I'm rubbing my heart as I speak. Mary says, "It's within you, John. It's within me. It's within all who will come after us, who follow my son Yeshua." That's the theme. That was the gospel that Paul took to the ends of the earth. No longer do you have to go to Jerusalem to find God. He says, "I'll come to you in a new way, which only the resurrection can make happen." Before, people like King David would say when they sinned, "Lord, please! Take not thy Holy Spirit from me!"[7] But once Jesus had risen from the grave, what's the first thing that happened in the upper room? The Spirit came down and said, "I will live in you, never to be taken from you." So everyone should take that message to the ends of the earth.

---

7. Psalm 51:11, author's paraphrase.

KATHIE: That's why we've written this book. We want the message of Paul to reach people today.

BRYAN: Right! I think Paul would be very glad about it because when he was in prison he said, "Bring me paper! Bring me pencils. I want to write!" And I think we've tried to write this book in the legacy of Paul, to honor his memory, but really to honor Jesus. And to use the written word like Paul did to proclaim what he proclaimed as well.

KATHIE: And he proclaimed one simple idea: Through faith in Yeshua, the presence of God can live within us.

BRYAN: We can be the temple of the living God.

KATHIE: What love he has for us! His love changes us from the inside out. Only the love of Yeshua can do something like that!

ACKNOWLEDGMENTS

Kathie and Bryan are grateful for the outstanding editorial work of Rachel Buller, Carrie Marrs, and Debbie Wickwire. In addition, Mrs. Christi Hurt, Kathie's executive assistant, provided outstanding coordination and service throughout the writing process. Last but not least, we are grateful for the leadership and vision provided by Kathie's son, Cody Gifford, a true intellectual and storyteller. This book wouldn't have been possible without great teamwork from everyone involved!

ABOUT THE AUTHORS

KATHIE LEE GIFFORD is the four-time Emmy Award–winning former cohost of the fourth hour of the *TODAY Show* alongside Hoda Kotb. Prior to her time at NBC News, Gifford served as the cohost of *Live with Regis and Kathie Lee* for fifteen years. In 2015 she was inducted into the Broadcasting and Cable Hall of Fame, and recently she was awarded a star on the Hollywood Walk of Fame.

A playwright, producer, singer, songwriter, and actress, Gifford has starred in numerous television programs and movies in her forty-five-year career. She has written several musicals, including Broadway's *Scandalous*, for which she received a Tony nomination in 2012 for Best Actress. In 2019 she made her directorial debut with *The God Who Sees* oratorio, shot in Israel and based on a song she cowrote with Grammy nominee Nicole C. Mullen. She has written and directed three more oratorios and will be releasing the collection of four as *The Way*.

Gifford has authored six *New York Times*–bestselling books, including *The God of the Way*; *It's Never Too Late*; *The Rock, the Road, and the Rabbi*; *Just When I Thought I'd Dropped My Last Egg*; *I Can't Believe I Said That*; and the popular children's book *Party Animals*. She has also recently released *Hello, Little Dreamer* (2020); *The Jesus I Know* (2021); and *Herod and Mary* (2024).

Gifford lends support to numerous children's organizations, including Childhelp, the International Justice Mission, and the Association to Benefit Children. She received an honorary doctorate from Marymount University for her humanitarian work in labor relations. Gifford is on Twitter/X and Instagram @KathieLGifford.

DR. BRYAN M. LITFIN is a professor of Bible and theology at Liberty University in Lynchburg, Virginia. Previously he served as a professor of theology at Moody Bible Institute in Chicago and an editor and writer at Moody Publishers.

Bryan received his PhD in religious studies from the University of Virginia, where he focused on the field of Christianity and Judaism in antiquity. His area of expertise is the early Christian writers of the ancient Roman era. He has a ThM in historical theology from Dallas Theological Seminary and an undergraduate degree from the University of Tennessee in print media and communications.

Litfin has published six adventure novels—three set in an imaginary future (the *Chiveis Trilogy*) and three in the ancient church (*Constantine's Empire* series). His nonfiction books include *The Story of the Trinity*, *Getting to Know the Church Fathers*, and *Early Christian Martyr Stories*. His book *After Acts* describes what happened to Jesus' apostles after their biblical stories ended. In addition, Litfin has published many book chapters and journal articles of academic scholarship. He is a member of the Evangelical Theological Society.

Bryan is married to Carolyn, and they have two adult children. He enjoys taking students on annual trips to Greece, Turkey, and other Mediterranean lands. The Litfins worship at Rivermont Evangelical Presbyterian Church in Lynchburg. Bryan can be reached via his website, bryanlitfin.com.

OTHER HCCP BOOKS BY KATHIE LEE GIFFORD

Kathie Lee Gifford reveals heartwarming, entertaining conversations between people and personalities who both agree and disagree about who Jesus is, his role throughout history, and his presence in our lives today.

Journey with Kathie Lee Gifford and Messianic Rabbi Jason Sobel into Israel and explore the deep roots of the Christian faith.

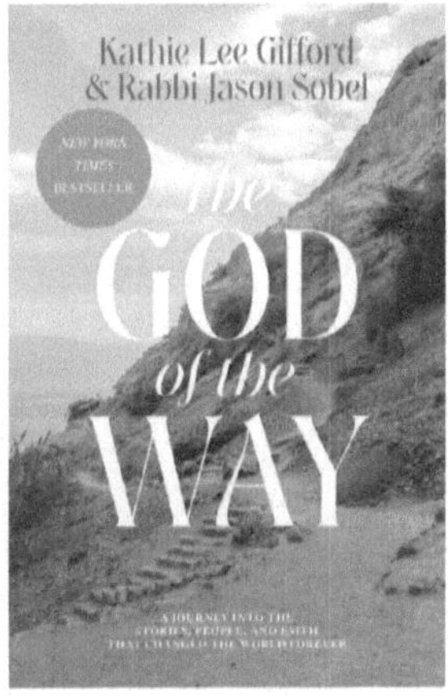

Dig deeper into God's Word, from the creation of the world through the desert and empty places, the Hebrew nation, and meet Jesus, the disciples, and his followers.

Connect with Kathie Lee on Twitter/X and Instagram @KathieLGifford.

OTHER BOOKS FROM BRYAN LITFIN

Christian Fiction the Way it Was Meant to Be

The Chiveis Trilogy

Nuclear war has ravaged the earth. Centuries from now, an alpine society has achieved a culture of swords and horses but has lost all memory of Christianity. Then a courageous army scout and a beautiful farmer's daughter find the ancient Scriptures of God. Can the one true faith reawaken in Chiveis?

Constantine's Empire Trilogy

Rome totters on the brink of war. Constantine's army is on the move. Will the barbarian warrior and the senator's daughter live to see the Empire bow the knee to Christ?

For more information, visit bryanlitfin.com.

OTHER BOOKS FROM BRYAN LITFIN

Historical Nonfiction about the Early Church

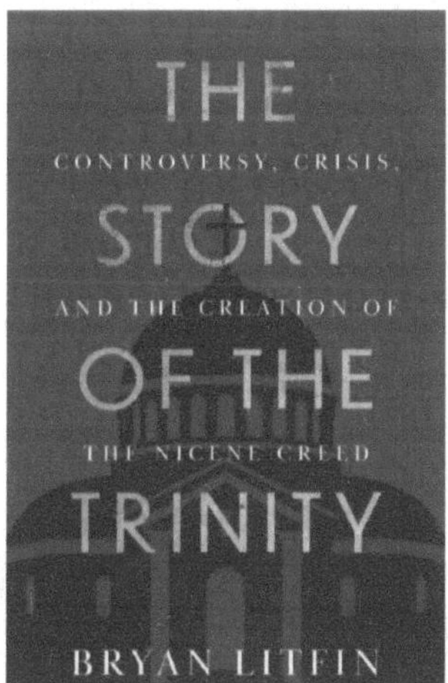

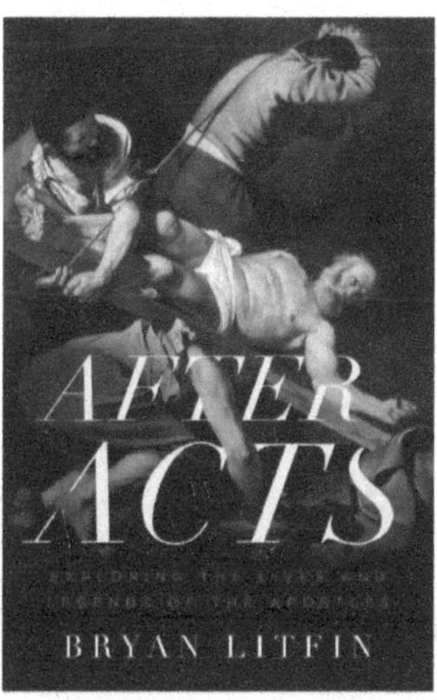

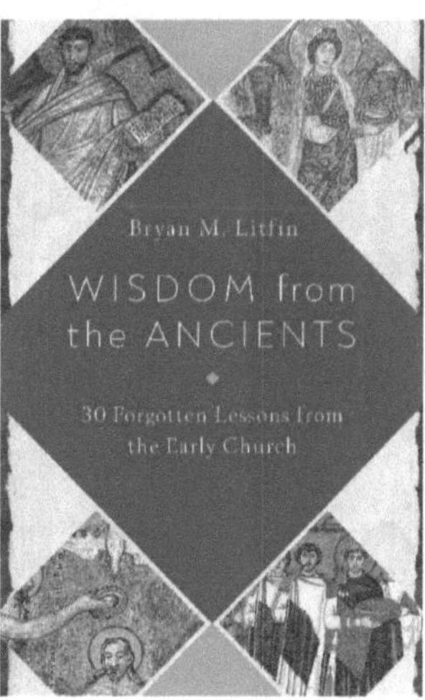

Discover the roots of your faith in the ancient church.
Get to know the early Christians who laid the foundations of church history!

For more information, visit bryanlitfin.com.

www.ingramcontent.com/pod-product-compliance
Lightning Source LLC
LaVergne TN
LVHW030918080826
845145LV00013B/2956

* 9 7 8 1 4 0 0 3 5 5 6 6 2 *